STUDENT CONDUCT PRACTICE

STUDENT CONDUCT
PRACTICE

The Complete Guide for
Student Affairs Professionals

Edited by

James M. Lancaster and Diane M. Waryold

Foreword by Linda Timm

Sty/us

STERLING, VIRGINIA

This book is endorsed by the Association for Student Judicial Affairs

Published in Association with the Association for Student Judicial Affairs

COPYRIGHT © 2008 BY
STYLUS PUBLISHING, LLC.

Published by Stylus Publishing, LLC
22883 Quicksilver Drive
Sterling, Virginia 20166-2102

Library of Congress Cataloging-in-Publication-Data
   Student conduct practice : the complete guide for student
   affairs professionals / edited
by James M. Lancaster and Diane M. Waryold ; foreword
by Linda Timm.—1st ed.
      p. cm.
   Includes bibliographical references and index.
   ISBN 978–1-57922–285–7 (cloth : alk. paper)—
   ISBN 978–1-57922–286–4 (pbk. : alk. paper)
      1. College discipline—United States. 2. College
students—United States—Discipline. I. Lancaster,
James M. II. Waryold, Diane M., 1959–
   LB2344.S78   2008
   378.1′95—dc22fw2007031390

13-digit ISBN: 978-1-57922-285-7 (cloth)
13-digit ISBN: 978-1-57922-286-4 (paper)

Printed in the United States of America

All first editions printed on acid free paper
that meets the American National Standards Institute
Z39-48 Standard.

> Bulk Purchases
>
> Quantity discounts are available for use in workshops
> and for staff development.
> Call 1-800-232-0223

First Edition, 2008

10 9 8 7 6 5 4 3 2 1

CONTENTS

ACKNOWLEDGEMENTS

T hose who work in student affairs, especially those working with conduct issues, face challenging times. Having met and worked with
many of these individuals, we are constantly impressed with their
dedication to helping their students while balancing personal and institutional concerns. Much of their work can be judged only by the longer-term
success of their students or, occasionally, by managing liability for themselves
and their institutions. Yet they persevere in the face of adversity and other
challenges. We are grateful for their dedication and for their commitment to
student growth and development

We are grateful to Dr. Bill Grace, founder, Center for Ethical Leadership, for permission to use the 4-V Model of Ethical Leadership Development in chapter 9.

We are also appreciative of the contributions of the many presenters,
authors, and practitioners who, over time, have helped to shape this profession and our own understanding of the field of conduct administration. We
are thankful to the founding members of the Association for Student Judicial
Affairs (ASJA), especially Don Gehring, for recognizing that student conduct
administration has a special place as a profession within student affairs. ASJA
has brought together a community of practice that challenges administrators
to strive for excellence in meeting diverse student need and emerging societal
demands.

FOREWORD

College campuses have always been communities grappling with the issues of contemporary society. We have always looked to the campuses as sources for answers through research, dialogue, and action. Historically, students have been fearless in their activism as evidenced by the role they played in the civil rights movement, the women's movement, and our political structures and in expressing their beliefs about war, apartheid, environmental concerns, and poverty. Many of us recall our own experiences in "acting out" when we saw injustice around us. Indeed, one of our greatest freedoms is our freedom of expression.

Students are also incredibly generous with their time and talent when it comes to community service and volunteerism. Wherever in the world there is crisis, be it tsunami, hurricane, fires, or poverty, students are there to provide support and care.

Yet, with all this good, every campus in this country also faces behavioral challenges. College campuses have always been communities in which students are held accountable for their actions. In a time when boundaries are being tested, personal values are conflicted, and futures look confusing and unsure, students have been challenged to follow rules and regulations so that the learning process on campus can move forward without disruption. We ask a lot of our students from the day they move onto campus, well beyond the academic expectations we hold for them. We bring together students from diverse backgrounds—racial, economic, geographic, every kind of difference one can think of—and they are placed in small living communities and expected to live together in relative harmony. Of course we know it won't work quite that way immediately, but here is an 18-year-old student, away from all things familiar, and now living with a group of total strangers (in most cases). So, when there are the inevitable, expected conflicts, how do we assist the students, in an educationally sound manner, to recognize how their behaviors are impacting others? How do we encourage growth, ethical decision making, and sensitivity to the differences among us? How do we ensure students' freedom of expression while protecting others from hurtful, uncivil behavior?

As a college president I may not be on the front lines as a conduct administrator anymore, but it is imperative that all of us in college administration understand the environment surrounding sound student conduct administration. All of us must be aware of the actions of our students, particularly those actions that may be signals to us of potential safety concerns. Our campus communities are not immune from the everyday life challenges of greater society. We know we have students who suffer from mental health issues, who experience violence, and who are feeling pressure to succeed at all costs. How can we, as educators, construct and utilize a conduct process to protect, support, and hold students accountable?

Each of the contributing authors in this book is currently or has been deeply involved in conduct administration. They know, from years of experience and study, what the contemporary issues are and how they may be best approached with students, carefully integrating theory with practice. Student conduct administration has moved from the faculty courts of years past to an array of processes structured to fit the issue at hand. Whether it is a student hearing panel, a mediation process, or a one-on-one conference, just to name a few, the processes are all grounded in the core principles of student development. Their dedication to student development is sincere and honest. It has been their lives' work as educators and practitioners. As such, I read this book with a high degree of confidence and see it as a guide to assist all of us working in colleges to understand the climate and processes necessary to assist students to grow and become our next generation of leaders.

Linda Timm, President
Mount Mary College

INTRODUCTION

James M. Lancaster and Diane M. Waryold

The subject of student conduct has been with us for as long as young persons have gathered in groups in educational settings. In that time, a variety of approaches have been taken to resolving misconduct when it occurs. Only recently have we come to think of those who administer resolution processes in student conduct as members of a group of professionals.

When Donald Gehring founded the Association for Student Judicial Affairs (ASJA) in 1988, it came as no surprise that the organization immediately attracted a large number of members. Even so, literature pertaining to student conduct has been presented most often in articles in various journals, occasionally in book form, and often from outside the practice itself. In 1998, William Kibler and Brent Paterson published an important compendium of such wisdom in their book *The Administration of Campus Discipline: Student, Organizational, and Community Issues*. This book featured chapters authored by leaders in the field. Topics included areas such as the distinction between the criminal justice system and campus student conduct, student conduct records, sexual assault, relationship violence, speech codes, student organizations, academic misconduct, use and misuse of computers, students and mental health, working with campus hearing panels, and alternative dispute resolution. Although some of these topics have remained in the forefront of student conduct practice, in other areas the profession of student conduct resolution has come far. Case law has further refined our understanding of rights and procedures, alternative practices to the traditional hearing model have emerged, and the position of conduct officer has become more specialized and professional and thus has changed from a part-time or transitory professional experience to a full-time and continuing professional choice for many.

The year 2008 is the twentieth anniversary of the founding of ASJA and coincides with the tenth anniversary of the earlier publication of *The Administration of Campus Discipline: Student, Organizational, and Community Issues*. It seems a proper time to revisit what has transpired in the undertaking of student conduct resolution. The current book seeks to fulfill that purpose. A variety of practitioners and faculty have sought to create in this book a current compendium of best practices and topical discussions that may be useful to students, new practitioners, and established professionals.

Part one of this book is dedicated to structural considerations in the practice of conduct resolution. In chapter 1, the editors of this book revisit the professional philosophy of conduct administration, seeking to understand and convey the various themes that have led to creation of this profession. On a related note in chapter 2, William Fischer and Vaughn Maatman consider what type of person and what personality types are most likely to become successful in the practice of conduct administration.

Felice Dublon, in chapter 3, examines issues of environment and governance in which the administrator of conduct must function. These issues, while not always amenable to control by administrators, must be held in careful regard if we are to understand our role as conduct administrators.

With chapter 4, we begin to examine some of the fundamental tools used in conduct administration. Edward Stoner II begins this examination by reviewing the elements of a model code of conduct, and he offers suggestions on using this code to assess your own practice. John Lowery follows in chapter 5 by discussing the laws, policies, and government mandates that affect our understanding and practice within legal boundaries. Eugene Zdziarski and Nona Wood, in chapter 6, offer guidance and advice on using the various forums for resolution that exist today for practitioners.

In chapters 7 through 9, we consider the "softer" and more philosophical and educational dimensions of conduct resolution. Gary Pavela opens this approach with a thoughtful discussion of why the educational and ethical dialogue must remain a constant concern of those addressing student conduct. In chapter 8, Matthew Lopez-Phillips and Susan Trageser take us on a journey across the office desk and into the lives of our students as they discuss student development, diversity, and social justice as daily concerns.

And in chapter 9, Elizabeth Baldizan asks that we consider ethical decision making in the context of our student conduct resolution work.

In part two, we begin examining current issues affecting conduct administration. William Kibler and Brent Paterson, authors of the earlier text *The Administration of Campus Discipline: Student, Organizational, and Community Issues*, here examine incivility as it occurs on college campuses and our attempts to manage such disruptions of the educational process. Related to these concerns are first amendment issues, the topic for Saundra Shuster, Lee Bird, and Mary Beth Mackin in chapter 12. The authors are careful to define what constitutes protected speech and acts while suggesting some remedies for those faced with the difficulties these topics present.

Mental health and student well-being are growing concerns on our campuses as greater numbers of more diverse students challenge our traditional notions of "typical" student needs. Gary Dickstein and Annie Nebeker Christensen consider these topics in chapter 13.

In chapters 14 and 15, Judith Haas and James Street offer insights for prevention of and response to student organizational conduct issues while Patrick Drinan and Tricia Bertram Gallant consider cases involving alleged academic integrity violations.

In chapter 16, we offer a look over our shoulders at where the profession has traveled as well as a commentary on the view ahead, including suggestions from current administrators. In all, we hope that those interested in the practice of student conduct resolution as a developmental and educational process will find this book a useful addition to their professional libraries.

PART ONE

STRUCTURAL CONSIDERATIONS

I

THE PROFESSIONAL PHILOSOPHY OF STUDENT CONDUCT ADMINISTRATION

Diane M. Waryold and James M. Lancaster

T he philosophy of student conduct administration has an unsettled past that has culminated in a more clearly defined and professional future. However, some suggest that the profession is still in its early adolescence. After all, it has only been a little over 20 years since the Association for Student Judicial Affairs (ASJA), the premier professional organization for "any professional employed at a postsecondary institution with the responsibility for, or an interest in student judicial affairs" (ASJA Constitution), was founded. Therefore, as an organized profession, student conduct administration is still very young by any historical yardstick. To compound this issue, for years, there has existed a deep-seated schism between other functional units of the university and student conduct administration. This schism has apparently been caused by a lack of understanding about and appreciation for the value of student conduct work. And, from outside the academy, there is a lack of understanding and sometimes an adversarial relationship between conduct administrators and external constituents. Unfortunately, it is rare for practitioners within the field to reflect on and publish research or write about the vital role student conduct administration plays within an institution. As a result, student conduct administration is often relegated to second-class status in which onlookers frequently remark that they dislike the negativity and stress associated with the work, so they keep their distance. Questions and remarks such as "Why would you choose this profession?" and "Oh, you are so brave," or "Are you on a power trip?" or "Don't you feel like a glorified baby sitter?" and student conduct is "A necessary institutional evil—someone has to do it," are sometimes difficult to endure. Conduct administrators need a thick skin and great courage to practice in a field that attracts such disillusionment and controversy. This is a tough field, and one must look deep within to discover what it is that is so compelling about the practice. No matter how often we have heard these comments, they still make us pause and reflect on what it is about student conduct work that we believe to be attractive, important, powerful, and special. This chapter explores the philosophy of student conduct administration—what it is and how it came to be. It examines student conduct as a profession that is indeed necessary and arguably one of the most important functional areas in student affairs practice.

Philosophy: What Is It and Why Is It Important?

The English word "philosophy" has its origin in Greek tradition. *Philosophia* can be broken down into two root words, loosely translated as *philos*, meaning friend or lover (love of), and *sophy*, meaning wisdom (http://wordinfo .info/words/index). Others have defined the word philosophy as an "examination of basic concepts—the branch of knowledge or academic study devoted to the systematic examination of basic concepts such as truth, existence, reality, causality, and freedom." Philosophy is also associated with schools of thought: "a particular system of thought or doctrine, guiding or underlying principles, a set of basic principles or concepts underlying a particular sphere of knowledge" and "a precept, or set of precepts, beliefs, principles, or aims, underlying somebody's practice or conduct" (http:// encarta.msn.com/dictionary_/). No matter how precisely one defines the word, we believe it all comes down to raison d'être, or the reasoning or basis on which our practice is grounded or the intention we attach to our work.

In their seminal work, *Critical Issues in Student Affairs*, Sandeen and Barr (2006), remark that the foundation of the student affairs profession has an assortment of origins.

> For some, the roots of the profession are in counseling and counseling theories; for others, the foundation of the profession is student development

theory and practice; and for still others, the appropriate foundation for student affairs is based on organizational theory, administration, and management. With such divergent points of view within the profession, the foundation can at times feel like it is built on quicksand. (p. 2)

A strong parallel can certainly be drawn for student conduct work as a functional unit within student affairs. One does not have to look far to discover applications within counseling, counseling theories, and student development. The fundamental purpose of student conduct work is to promote growth and development in students while protecting the interests of the larger campus community. ASJA (1987) has promulgated the purpose of student conduct in its constitution, which states:

> The mission of this Association shall be to facilitate the integration of student development concepts with principles of judicial practice in a postsecondary educational setting, and to promote, encourage and support student development professionals who have responsibility for student judicial affairs. (p. 1)

Effective practice also requires administrators to think carefully about creating a safe environment in which students are encouraged to talk about and explore the issues that challenge their life and threaten their success in college. In the student conduct process, students are empowered through counseling and/or helping skills to gain greater self understanding, which in turn leads to accepting responsibility for their actions and changes in their behaviors. Organizational theory, administration, and management are also integral parts of the process. Careful attention to the method in which the student conduct process is carried out and the climate of learning that is created through such attention to these details is essential to sound practice. Chapter 3, on environment and governance, speaks to the importance of this foundational piece. But with this said, Sandeen and Barr (2006) make it clear that

> The foundation of any profession is formed from a shared philosophy about what needs to be done, a shared understanding of the theoretical constructs that inform the practice of the profession, the application of the accumulated knowledge of the members to the tasks that need to be accomplished, and the ability of the practitioners of the profession to effectively link their theoretical knowledge, practical wisdom, and skills to larger organizations and society. (p. 1)

It is not enough simply to identify the principles and concepts that form the basis for the philosophy of student conduct administration. Evans, Forney, and Guido-DiBrito (1998) contend that,

> in order to be most productive and useful, student affairs professionals should consider the following questions when utilizing student development theory: "(a) what interpersonal and intrapersonal changes occur while the student is in college; (b) what factors lead to this development; (c) what aspects of the college environment encourage or retard growth; and (d) what developmental outcomes should we strive to achieve in college?" These questions allow professionals to begin connecting theory and practice. (p. 5)

Student conduct administration as a functional unit of student affairs is ripe with opportunities to educate the student, and student conduct administrators would be well served to keep these questions in mind as they interact with students. Chapter 16 discusses in depth the salient philosophical beliefs that inform our practice.

The remainder of this chapter explores the historical context of our work, the milestones in our short history, and the educational needs of the present-day student.

Historical Context of Student Conduct Administration

Student conduct administration, as with many other service-oriented professions, evolved out of need. As is stated in chapters 11 and 16 of this text, student behavior (or misbehavior) has always been a part of the academy. It is the demographics of the student population and the needs of the population that have compelled the structure and response to such behaviors to change and evolve over time.

In the early days, young and affluent male students attended college to train as clergy and promote Christianity. Morality was central to what was taught, and live-in tutors had a tight hold on these youthful students, allowing them very few freedoms (Rudolph, 1962). The president of the college, and later the faculty tutors, were responsible for advising students about such things as their "moral life and intellectual habits." They acted *in loco parentis*, or "in place of a parent," as fashioned by British common law. Student affairs as a profession in the United States can be traced back to the first dean of men at Harvard University, when LeBaron Russell Briggs was appointed in 1870 to relieve the president and faculty of the above mentioned duties (Appleton, Briggs, & Rhatigan, 1978, p. 13). Several years later, the first dean of women, Alice Freeman Palmer, was appointed at the University of Chicago. It is interesting to note, however, that Palmer ended up serving in this role after she had already served as president of Wellesley College (for women). Palmer had resigned her position as president of Wellesley to follow her heart (she had fallen in love with George Palmer, a philosophy professor at Harvard). In her role as dean of women at Chicago, Palmer advocated for women in higher education and was one of the founding mothers of the American Association of University Women. While Palmer served as dean of women at Chicago, the enrollment of women doubled and had climbed to 48% of the total enrollment by the time that she left this post. Meanwhile, enrollment of women on other campuses across the nation was concentrated primarily in women's colleges, and coeducational enrollment paled in comparison (Bordin, 1993, p. 5).

The land-grant movement (a result of the original Morrill Act of 1862) created federal support for the creation of the land-grant colleges and universities in an attempt to open up institutions of higher learning to the working class and to meet the needs of a growing industrialized nation (Kerr, 1982). The proliferation of public higher education by way of the creation of public junior colleges, teachers' colleges or normal schools, and the establishment of new technical colleges opened the door to a more diverse student population (Thelin, 2004, p. 1). With increased diversity and unprecedented expansion, tensions among students, faculty, and administration began to emerge. Conflicts turned into "a battleground of a protracted generational war" (Thelin, 2004, p. 1) during the 1960s and the era of student activism. In response to the emerging social and legal environments, colleges began to treat students as so-called mature"adults." Patrick Love, in his essay, titled *Considering a Career in Student Affairs* (on the ACPA website) suggests

> The number and type of advising, counseling, administrative, and management positions continued to increase throughout the 20th century to meet the evolving needs of institutions and the students who attend them. Other factors that contributed to the development of the field of student affairs include the proliferation of colleges and universities during the late 19th

and throughout the 20th century, the inclusion of women and students of color, the rise in the importance of extracurricular activities, and research conducted on the experience and development of college students. More recent trends influencing the field include the expansion and integration of developmental theory, refocusing on the learning experiences of students, and exploring the role and enhancement of student engagement. (http://www.myacpa.org/c12/career.htm

With this change in demographics came a need for change in the purpose of higher education and the creation of the student personnel movement and the field of student affairs as we know it today. As evidenced in many of the early documents, such as the Student Personnel Point of View (Student Affairs Administrators in Higher Education, 1937), and a subsequent 1949 revision of this document, institutions of higher learning were called on to provide services through functional areas to assist in the development of the "whole person." Many changes have occurred since that time in student demographics as well as in college and university management and organization. The practice of student conduct administration has changed with the times and in response to student needs. The remainder of this chapter discusses these contemporary needs.

The Needs of the Present Day: "Information Age Student"

The educational needs of postindustrial society in the 21st century are vastly different from those in the past. We are living in tumultuous times in which the world continues to change right before our eyes, and landmark events set the agenda for our work. Student conduct administration professionals are in a strategic position as they grapple with how to respond to the ills of society while at the same time convincing students that these ills may be overcome. There are days in which these tumultuous times may seem overwhelming; a snapshot of today's news speaks of a major international airport evacuation due to a bomb threat, sex abuse payouts by the Catholic Church, a teen killed in an auto accident while possibly text messaging a friend, an earthquake hitting Asia, a new invention in the works—a sneaker with a global positioning system (GPS) device, salmonella found in food, global warming, al Qaeda regrouping and intent on attacking the United States, immigration reform debated, and a 19-year-old charged in an online sex ring.

The chaotic and frenzied nature of our world has undoubtedly affected how individuals and families function. The chapters in this book on such topics as incivility on campus (chapter 11) and addressing student mental health (chapter 13) attest to the fact that student needs are at issue. Students, as with other citizens in the United States, live in a culture of fear. They are barraged with fear-producing media such as the headlines noted. It is natural to fear the things we cannot control. And more and more, students are feeling the impact of this perceived loss in control as world events are presented as violent and unstable.

Thomas (2004) describes our students as "special, sheltered, confident, team oriented, conventional, pressured and achieving." Chapter 10 speaks to the impact of technology on students. Student conduct administrators are well advised to note the social and ecological perspective of what affects human behavior and to take this into account when talking with students. Student bodies are more diverse than ever, and they present challenges that reflect the complexity of today's world. This demands that student conduct administrators go about their work with thoughtfulness and intention. While we cannot correct the ills of society, we can use education to our best advantage and help to instill hope within our students through building positive relationships with them during the student conduct process. Just as we ask our students to act as adults, so should those in the profession of student conduct administration. We have matured as a profession, and it is up to each individual within the profession to demand the respect that has been earned as we enter adulthood. Whether or not we like it, we must accept that our students will continue to look to us as a stabilizing force. They will follow our lead and place their trust and faith in our ability to guide them. As the late Melvene Draheim Hardee stated during an energetic lecture in a doctoral course, "dreams are what students are made of" (M. D. Hardee, personal communication, 1986). Fear can have an immobilizing impact on these dreams, and student conduct administrators are in a strategic position to empower students to overcome their fears and make their dreams come true.

References

Appleton, J. R., Briggs, C. M., & Rhatigan, J. J. (1978). *Pieces of eight: The rites, roles and styles of the dean by eight who have been there.* Portland, OR: NASPA.

Association for Student Judicial Affairs (ASJA). (1987). *ASJA constitution*. Retrieved July 2, 2007, from http://www.asjaonline.org/attachments/files/1/ASJAConstitution.pdf

Bordin, R. (1993). *Alice Freeman Palmer. The evolution of a new woman*. Ann Arbor: University of Michigan Press.

College Student Educators International (ACPA). *Considering a career in student affairs*. Retrieved July 3, 2007, from http:// www .myacpa .org/ c12/ career.htm

Evans, N. J., Forney, D., & Guido-DiBrito, F. (1998). *Student development in college: Theory, research and practice*. San Francisco: Jossey-Bass

Kerr, C. (1982). *The uses of the University* (3rd ed.). Cambridge, MA: Harvard University Press.

Rudolph, F. (1962). *The American college and university: A history*. New York: Knopf Publications in Education.

Sandeen, A., & Barr, M. (2006). *Critical issues for student affairs: Challenges and opportunities*. San Francisco: Jossey-Bass

Student Affairs Administrators in Higher Education (NASPA). (1937). *Student personnel point of view*. Retrieved July 2, 2007, from http://www.naspa.org/pubs/StudAff_1937.pdf

Thelin, J. R. (2004). *A history of American higher education*. Baltimore, Maryland: Johns Hopkins University Press.

Thomas, B. (2004). *Summary of "Millennials go to college."* Unpublished paper.

2

TEMPERAMENT FOR PRACTICE

The Effective Student Conduct Practitioner

William Fischer and Vaughn Maatman

What goes into making an effective student conduct practitioner? How would you describe the best temperament for practice—that combination of knowledge, skills, and attitudes—that leads to effectiveness?

Those questions and others in the same vein have been near the center of the student conduct profession and the Association of Student Judicial Affairs (ASJA), since their inception. Indeed, it is only because ASJA has insistently asked those questions and attempted answers for the last 20 years that we can begin to call what we do as student conduct practitioners a profession.

As is noted elsewhere in this book, student conduct practitioners stand in cross-currents. As the concept of *in loco parentis* wanes, and increased specialization in higher education and increased litigation surrounding student actions and behaviors increases, deans and directors responsible for responding to student conduct on their campuses find that they need to be adept educators attuned to student development, need to be knowledgeable about legal developments in higher education, and need to develop mediation and conflict resolution skills. Matters between accusing and accused students raise concerns about due process and fundamental fairness, confidentiality, and appropriate sanctioning, not to mention the appropriate involvement of parents and attorneys. Student conduct practitioners often find themselves at the intersections of competing value systems—institutional, legal, ethical, and individual. Our profession has evolved, thanks in no small measure to individuals and organizations that have attempted to describe effective function in those cross-currents and at those intersections. Prompted by behaviors on campus, cultural trends, and the development of case law that follows on those behaviors or trends, approaches to developing temperament and function have been articulated in a variety of ways.

The Donald D. Gehring Academy for Student Conduct Administration (named for the founder of ASJA) has provided education and training in basic and advanced competencies, and beginning and advanced mediation skills for student conduct practitioners. The basic competencies that have been identified through research and practice and must be learned and understood include the governance and environment of the institution in which the professional works, the "mechanics" of student conduct administration and operations, methods of adjudication of student conduct matters, the essential components of a comprehensive and well-written student code of conduct, professional ethics, student development theories, multiculturalism, and relevant laws, policies, and legal mandates affecting the profession.

As discussed in chapter 16, over time and with research and practice, we have come to understand what makes professionals effective in their practice. Examples include ensuring that campus hearing bodies reflect the diversity of their respective institutions; that basic fundamental values of fairness, respect, and integrity are affirmed by serving as the foundations of conduct processes; that cases are fully heard before being decided; that focusing on education and character development are critical in imposing sanctions; and that serving as role models for the behaviors we seek in our students, including respect for self and others, civility, integrity, and attentiveness, is among our most important educational and developmental roles.

This chapter attempts to synthesize experience from the field, literature, and the learning of the last 20 years from our profession about what constitutes the temperament of effective student conduct practitioners. A number of critical questions prompted this synthesis:

1. How is temperament defined?
2. How is effectiveness defined and measured for a student conduct practitioner?
3. To what extent does temperament—that combination of attitude, knowledge and skills—contribute to effectiveness?
4. Is the temperament inherent in some, or can it be developed in all?

The issue of developing temperament—the knowledge, skills, and attitudes that lend themselves to effectiveness in conduct administration —naturally leads to questions of education and preparation. What combination of philosophy, study, experience, personality, and reflection create the temperament of the successful student conduct practitioner? Perhaps more important, can we describe the temperament of the effective student conduct practitioner in terms of the *desired outcomes* of that education and experience? In short, what knowledge, skills, and attitudes are demonstrated by effective practitioners in the field?

Knowledge

When one thinks of the variety of tools needed for effectiveness as a practitioner in student conduct, knowledge might seem an obvious foundation. But the term "knowledge" is overarching and can encompass a variety of components, including formalized training and education received both inside and outside the classroom, experience at a variety of institutions, knowledge of self and of others, institutional cultures and mores, and gaining wisdom from listening to the stories and experiences of others, including colleagues and students.

In considering "formalized" training, a variety of options must be considered. Certainly, an advanced degree is required for most, if not all, positions in student conduct. A brief "scan" of the World Wide Web suggests that a master's or doctoral degree in student development or higher education administration or law—with field experience in student conduct administration—is a common requirement for most positions in student conduct administration. But as Blimling (2002) points out, most career student affairs administrators did not begin their college work intending to become a senior practitioner in the field. However, over the years, with the advent of law and policy considerations and their impact on the field, conduct administration as a subset of student affairs administration began to require individuals with degrees "appropriate" to the management of what was becoming a high-liability function within institutions. Thus, while the proper graduate degree is generally considered a prerequisite today, in years past one might have entered student affairs and student conduct work from a variety of undergraduate and master's preparation programs. Regardless of the degree attained, it remains vital that the student conduct practitioner have a working knowledge of legal, policy, developmental, and educational implications for the field. Beyond degree preparation, a multitude of seminars, workshops, and conferences can provide the requisite level of knowledge needed for effective practice.

As noted in chapter 1, the field of student conduct administration is a dynamic one. Therefore, continuing education, training, and development have now become essential to stay current with the changing demographics of the student population we serve, as well as best practices and legal developments in the field. One example of this is the increase in the number of individuals adopting conflict resolution programs and services and other alternative practices. Such alternatives have become invaluable in shaping and educating our students about violence prevention, understanding the dynamics of conflict, and how to resolve such conflict in meaningful and productive ways. Since many professionals in the field may lack sufficient education and training for such programs, formalized training programs in mediation and other practices are becoming popular vehicles for professionals who seek to incorporate such alternatives into their practice. For a more complete discussion of alternative forums of adjudication, see chapter 6.

Mediation training programs are only one example of the value of continuing education. It is also essential to stay current in the field through attending conferences, institutes, workshops, and seminars on a variety of topics sponsored by higher education associations. ASJA sponsors an annual conference and a summer academy in addition to other professional development opportunities. The academy has become well known in the field for offering basic training to new professionals in the critical competencies needed for effective practice. It also offers an advanced seminar focusing on relevant topics for the more senior professional, and a mediation training seminar for those professionals seeking knowledge of the mediation field.

Understanding student development theories is another necessary ingredient for those working with student behavioral issues. A central challenge of student conduct work often involves the dichotomy between the institutional community's standards of appropriate behavior and a student's understanding of and deviation from such standards. Appreciating where the student is in terms of his or her stage of development can be most helpful, not only in knowing the student's particular needs, but also in understanding how to help the student grow in an appropriately developmental manner. An example of this might involve helping a self-absorbed student offender move to an understanding and appreciation of the impact of his or her behavior on others in the living/learning community. Student development theories can be learned and understood during an individual's course of study in the typical master's or doctoral program in higher education administration. For those individuals working in the student conduct field who have an advanced degree in other disciplines (e.g., law), it is imperative to become educated about such theories by successfully completing a course on the subject or through other workshop or conference offerings.

As the U.S. population continues to become more culturally diverse, its institutional communities of higher education will experience the same population shifts. To achieve a positive and productive living and learning environment, student conduct practitioners will be required to have knowledge of and experience in working with such culturally diverse communities. Understanding what different individuals value, respective life stories, and the communication dynamics among different cultures will be critical in maintaining a welcoming and positive living and learning campus environment. The seasoned student conduct practitioner will need to understand the dynamics underlying the cross-cultural challenges that sometimes occur in such communities. Administrators will be expected to respond to such conflicts through educational and developmental interventions with students that assist them in better understanding and appreciating the richness represented by a culturally diverse community. Conduct administrators need to recognize that each time they interact with a student, this interface is a cross-cultural experience. Knowledge of and experience with such considerations will increasingly become a requirement for consideration in recruiting student conduct professionals. Such knowledge and experience can be attained through the formal education process and through continuing education seminars, institutes, workshops, conferences, and exposure to different cultures.

Wisdom—characterized by insight, sound judgment, reflection, and learning through time—is a form of knowledge that comes from a variety of sources. Work experience can offer one means of developing such knowledge. An individual with broad-based experience at both public and private institutions with large, medium, or small populations can bring enhanced wisdom to work at his or her current institution. Institutions seeking positive change may welcome individuals with such diverse experience, as they may bring new perspectives to designing and creating more appropriate systems, programs, and services in the administration of student affairs and of student conduct in particular. Such experience provides the opportunity to view situations through a wider lens and to discern more possibilities for solutions.

It is also possible that one might face adversity from fellow colleagues who are resistant to change or any form of restructure or new design for their operations. Such individuals typically are hesitant to step out of their "comfort zones." This can be detrimental to effecting positive change in an organization. A wise student conduct practitioner first seeks knowledge by learning about the culture and dynamics of the institution's community before introducing new ideas, programs, or services from prior experiences in other institutions. One cannot assume that what has worked at one institution will work at all institutions. The phrase, "one size fits all," does not apply to conduct administration. Many practitioners learn this either through their own experience or through seeking counsel and guidance in advance from professional colleagues.

Knowing an institution's mission, goals, and values is most helpful before deciding to join that community as a professional staff member. Such knowledge helps inform and guide the decision whether to accept a position and, therefore, to become a supportive community member to further the institution's mission and goals. Once there, a professional should seek to learn as much as possible about others in the community and how they work to accomplish the mission and goals. Familiarity with mission and goals will also be helpful when working with students and their behavioral issues. Educational dialogue with the student can focus on how one's behavior may be inconsistent with an institution's core values. The student then has the opportunity to reflect on such behavior and make a knowledge-based choice about whether to modify behavior to support the institution's mission or withdraw from the community, either voluntarily or involuntarily.

Self-knowledge is another critical ingredient for success as a student conduct practitioner. This includes the ability to identify one's strengths, areas of challenge, and limitations. Such self-awareness can serve as the foundation for growth and development in one's position—through mentoring, continuing education, or other development opportunities. Knowledge of one's core values is helpful in determining whether a particular institution is a good "fit" for that individual as a professional. Such knowledge is also helpful when working with students whose values may be inconsistent with your own. A student's behavior that is grounded in his or her core value system is difficult to change. It is important to understand this, and to recognize when your value system is incongruent with the student with whom you are interacting. Such knowledge can help you remain objective and fair by allowing you to understand where the student's thinking originates and where your own shadows and biases may exist. The ability to listen to oneself when feeling certain negative emotions, including frustration, discouragement, exhaustion, and impatience, is critical. Looking within yourself to determine the source of such emotion is an important step in learning to help students who may suffer similar feelings. Such feelings may be isolated incidents involving a negative interaction or broader reactions to the culture that surrounds us. Such feelings, in addition to being important barometers of mood, may reflect the need for "time out" for a brief interval, a vacation, or even a sabbatical. While we recognize such needs in our troubled students, we sometimes miss the same need in ourselves. It is also important to be aware of when such emotions may suggest that you are the wrong fit for the position or, more important, that you need to move in a different career direction or focus, whether it be student affairs, higher education, or an alternate career path.

Skills

The authors of this chapter cumulatively have decades of experience in the field and with ASJA. Yet, without fail, we come away from each conference or institute with the thought that there is an area of skill development in which we could use more work, or a new area that deserves our attention. The skills the modern student conduct practitioner requires comprise an almost endless list. Each area of knowledge implies at least one skill set, and each basic competency taught at the Gehring Academy prompts its own area of necessary skill development.

Here is where recognition of transferable skills becomes useful, especially for the individual new to the profession or to a particular administrative position. The following sections identify common "families" or broad categories of aptitudes or abilities the most seasoned and successful student conduct practitioners possess. These impressions are based on our own experiences and those of other colleagues with whom we have spoken over the years.

Collaboration

The practice of student conduct administration can be a lonely endeavor. Within a relatively new profession where theory and practice are evolving rapidly, even the best practitioners find themselves explaining the "why" or "how" of what they do to those less knowledgeable or less experienced or to those who take exception to the methods we use in our practice. In a society attuned to law, debate, and litigation, the student conduct practitioner stands in the midst of competing value systems, trying to resolve often heated issues without succumbing to the heat (Lancaster & Cooper, 1998). For this reason, student conduct practitioners must be skillful collaborators and bridge builders. The first family of skills therefore has to do with connecting in productive ways with others on campus, within the profession, and with our legal colleagues to engage in collaborative efforts to create campus climates where naming and discussing the values of the academy are the order of the day. Student conduct practitioners need to be able to skillfully engage others in such dialogue in a way that clarifies institutional values and makes discussing those values and addressing conduct issues a productive rather than a disruptive process. This means one has to assist in the creation of an ethical community that values a fundamentally fair conduct process and fair treatment within that process, even when the heat is on and others may be pushing for action that may not honor due process, fairness, development, and education. This is more than publishing a student handbook and conduct code so "everyone knows what the standards are." The most skillful of practitioners are those who build relationships with a diverse group of individuals on their campus who can subsequently serve as allies in the promotion of institutional values, ethical dialogue, and ethical treatment. The ability to enlist and grow the number of people on campus who believe they are stakeholders in creating a community of integrity is critical, not only to what happens in a student conduct office, but also to creating an educational environment that produces graduates who are prepared to enter workplaces and relationships as responsible citizens.

Cognitive Diversity

A second skill, critical to the first, is the ability to think in multiple frames and broadly about complex problems. This demonstrates an ability that reflects what Howard Gardner (1983) has termed cognitive diversity. In application to practice in student conduct work, it represents the ability to distinguish among and appropriately synthesize institutional values, policy, law, and ethical practice. This is a learned ability; for young or new professionals in our field, the overlap of values, ethics, policy, and law creates a blur that often prompts a "these are the regulations" approach to dealing with students and the temptation to shape any action simply to avoid litigation. The relationship between personal and institutional values, institutional policy, and the law is dynamic, with much pushing and pulling. We speak of "gray areas" in our practice, and it is incumbent upon us to define the shades of gray and what role values, policy, and law play in our practice. Where do they intersect? Where do they diverge? This implies again that the student conduct administrator needs to be able to articulate his or her institutional missions, personal and professional values, policies, and intersections with law—and each one needs to be able to articulate those intersections as he or she mentors younger staff, deals with students and faculty colleagues, and engages institutional presidents and institutional legal counsel.

An important ancillary to this skill is the ability to adapt and be flexible within a particular institution's culture and environment. This is more than knowing the differences among student conduct practices at various institutions. This has to do with knowing thoroughly one's own set of values and ethical expectations, understanding the *operational* culture of an institution—how things work and why—and adapting one's approach to function effectively with persons within that culture. It represents an ability to think about challenges in a broader way, relying not on a single intellectual approach but on a diversity of approaches and understanding this diversity when it appears in others.

Transformative Teaching

A third broad category of skills has to do with becoming a good educator. Volumes have been written on this topic, and workshops abound, but few skills within this family are basic, and without which the student conduct practitioner is bound to be frustrated and frustrating. Good education is connective and relational, akin to good mentoring or the best of friendships. It may sound like a cliché, but the ability to listen well is foundational. Careful listening does not just yield content, facts, and what happened or was said, but also uncovers fear, psychosocial or ethical underdevelopment, conflicts between truth and loyalty, and the need to acknowledge wrongdoing and be forgiven. Being heard in this way is powerful in itself. When coupled with the twin ability of skillfully prompting a transition from one perceptual context to another, of deepening and broadening understanding, and moving to more mature insight, listening becomes a tool for transformation and development.

By way of example, a colleague shared a conversation with a first-year male athlete who observed the hazing of another first-year teammate by older members of the team. The teammate was harmed by the hazing. In his own eyes, the student had to choose between sharing what he knew to protect another, thereby challenging team culture and potentially setting himself up to be ostracized, or protecting his teammates, and perhaps himself, by observing the code of silence that was a part of that team's culture. Obviously, this creates a classic dilemma between two competing values—loyalty and truth (Kidder, 2003). The student acknowledged that he was bothered by what happened and troubled by the power he gave his teammates over him, and he very much wanted to communicate how sorry he was for what happened to the student who was harmed. By careful listening, the professional colleague heard the psychosocial and ethical development issues involved, saw clearly the conflict between the student's own values and the team's, was able to perceive the emotions pulling the student in multiple directions, and understood the student's genuine need to "get it off his chest"—to confess, accept consequences, and set things right and repair relationships. The first-year student could certainly feel all of this, but could not organize it intellectually or articulate it. In a concerned and caring manner, the professional colleague helped the student see the situation in its multiple layers and nuances—not just from the perspective of feeling caught between two opposing forces, but from a variety of perspectives; ethical, emotional, developmental, interpersonal, and athletic, and framed the student's alternatives as a part of his education and preparation for a future where similar issues would come his way. In the end, by listening respectfully and carefully, and by gently and skillfully framing dilemmas and choices from several angles, this colleague facilitated a resolution for the first-year student and his teammates. Relief was palpable. A more mature commitment to responsible and courageous choices was made possible. A mere policy or law approach to this situation would not have sufficed; a linkage between careful listening and an ability to prompt transitions from one perspective to another was transformative.

Basic Competency

A fourth broad area is to develop skills in each of the "basic competency" knowledge and skill areas listed on page 15. The Training Institute of the Gehring Academy, offered annually, is a good way for new and seasoned professionals to acquire, refresh, and tune up their skills. Of particular note are the skills related to conflict resolution and mediation. Broadly speaking, the student conduct practitioner's job is about conflict resolution in a number of spheres; between parties, between individuals and a community, between competing value systems, and sometimes between oneself and others over matters of policy, law, or process. Conflict resolution and mediation encompass a number of useful abilities that are transferable to situations across the board in handling student conduct—skillful listening, attention to process, and identifying common values and common ground on which to build a compromise or agreement between aggrieved parties. Becoming skillful in the scrupulous application of fundamental fairness principles in the resolution process and listening carefully for and identifying out loud the collision of values or the underlying issues between parties locking horns often helps bring a disagreement into sharper and a more realistic focus. Skillfully helping parties zoom in on points of frustration and homing in on potential options and choices not only helps defuse highly charged disputes, but also empowers parties to take control of a conflict they may feel is beyond their influence. Skillfully mediating conflict may be among the most useful and effective tools in the practice of the conduct officer's craft.

Professional Maturity

It could be argued that the fifth skill area is both innate and the product of experience and practice. Certainly it is a sign of professional maturity. Mature professionals in the field are able to separate out personal feelings about someone or something to suspend judgment and remain objective. They can engage persons and problems deeply, and then "leave it at the office." As we have said, the student conduct practitioner invariably stands at the intersections of values, policies, behavior, individuals, and community. The conflicts at those intersections are complex, often emotional, laden with biases, and sometimes very heated. How and what is done is frequently scrutinized within one's institution and by external third parties such as parents or courts. At some point in his or her career, the student conduct practitioner is likely be threatened with legal action, to be involved in legal maneuvering, or to be the direct target of legal action. Keeping one's balance while keeping one's cool in these kinds of cross-currents can be challenging. It is harder still not to allow this kind of turmoil to drift over into one's personal life and relationships. Burnout in our field is a reality, and many of our most experienced practitioners move into other positions in student development/ student affairs prompted by what can be a significant stress load. Using friends and colleagues to sound out complex issues (while appropriately protecting confidentiality!) and to refresh perspective is vital. The most effective practitioners, and those who last in the field, are those who have nurtured the ability of deep engagement with people and problems, while maintaining the ability to remain objective in spite of temptations to the contrary, and who master the ability to separate professional and personal life in a way that maintains balance.

Temperament and Attitude

While some specialized knowledge and skills are critical, temperament and attitude may be at the heart of a student conduct practitioner's effectiveness for reasons we hope become clear in this section. For our purposes, we use the following definition of temperament and attitude: "The combination of mental, physical and emotional traits of a person; natural disposition" (http://dictionary.reference.com/browse/temperament). Temperament and attitude reflect one's state of mind involving beliefs and feelings and values and dispositions to act in certain ways.

Temperament and attitude are arguably inherent as they relate to possession of certain personality traits and characteristics that are either learned during the personal growth and maturation process or possessed on an innate level. However, we also believe temperament and attitude can be developed through experience gained as a practitioner, and through an understanding of student development theories and principles, learned both inside and outside of the classroom. For the reflective practitioner, over time practice provides the opportunity to learn from professional experiences, mistakes made, and observing other practitioners' traits and characteristics in pursuit of their own effectiveness.

Perhaps primary in the definition of temperament is a willingness to stand at the intersection of conflicting value and emotions and, with fortitude, attempt to reconcile those differences through the application of a particular institution's values and standards of conduct. Good practitioners find such conflict interesting and learn not to take such difference or conflict personally. Of course, practitioners asked to act in ways that violate their own deeply held convictions have a longer-term professional career decision to make. But in the everyday give and take of contradiction, the practitioner must be predisposed to see difference and conflict as a place where education can occur, and to see such challenges as a healthy part of the change and growth process. Those who remain conflicted and view adversity as a negative phenomenon do not last long in this field. Those who do remain in the field demonstrate a *desire* to hold values in tension, which provides a reasonable check and balance *and* clarity in the conduct decision-making process. This requires clarity of one's own values and ethical courage while standing at that intersection of conflict. This is what Parker Palmer discusses in referencing Niels Bohr's argument on behalf of the power of paradox—the power to hold competing ideas in tension—both/and rather than either/or—in the pursuit of truth (Palmer, 1998).

A helpful exercise in this regard is what Robert Nash, of the University of Vermont, describes as a pedagogical tool he uses regularly when teaching:

1. First find the truth in what you oppose.
2. Find the error in what you espouse.
3. Then, and only then, declare the truth in what you espouse and the error in what you oppose (Nash, 2002).

Such an exercise helps students see that you, the practitioner, are fair and balanced in your approach and prompts them to be the same.

A second useful attitude is a toleration of ambiguity in the pursuit of clarity. Given that one needs to be committed to holding values in tension, clarity can sometimes be elusive. With students, who often see things dualistically, or who tend to resolve matters in an either/or fashion, learning tolerance for ambiguity from a seasoned practitioner is a valuable lesson. A toleration of ambiguity is a balancing process founded in the commitment to suspend judgment until a decision is required. To that end, editions of the ASJA Law and Policy Report authored by Gary Pavela (2002), one of the very wise and seasoned men in our field, always end with a quote from Alfred P. Murrah: "Hear the case before you decide it."(Pavela, personal communication).

Such a toleration of ambiguity and suspension of judgment requires intentionality in ensuring that an individual is treated with fairness, dignity, and respect, regardless of the alleged infraction or the outcome. Intentionality in this regard provides opportunities for individuals to present and share their stories and perspectives. We advocate regularly, during or at the end of any conversation about conduct with students, asking, "Do you feel you have been heard? Do you think you have been treated fairly?" The willingness to ask for and receive feedback indicates a predisposition to treat others as one would like to be treated and demonstrates a commitment to fairness.

Empathy—the desire and ability to stand in another's shoes—and humility—the importance of acknowledging limitations or acknowledging mistakes and learning from them—are twin attitudes in the face of complexity that enable the practitioner to remain approachable and to be perceived as what a colleague used to describe as "caringly human." This includes the willingness to second-guess oneself, to be a "compassionate doubter" in spite of temptations or pressures to behave otherwise. This allows one to focus on the holistic development of an individual through education (including appropriate consequences) and, when appropriate, to extend mercy to problem students. As one of the authors of this chapter regularly reminds himself, "If we ever get to the point where we cannot extend another chance or cannot question our own decisions, it's time to find something else to do."

Additionally, one needs to have a predisposition to find developing the competencies of our field an interesting and engaging process. This requires a commitment to one's personal *and* professional growth, for the linkages between these things when discussing temperament cannot be overstressed. In a field that is rapidly evolving, our best colleagues have a drive to discover and develop the best practices, and to do so with an empathy and humility in collegial relations, too. It's what makes membership in ASJA and attendance at its conferences exciting and refreshing.

Finally, as noted before, the burnout in our field—where standing at the intersections of competing value systems, where a toleration of ambiguity and suspension of judgment is required, where empathy and humility communicate fairness and humanness—is high. Two additional traits are required. One needs courage under fire, an ability to stand strong in times of adversity and pressure from a variety of constituents, both political and nonpolitical in nature, coupled with persistence in the face of discouragement. Courage and persistence are born of hope in the ability of persons to change and grow when there are signs to the contrary. It is vitally important to find ways to sustain that hope in oneself and one's work, and to nurture that hope in colleagues within one's institution and within our field.

Reflective Practice

It is impossible to overstate the importance of reflection in our work as conduct officers. We are challenged to reflect on our beliefs, on the vitality of our knowledge, on the development and artful use of our skills, and on how such reflection can help in further nurturing the attitudes that sustain us for the long haul. In developing their reflective judgment model, King and Kitchener (1994), suggest that difficult decisions require a synthesis of abilities. One should use critical thinking, along with experience, study, and reflection, to understand and to make decisions in complex situations with inherently competing values. A reflective practice is, in short, exercising reflective judgment as an opportunity to assess what we as professionals know (and do not know), what we intuit, where this knowing comes from, and in what context this knowing becomes a truth that we can rely on in the face of challenging and difficult decisions. Without reflection, there can be no critical skills and abilities in any meaningful sense. We might possess certain tools, but without reflection, without the time to process what we experience juxtaposed against prior knowledge and beliefs, these tools become mechanical and no better than a simplistic formula for moving from one step to another without real understanding of how we arrived at our final destination as decision makers. Worse, the absence of reflection, so often typical of the students we see in conduct work, makes any guidance we offer to these students hollow and duplicitous—virtually telling students to "do as we say, not as we do." Students easily detect such duplicity in our work, which makes everything else we seek to accomplish meaningless in their eyes.

Conclusion

Further chapters explore the critical competency areas about which student conduct practitioners must be knowledgeable through education and professional experience as well as current issues affecting the field. This chapter has focused on the practitioner as an individual, discussing the temperament—that combination of knowledge, skills, and attitudes—needed to guide and direct the individual to maximize the potential for success in the field.

The knowledge component is developed through formal education, continuing education, and the practice itself. Such a component also requires (1) respect and appreciation for wisdom, gleaned through one's own professional experiences and learning from others' experiences; (2) being attuned to the inner self and the variety of emotions that one may feel and experience during practice; and (3) more important, knowing how to manage such emotions and what they might mean in terms of one's own growth and development.

The skill set can be built on the knowledge base that serves as a foundation. The ability to work collaboratively on campus and build relationships becomes critical for success, since it will create a supportive environment for professional success in the position. Learning and being comfortable with the shades of gray where institutional values, law and policy issues, and ethical dimensions often converge is important when analyzing particular behaviors. Knowing when and how to seize on the teachable moment, along with appropriate educational content, creates precision in the practice. In addition, professional maturity—obtained through consistent practice over time—makes for a seasoned and skilled practitioner.

Finally, taken with the need for reflective practice, the attitudinal aspects of temperament certainly play an important role on the continuum for success. The desire to educate students and develop character, the ability to be empathetic, manage conflict, tolerate ambiguity, and embrace values of fairness, dignity, and respect—these are just a few components encompassing the disposition most likely to be successful in the field.

A final question arises: how do we assess our effectiveness? Can it be measured? The answer is yes. Assessment measures that quickly come to mind come from the conventional approaches that include internal campus reviews and retention of consultants external to the university to facilitate the review process—using perhaps a set of defined standards (such as the Council for Advancement of Standards in Higher Education, as one example). But perhaps the best measure of assessment comes from speaking directly with those individuals who have personal experience with a student conduct office and its professional staff. If they were asked, What would your colleagues and constituencies on campus say of you and your department?

Would they perceive a system where integrity and consistency are grounded core values—reflected in both the department and its professional staff? What would the student and his or her parent say? Were they treated with respect, dignity, and fairness, even in light of an adverse decision? The answers to these and other similar questions may provide the best insight in assessing our own individual impact and effectiveness in this field.

H. Jackson Brown Jr. some years ago became known for what some might have viewed as a simplistic, little book of platitudes. As is often the case, there is wisdom in the most simplistic ideas. Paraphrasing one of Brown's ideas provides excellent guidance to the kind of temperament that leads to successful conduct practice: Practice so that when your students think of fairness and integrity, they think of you (Brown, 2007). At the end of our careers, no finer measure of our temperament and fitness for our work could be found than to hear such words from the students we serve.

References

Association for Student Judicial Affairs (ASJA). (2007). Retrieved July 20, 2007, from http://asjaacademy.tamu.edu/Curriculum.htm#Training_Institute

Blimling, G. (2002). Reflections on career development among student affairs leaders. In J. Dalton & M. McClinton (Eds.), *The art and practical wisdom of student affairs leadership. New Directions for Student Services* (pp. 27–36). San Francisco: Jossey-Bass.

Brown, H. (2007). Retrieved July 20, 2007, from http://thinkexist.com/quotation/live_so_that_when_your_children_think_of_fairness/152997.html

Gardner, H. (1983). *Frames of mind: The theory of multiple intelligences.* New York: Basic Books.

Kidder, R. (2003). *How good people make tough choices.* New York: HarperCollins.

King, P., & Kitchener, K. (1994). *Developing reflective judgment.* San Francisco: Jossey-Bass.

Lancaster, J., & Cooper. D. (1998). Standing at the intersection: Reconsidering the balance in administration. *New Directions for Student Services, 82,* 95–106.

Nash, R. (2002). *"Real world" ethics: Frameworks for educators and human service professionals* (2nd ed.). New York: Teachers College Press.

Palmer, P. (1998). *The courage to teach.* San Francisco: Jossey-Bass.

Pavela, Gary. (2002). Ten principles for members of student conduct hearing boards. *ASJA Law and Policy Report, 73.*

3

DEMYSTIFYING GOVERNANCE

The Influential Practitioner

Felice Dublon

How much interest is there in examining *governance structures* and *learning environments* in higher education? A recent search on Amazon's website yielded a list of over 800 and 1,400 books, respectively. An online query of higher education's familiar search engine, ERIC (Educational Resources Information Center), generated more than 4,000 results. Given the magnitude of documented resources and the specific focus of this book on contemporary student conduct issues, no determination of one perfect structure can be expected. Instead, the question is, how can we as practitioners working with students best identify and then navigate the structure within which we work?

As context for understanding the role of governance, a review of applicable organizational theory is followed by a brief account of how the concept of governance in higher education evolved in the United States, and how that evolution was often shaped by student conduct issues.

Despite the obvious interest in the study of governance as the process by which power is understood, it may be far less critical to achieving an understanding of how colleges actually affect students. Instead, it may well be the long-term integration of environmental assessment into campus planning that enables those who manage student conduct issues to harness this knowledge and build communities that promote positive behaviors.

The Unique Structure That Defines Educational Organizations

Most of us recognize governance on our own campuses as "[t]he process or art with which scholars, students, teachers, administrators, and trustees associated together in a college or university establish and carry out the rules and regulations that minimize conflict, facilitate their collaboration, and preserve essential 'individual freedom'" (Corson, 1960, pp. 12–13).

A more provocative and perhaps more descriptive perspective is argued by Robert Birnbaum (1988), who explains how institutions of higher education differ from other organizations through governance, which he defines as,

> [t]he structures and processes through which institutional participants interact with and influence each other and communicate with the larger environment. A governance system is an institution's answer—at least temporarily—to the enduring question that became a plaintive cry during the campus crisis in the late 1960s and early 1970s: "Who's in charge here?" (p. 4)

He goes on to explain how American colleges and universities may well be the most paradoxical of organizations: "to at least some extent our colleges and universities are successful *because* they are poorly managed, at least as *management* is often defined in other complex organizations" (p. 4).

Earlier, Cohen and March (1974) portrayed academic organizations as "organized anarchies," describing the institutional environment as a place where no one person or group had much power, where each person makes decisions autonomously, and

> [t]eachers decide if, when, and what to teach. Students decide if, when, and what to learn. Legislators and donors decide if, when, and what to support . . . . The "decisions" of the system are a consequence produced by the system but intended by no one and decisively controlled by no one. (pp. 33–34)

Baldridge, Curtis, Ecker, and Riley (1977) contend that unlike the well-organized bureaucracy or the academic organization modeled on consensus building, the organized anarchy is one where,

[l]eaders are relatively weak and decisions are made by individual action. Since the organization's goals are ambiguous, decisions are often the by-products of unintended and unplanned activity. In such fluid circumstances, presidents and other institutional leaders serve primarily as catalysts or facilitators of an ongoing process. . . . They do not command, but negotiate. (p. 131)

In his analysis of complex academic organizations, Karl Weick (1976) describes such anarchies in the context of "loosely coupled systems." In such an analysis, it is important for student affairs' practitioners to realize that

> in a loosely coupled system there is more room available for self-determination by the actors. If it is argued that a sense of efficacy is crucial for human beings, then a sense of efficacy might be greater in a loosely coupled system with autonomous units than it would be in a tightly coupled system where discretion is limited. (p. 41)

For anyone working within higher education, such thought-provoking assessment certainly elicits a nod of understanding. We recognize that to function successfully in such a setting, one must be comfortable with ambiguity, challenged by complexity, and intrigued by the human condition. So, too, we trust that the effort—the hours, the anxiety, the sacrifices inherent in most student affairs' roles—will be rewarded as we, in our role as educators, challenge students to share in the responsibility of their learning and, ultimately, their transition to global inhabitants. It should also produce a certain sense of relief that despite the existence of formal, organizational structures and shifts in governance, the individual determined to make a difference has the power to effect change.

The Impact of Students on Governance

No history of governance would be complete without reference to Brubacher and Rudy's *Higher Education in Transition* (1976), in which we are reminded that changes in college governance have often been inextricably tied to issues of student conduct and preparation for civility.

> The colonial American college was in many ways a blood brother to its English model. Like the latter, it upheld the tradition of a prescribed liberal-arts curriculum, based upon a primarily classical preparatory course;

it was more deeply concerned with the forming of character than the fostering of research; it placed great value on a residential pattern of life for students; and it was concerned primarily with training a special elite for community leadership. (p. 23)

The authors go on to describe Thomas Jefferson's notable presidency at the University of Virginia as one characterized by student-led rebellions, a result of his support of an experiment with student self-governance. After the Civil War, the movement away from rigorous discipline toward treating students as young adults resulted in fewer such uprisings (Brubacher & Rudy, 1976, p. 55). Yet, college governance structures were created to manage student conduct in an environment separate from external entities.

Bickel and Lake (1999) argue convincingly that, before 1960, *in loco parentis* located authority in the university, not in the courts and certainly not with students. In examining how contemporary approaches to student behavior evolved, they point out that, "in its *disciplinary* role, the university was like a family—a father—to its students. It gave them guidance and set rules and enforceable boundaries" (p. 30). Furthermore,

The demise of *in loco parentis* was hastened by the fact that university life in the 1960s (and 1970s) became a focal point of the major social issues of the time. This is because the 1960s civil rights movement raised questions of basic civil rights and the bargains struck between universities and students. (p. 36)

Many of those in student affairs leadership positions today recall the upheaval of the 1960s and how, as either participants in or observers of history, students formed their views on the importance of collaboration in building community based on those experiences. After the sit-ins initiated through civil rights proponents in the South, after the free speech movement in fall of 1964, and after the escalation and eventual denouement of the war in Vietnam, those faculty and staff now responsible for overseeing the professional practice of student affairs were faced with the challenge of balancing students' rights and responsibilities in a context that now included external scrutiny from the media, government, family, and governing boards.

Today, the management skills required to address growing interest on the part of all constituents need retooling as shared governance structures—

where faculty, staff, students, parents, and governing boards work collaboratively—must compete with an emphasis on corporate practices, with
pressure for greater accountability and identifiable revenue streams. With
many institutions either reliant on tuition or susceptible to state-regulated
legislative initiatives, what kinds of governance structures can we anticipate
in the future? And perhaps more important, how will those structures affect
our readiness to address student conduct on campus?

An almost universal and reassuring response suggests that the opportunity to operate successfully within any structure is possible and that

> [t]he relationship of the student affairs organization to the institutional or-
> ganization as a whole is very important, but it is not as critical to the suc-
> cess of student affairs as the relationships, coalitions, and cooperative
> programs that can be developed. Student affairs does not become effective
> on a campus as a result of the power arrangements described on an organi-
> zational chart; it earns its role by successfully accomplishing tasks deemed
> important to the institution. (Sandeen, 1996, p. 436)

Beyond Governance: Know Your Students, Impact Your Campus

In 1977, Alexander Astin published his seminal text, *Four Critical Years*,
which has since been called the most frequently cited work in the higher
education literature. In his follow-up text, *What Matters in College? Four
Critical Years Revisited* (1993), Astin presents an important sequel study of
how students change in college—and discloses how colleges can foster student development. Based on a study of more than 20,000 students, 25,000
faculty members, and 200 institutions, the book shows how variables such
as academic programs, faculty, and student peer groups affect the college
experience. Astin studies more than 190 environmental characteristics of institutions and explains how these attributes can influence everything from
students' self-concept, behavior, values, and academic development, to their
overall satisfaction with college life. He further submits that governance
structures, in and of themselves, are not the primary determinant of outcomes. Astin's research suggests that the traditional model of undergraduate
education, based on the British model, fosters student-to-student and student-
to-faculty interactions and

leads to favorable educational results across a broad spectrum of cognitive and affective outcomes and in most areas of student satisfaction. Perhaps most important, however, is the finding that institutional *structure*, as such, is not the key ingredient; rather, it is the kinds of peer groups and faculty environments that tend to emerge under these different structures. (p. 413)

His findings of particular interest to those working directly with students on conduct issues, concluded that

the student's peer group is the single most potent source of influence on growth and development during the undergraduate years . . . students' values, beliefs, and aspirations tend to change in the direction of the dominant values, beliefs, and aspirations of the peer group. (p. 398)

Furthermore, "next to the peer group, the faculty represents the most significant aspect of the student's undergraduate development" (p. 410).

By far the strongest environmental effect on student satisfaction with faculty involves the environmental measure Student Orientation of the Faculty . . . the item content that would be associated with this high score [includes] . . . faculty are interested in students' academic problems, faculty are interested in students' personal problems . . . and there are frequent opportunities for student-faculty interaction. (p. 281)

An interpretation of Astin's findings should not, of course, suggest a dismissal of the role of governance; rather, one can derive some assurance from the research that demonstrates the primary impact of collaborations among all parties. His research on environmental effects and their impact on student outcomes is also useful in any discussion of student conduct outcomes. It is not surprising that the lowest levels of satisfaction result from regulations governing campus life, along with almost all of the support services typically associated with student affairs: academic advising, career counseling, financial, and job placement (p. 310).

In 1991, Pascarella and Terenzini published a synthesis of over 2,600 studies on college impact, followed by their 2005 review of the research on the impact of college on students. Their conclusions are closely aligned with Astin's findings:

Critical thinking, analytic competencies, and general intellectual development thrive in college environments that emphasize close relationships and frequent interaction between faculty and students as well as faculty concern about student growth and development. . . . Student perceptions that faculty members care about them and about teaching, as well as faculty accessibility to students, all promote persistence and degree completion even after adjustments for a variety of precollege characteristics, including ability. (p. 600)

They also refer to a

growing body of empirical support for the proposition . . . that students change in holistic ways and that these changes have their origins in multiple influences in both the academic and nonacademic domains of students' lives. The research published since 1990 persuades us more than ever that students' in- and out-of-class lives are interconnected in complex ways we are only beginning to understand. (p. 603)

Building Communities That Promote Positive Behaviors

What assumptions can be made vis-à-vis the influence of college governance and environments on student conduct? How can those working with students on conduct issues, in roles ranging from student conduct administrator to dean of students, from faculty hearing panel member to faculty member engaged in the classroom, interpret their own academic organization and their unique climate of learning to influence student behavior? If the research shows that the lowest levels of student satisfaction with college stem from regulations governing campus life, what options exist to both change perception and positively impact behavior?

College Impact Research Shows That Faculty and Student Affairs' Connectivity and Involvement Are Key to Everything From Student Persistence to Satisfaction.

The research is replete with references to the importance of collaboration. Within the student affairs' profession, documents, such as the American College Personnel Association's *The Student Learning Imperative: Implications for Student Affairs* (1996), affirm the central role student affairs' educators play in the intentional process of active learning. It assumes that greater student involvement yields greater student learning and success.

Student affairs professionals attempt to make "seamless" what are often perceived by students to be disjointed, unconnected experiences by bridging organizational boundaries and forging collaborative partnerships with faculty and others to enhance student learning. (p. 3)

Steffes and Keeling (2006) drive home the importance of "respectful" collaboration between academic and student affairs educators, saying,

> both the unconscious processing of new material and the intentional or happenstance application and testing of knowledge will, more likely than not, occur outside the classroom and laboratory, in the active context of students' lives. Thinking separately of curriculum and co-curriculum has only administrative value; it is, in fact, counterproductive to continue working with those terms and the assumptions that underlie them. (p. 70)

Although not often mentioned as representative of collaboration, the disciplinary hearing panel comprised of students, faculty, and staff is most certainly a model. Student participants engage directly with faculty and staff on an even playing field, challenging their peers and often examining and affirming their own values. These students also become ambassadors for change, not only as opinion leaders among their fellow students but also as alumni who, with time, reflect on the value of their college education taken as a whole.

Citizenship Can Be Taught.

Gary Pavela, the former director of judicial programs at the University of Maryland and a widely respected authority on college student behavior, recommends how educators can promote better values and subsequently better conduct by students:

- Values are formed in communities, especially communities with a purpose.
- Truth and virtue can be affirmed, even in a skeptical age.
- A commitment to civility—and the self-restraint essential to civility—serves an additional underlying purpose: happiness.
- Civility is learned by instruction, and by example.
- Civility is promoted when values and good manners are discussed and affirmed—especially by peers.

- Civility is developed and enhanced by cooperative action (1997, pp. 601–603).

Twenty years ago, the National Association of Student Personnel Administrators (NASPA) (1987) issued a statement on the 50th anniversary of *The Student Personnel Point of View*. The document affirmed again that citizenship should be taught:

> A democracy requires the informed involvement of citizens. Citizenship is complex; thus, students benefit from a practical as well as an academic understanding of civic responsibilities. Active participation in institutional governance, community service, and collective management of their own affairs contributes significantly to students' understanding and appreciation of civic responsibilities. (p. 11)

Recognize That Assessment Is Most Useful When Viewed as the Convergence of Intuition and Empiricism.

In a recent interview, J. Bryant, senior director of retention solutions, and D. Trites, senior consultant at Noel-Levitz, summarized what they had learned about the power of data-driven decision making through their work with over 500 college clients each year:

- Data derived from student surveys give campus leaders the confidence to focus on what matters to students and helps them prioritize their decisions.
- When raw data are examined within the campus context of ideas and intuition, they become information. When information is used to make improvements, it becomes knowledge and becomes a powerful tool for doing well.
- Shared with college trustees, data and the recommendations resulting from their analysis encourage additional dialogue in a setting where, "what gets measured, gets done."
- Over time, if the data result in action, students will perceive the institution as taking them seriously, that their views were valued, yielding higher levels of satisfaction and engagement, both proxies for learning (personal communication, April 10, 2007).

If the use of survey data is equated with the science portion of the equation, observational practices may be viewed as the "art." An excellent example of how keen examination can unearth the essence of a campus can be found in Loren Pope's *Colleges That Change Lives* (2006), in which the author's observations of the "look and feel" of 40 exemplary college profiles reveal the importance placed on community and collaborative practices. This type of descriptive technique is available to anyone interested in communicating his or her perceptions of the college experience on his or her respective campus, particularly if student input is given voice.

As Upcraft and Schuh (1996) state,

> since each student has a unique environment, there is no way to know how the environment has facilitated or inhibited an individual's growth and development without having a discussion with that student . . . the simplest of all, and perhaps most effective, being to talk to individual students and listen to what they have to say. This approach is time-consuming . . . but one can learn the most about the lives of students by talking with them. (p. 188)

Embrace Creativity, Originality, Critical Thinking, Intellectual Curiosity.

There is great latitude in addressing student behavior on one's campus. We are remarkably free to modify or reform how student behavior is governed according to whatever set of values we choose to pursue, including rules and regulations and responsibilities that govern student conduct. Although state, federal, and municipal law for both public and private institutions must be incorporated, how that is accomplished should take into serious consideration an assessment of one's mission, culture, and climate. A useful exercise is to review the conduct codes of comparable colleges with key staff, faculty, and students, then proceed through a case study using that code to simulate a conduct issue on campus and assess its appropriateness and acceptance by the community. Ed Stoner's chapter in this book guides you through this process and offers more useful hints in using your code effectively.

Another particularly useful guide to writing a tailored code of conduct is Stoner and Lowery's (2004) *Navigating Past the "Spirit of Insubordination": A Twenty-First Century Model Student Conduct Code*, in which the authors offer a model student conduct code that makes a compelling case for a commonsense approach to the student disciplinary process. The private college can use the code to reinforce those values most important to its mission without the encumbrances faced by the public sector. Assuming the process is neither "arbitrary nor capricious," the private school dean or student conduct administrator can structure everything from how a student is informed about his or her misconduct to who is involved in the process. Beyond the essential need for fairness, the participants can use this encounter with a student to reveal their commitment to the institution and its values and to confront inappropriate behavior.

Inform Students That They Share Responsibility for Their Success.

Not unlike the mission statement that encapsulates the overall goals of an institution, so too, a statement on shared responsibility can set the stage for conversations with students about their conduct. Such a statement also emphasizes the central function of the college, one that stresses educational values, as opposed to legal standards. Reminding students involved in conduct cases that the creation of a climate of learning is a shared responsibility characteristic of student self-governance minimizes the perception that students are about to "go to trial" or "go before a judge."

What follows are two examples of student handbook statements that introduce students to their student rights and responsibilities. They illustrate how the unique characteristics of each institution—one private, one public—convey an option available to any college wishing to communicate its core values.

Example One: Private College

The School of the Art Institute of Chicago is a diverse community of artists and scholars that celebrates both individual freedom and a strong sense of shared community values and responsibility. Students who enter this intellectual and social community make a commitment to an exchange of ideas and acknowledge that living and working within a community requires compromise and sensitivity to others. A strong community depends on respect for the rights of others, considerate behavior, and good judgment. Students are expected to maintain high standards of personal conduct; behavior should reflect maturity and respect for the rights of all members of the community. The School of the Art Institute of Chicago affirms that the responsibility to create an environment conducive to the freedom to learn is shared by all members of the academic community. These policies and procedures were developed to support such learning. (The School of the Art Institute of Chicago, 2007, p. 33)

Example Two: Public University

To be a student at Illinois State University, we expect you to recognize the strength of personal differences, while respecting institutional values. You are encouraged to think and act for yourself, as that is the purpose of higher education. However, we expect you to understand that the University has non-negotiable values in which it believes strongly. These values include: Character, Conscience, Civility, Citizenship, An Appreciation of Diversity, Individual and Social Responsibility.

These values are the hallmark of the University, and will be protected diligently. Each person has the right and ability to make decisions about his or her own conduct. Just as importantly, each person has the responsibility to accept the consequences of those decisions. When individual behavior conflicts with the values of the University, the individual must choose whether to adapt his or her behavior to meet the needs of the community or to leave the University. This decision, among others, assists each person to determine who he or she is with respect to the rest of society. (Illinois State University Code of Student Conduct, 2002, p. 2)

Trust Students. Trust Yourself.

Even with more data than any civilization has ever had to work with, no one can accurately predict what the student culture will look like in the future. Information gathered from both observational and empirical assessments, however, can better prepare us if it is considered in terms of what students themselves are telling us. And what they say is that the cumbersome rules and regulations burdening many college and university conduct codes are obstacles to hearing the more substantive issues facing them. Often, the opportunity to hear from students comes during either the investigation of misconduct or the student conduct hearing process itself, when they reveal much about the origins of their difficulties. This can also become the one chance to change a behavior. Although the desired result—an educational process that alters behavior—does not always occur, the school once again clarifies its position and its commitment to fundamental principles of fairness.

In the private college setting, for example, codes of student conduct, while often emulating public school codes, need not be constrained by constitutional restrictions. Thus the distrust in systems, particularly judicial and legal systems as portrayed recently in the popular press, can be avoided if a college does not rely on its onerous mechanics to deal with the student condition.

In a recent conversation with two past presidents of ASJA, I asked for their perspectives on the importance of trust. Dr. E. Baldizan, director of the Jean Nidetch Women's Center at the University of Nevada, Las Vegas, and Dr. D. Gregory, assistant professor of higher education at the College of William and Mary (personal communication, March 22, 2007), both remarked on the need to be in sync with their own values, to take what Dr. Baldizan called, "harmonious action," or project leadership consistent with ones' own values. For those responsible for student conduct issues, such action thus sets the tone for developing open, honest relationships. As Dr. Baldizan summarized, "Relationships that resonate with core values are premised on first recognizing those values; they set the foundation for trust-building, a powerful and critical cornerstone that enables us to both hear the issues and the voices of our students" (personal communication, June 25, 2007).

As F. Scott Fitzgerald (1945), aptly stated in *The Crack-Up*, "the test of a first-rate intelligence is the ability to hold two opposed ideas in the mind at the same time, and still retain the ability to function." Perhaps nowhere is Fitzgerald's wisdom needed more than when climate and governance converge, when the college is faced with a high-profile case involving a student, a case that typically draws unwanted media attention, places the institution under intense scrutiny by constituents ranging from governing boards to parents, and raises questions about the overall management of the institution. Elements of such cases typically include student misconduct that may or may not violate federal, state, or local law; misunderstanding of the institution's code of conduct and the relationship of that code to external legal proceedings; misunderstanding of why laws such as Family Educational Rights and Privacy Act of 1974 (FERPA) prevent disclosure and, in tandem, the assumption that the institution is hiding information; disbelief that the institution could not control the student or students, specifically those formally responsible for student conduct; questioning of all decision making, including everything from why the student was admitted to the decision to expel the student—or permit him or her to remain. The reaction to and subsequent management of a crisis draws attention to how an institution is governed and whether that authoritative body has made the "right" decision.

Issues centered on student behaviors almost always force one to juggle emergent facts, opinions, and expectations in the context of providing all involved with a meaningful, educational moment. The best-prepared professional is one who can sit comfortably with conflicting information while simultaneously directing a process perceived as fair and nonjudgmental. This state of being requires confidence not only in one's own decision-making process but also in one's understanding of the campus and whether a working trust has been established with students, faculty, and staff colleagues allowing all parties to seek common ground.

Which brings us back to the question, who is in charge? Regardless of your institutional role or the particular governance structure regulating your campus, with a desire to collaborate and the intellectual will to positively affect student behavior, the answer, in no small part, can be—you.

References

American College Personnel Association. (1996). *The student learning imperative: Implications for student affairs.* Washington, DC: Author. Retrieved May 27, 2007, from www.myacpa.org/sli/sli.htm

Astin, A. W. (1993). *What matters in college? Four critical years revisited.* San Francisco: Jossey-Bass.

Baldridge, V., Curtis, D., Ecker, G., & Riley, G. (1977). Alternative models of governance in higher education. In M. Christopher Brown II (Ed.), *Organization and governance in higher education* (pp. 128–142). Boston: Pearson Custom Publishing.

Bickel, R. D., & Lake, P. F. (1999). *The rights and responsibilities of the modern university: Who assumes the risks of college life?* Durham, NC: Carolina Academic Press.

Birnbaum, R. (1988). *How colleges work.* San Francisco: Jossey-Bass.

Brubacher, J., & Rudy, W. (1976). *Higher Education in transition: A history of American colleges and universities, 1636–1976* (3rd ed.). New York: Harper and Row.

Cohen, M. D., & March, J. G. (1974). *Leadership and ambiguity: The American college president.* New York: McGraw-Hill.

Corson, J. J. (1960). *Governance of college and universities.* New York: McGraw-Hill.

Fitzgerald, F. S. (1945). The crack-up. In E. Wilson (Ed.), *The crack-up with other uncollected pieces, note-books, and unpublished letters* (pp. 69–84). New York: New Directions.

Illinois State University Code of Student Conduct. (2002, July 1). Retrieved June 25, 2007, from www.deanofstudents.ilstu.edu/downloads/crr/code-of-student-conduct.pdf

National Association of Student Personnel Administrators (1987). *A perspective on student affairs.* Washington, DC: Author. Retrieved May 27, 2007, from www.naspa.org/pubs/StudAff_1987.pdf

Pascarella, E. T., & Terenzini, P. T. (2005). *How college affects students: A third decade of research* (vol. 2). San Francisco: Jossey-Bass.

Pavela, G. (1997). *Synfax Weekly Report, 9*(18), 601–603.

Pope, Loren. (2006). *Colleges that change lives.* New York: Penguin Books.

Sandeen, A. (1996). Organization, functions, and standards of practice. In S. R. Komives, D. B. Woodard, & Associates (Eds.), *Student services: A handbook for the profession* (3rd ed., pp. 435–457). San Francisco: Jossey-Bass.

The School of the Art Institute of Chicago Student Handbook 2007–2008. (2007). Retrieved September 3, 2007, from www.saic.edu/life/policies/index.html#handbook

Steffes, J., & Keeling, R. P. (2006). Creating strategies for collaboration. In R. P. Keeling (Ed.), *Learning reconsidered 2* (p. 70). Washington, DC: Authors.

Stoner, E. N., II, & Lowery, J. W. (2004). Navigating past the "spirit of insubordination": A twenty-first century model student conduct code. *The Journal of College and University Law, 31*(1).

Upcraft, M. L., & Schuh, J. H. (1996). *Assessment in student affairs.* San Francisco: Jossey-Bass.

Weick, K. (1976). Educational organizations as loosely coupled systems. In M. Christopher Brown II (Ed.) (2000), *Organization and governance in higher education* (pp. 36–49). Boston: Pearson Custom Publishing.

4

REVISING YOUR STUDENT CONDUCT CODE

Edward N. Stoner II

T homas Jefferson's 1822 lament to a fellow college leader sounds as if it had been written, instead, in the 21st century: "The article of [student] discipline," he wrote, "is the most difficult in American education."[1]

It is true today, yet we now have nearly two centuries of experience in dealing with the behaviors of college students. We also have many good ideas of "best practices" to follow in this effort. One critical best practice is to review your student conduct code periodically to bring it up to date with current best practices in student affairs. Such a review also enables you to keep your conduct code current with the latest innovative misbehaviors by college students.

On many campuses, such reviews occur on an ongoing basis, often annually. If that is not your practice, it is a good alternative to review your conduct code on a regular schedule—for example, a careful review at least once every three years. On the other hand, it may be time for you to undertake a complete review and overhaul of your student conduct code.

Fortunately, the process we use in revising our campus student conduct code is similar whether you are doing so as part of a continuing updating process or you are doing a top-to-bottom revision. In any event, the process you use can have a very important impact on your new code's success.

As with any "policy" adopted on campus, one cannot simply sit down and write or revise a student conduct code and expect it to be adopted and accepted. It is both the beauty and challenge of life on campus that it takes many small steps (and quite a bit of time) to put a new or updated student conduct code into place. To use this deliberate process to our advantage, we can identify a number of steps to consider as part of any student code revision process, including gathering resources for the project, identifying persons to include as part of the working revision team, selecting persons to include as resources during the team's work, listing current issues on campus, working with current issues arising in student affairs work nationwide and, of course, doing the work itself. Let us discuss each of these in turn.

The primary responsibility for writing and revising a student conduct code usually lies with the office of the senior student affairs officer (SSAO). This is natural enough, inasmuch as the SSAO is the officer primarily charged with creating a positive living and learning environment on campus.

Gathering Resources

The SSAO normally assigns someone—perhaps the person directly responsible for administering the campus conduct code itself—to the first task, gathering resource materials.

There are many resources available, but let me suggest a few that you—and the persons who work with you on the project—might find helpful. First, of course, you might consider earlier works about how to go about revising your student conduct code (Stoner, 2000).

Statistics from your campus's Jeanne Clery Disclosure of Campus Security Policy and Campus Crime Statistics Act report may provide you with a sense of the frequency of crime on campus. These data are, however, only the tip of the iceberg, because these figures are aimed only at criminal law violations. These statistics do not speak so directly to all of the campus conduct we must address in trying to provide a living and learning environment that is as good as possible.

Even more helpful are reports showing the number and type of violations you have dealt with under your student conduct code during the last three years. These statistics are most helpful if they are broken down by semester, type of student conduct code violation, and location (such as by residence hall or whether the violations occurred off campus). If you are fortunate enough to be able to gather this information over three years, you may be able to identify both trends in offenses and sanctioning approaches that do or do not work.

Equally important (but, we hope, smaller in number) is the number of students who have been suspended or expelled. Surely, many of these situations are unique. Nevertheless, it is important to identify each and to note what type of violation (and sanction) was involved. If your resources enable you to do so, it is helpful to review each of these serious matters with an administrator who is familiar with the situation. If it is possible, note whether the code facilitated the "right" result and sanction to be reached and whether that situation highlighted any problems with the code. When your working group does its work, it will come back to these "problems" you have identified to determine whether different code language is needed, different approaches are needed even under the existing code, or, perhaps, both.

It is also important to gather this history so those working on the new code have the right perspective on the problems facing the student affairs professionals who deal with student behavior issues day to day.

Every code violation is important, of course. Misconduct shows that the offending student is not getting full benefit from the opportunity to develop in a positive living and learning environment. Just as important, though, violations show how the environment is endangered for direct victims of the misconduct (such as another student who was assaulted) or indirect victims (such as the rest of the community affected by the misconduct, including other students and employees of the institution).

It is important to remember each of these parts of the living and learning environment as we analyze what will make our code more effective: the offending student, students directly affected by the offending student's actions, and the rest of the academic community. Unlike criminal law perspectives in which the defendant is most important, each of these three "constituencies" (offender, victim, campus) is equally important on campus when we consider improving our student conduct code.

That said, let me emphasize two particular types of code violations about which you should have an accurate history before beginning to revise your code: underage alcohol violations and sexual misconduct.

On every campus, it is important to gather statistics on alcohol offenses because such violations are common and often lead to other serious offenses, such as sexual assaults. Moreover, many campuses struggle continuously with how to deal with underage alcohol issues. It is important to understand exactly how serious this issue is on your campus. Because alcohol offenses undermine the living and learning environment for so many students, they cannot be ignored. You must focus on how your student conduct code can help you to deal with this most serious of issues.

Sexual assault statistics also can be very revealing. These involve the most difficult and sensitive cases. How your campus handles them can reveal much about the effectiveness of your campus conduct code. As with all statistics, it is important to review sexual misconduct thoughtfully; for example, a campus with one or no reported sexual conduct violations may appear at first to have the problem well in hand. More digging, however, may reveal that students do not report sexual conduct problems because there is a perception that the campus system does not deal with them well or fairly. So gather your statistics and consider them carefully! Be sure to include the groups in your community and on your campus who deal with victims of sexual assault. They will help you to comprehend the significance of the reported numbers of sexual offenses and the effectiveness of your programs.

If you have not already done so, it is critical to identify those matters that did not turn out right—either because you think the wrong decision was reached about whether the student was responsible for violating campus rules or because the wrong sanction (or an ineffective one) was imposed. These matters should be identified and explained to your working group (without personally identifiable information, of course) so you can use them to learn how to improve your code or practices.

Another type of helpful statistic is to know how many matters were appealed and how many appeals were sustained. If many were sustained, this is an obvious clue that you need to fix something. It could be that the hearing panels are not trained properly, so they are not following the process. It could be that the appeals board misunderstands its role and is mistakenly trying to rehear the matter. Or it might indicate something else entirely. But if you have more than a small handful of appeals sustained, you need to look at each one carefully.

In addition, it is helpful to know how long it takes to process matters under your student code. The key concept here is promptness. A good goal is to try to complete the large majority of matters within 7 days and all matters (including the appeal) within 30 days. If you are not achieving this, study carefully what the reasons are for the delays and what can be done to expedite matters.

Other resources you might consider include model student conduct codes. You may benefit from carefully reading more than one because no

single model will fit your campus history and social system perfectly. Gary
Pavela (2000) has done excellent work in this area, and our Model Student
Conduct Code (Stoner & Lowery, 2004) also provides a basis for your
review.

Here is how Dr. Lowery and I hope you use our model code (see appendix
4A). First, there is a section setting forth in narrative fashion the history of
student discipline on campus from the days of Thomas Jefferson. It has not
gotten any easier since Jefferson struggled with it in the 1820s. On the other
hand, courts still do as they always have done, deferring to educators who are
doing what they said they would do and who are exercising their educational
judgment when college students engage in misconduct. Knowing this history
will give you comfort as you address even the most troubling of issues.

Second, the model code is a literal model of how a student conduct code
might be worded. You may use it as a checklist of topics to be included (or
those not needed in the environment on your campus). If you use it this
way, we hope you will not accidentally "miss" any issue—most are far easier
to resolve in drafting than they are when you have an actual case.

Finally, there is a model hearing script in our model code that illustrates
how you can have a fact-finding process that reflects the values of your institution, does not mimic a court of law, and does not revictimize or traumatize
students who are part of the process. All of this is a resource for you when
you begin to draft or to revise your own code.

A different type of resource is to attend the Gehring Institute. Every
summer, the Association for Student Judicial Affairs (ASJA) sponsors the
Donald D. Gehring Academy for Student Conduct Administrators where
student affairs professionals nationwide gather to learn about and to discuss
best practices in student discipline and the use of student conduct codes (for
more information, see www.asjaonline.org). It is an excellent practice to send
someone from your student affairs office to this academy the summer before
you begin drafting your code. You will come away with excellent ideas and
will meet many other student affairs professionals struggling with the same
challenges you face.

The Working Group

Now that you have gathered your resources, you need to determine who will
work on the project. When revising your conduct code, it is important to

involve people from all over campus. This will make your work product better informed and help it to gain acceptance more easily. To get your work finished, however, it is better to have a small working group, so you need to balance both concerns. Here is a suggestion that has worked for me.

First, assemble a small working group of people who can get the project done. The group might include the campus discipline officer, a student or two (e.g., someone who has served on a campus hearing board and someone from student government), a faculty member who has been involved in campus discipline, and someone from campus security/police. One person is assigned to do the writing and, of course, you may add others depending on who has the talent and interest. It is helpful to keep the group to 10 people or fewer. If your group is larger, scheduling meetings will become difficult and agreeing on approaches will be daunting.

As you proceed through the process, invite others from a broad spectrum of the campus to attend one or more meetings of your group. You can explain to them what you are doing and ask for their opinions. You will get a lot of good input, and including people from all sectors of campus will help to educate everyone about what you are trying to accomplish with your student code.

Here are some key stakeholders that you might consider involving: a group of campus security officers; the athletics director and administrators (coaches); residence hall advisors; students, faculty, and administrators who have served on campus hearing boards and appeal boards; a concerned member of the Board of Trustees who is responsible for student matters; students from various organizations (from Greek life to campus sexual assault personnel); counseling center leaders; a campus media spokesperson; and even, perhaps, an outside expert if you know one who understands student codes.

If you are able to involve the campus attorney who will represent you later if there is a dispute, it is very important to involve that person at the drafting stage. This person will give you valuable insights and will be more effective in defending the results of your process if he or she is included during the revision process. On the other hand, you must be very careful about involving law school professors. Regrettably, they often know little about student affairs and think you should be trying to write a mock criminal law process, when that is the polar opposite of what you are trying to create.

Starting the Work

How you go about doing the work varies, depending on the task before you. If you are merely addressing several discrete problems, perhaps you may simply dive in and address each one in turn. Eventually, that is what you will do in any event.

If you are engaged in a more major revision, however, a good starting place is for the working group to write a statement about what the student code seeks to accomplish. The end product may not be lengthy, but it will tie your work into the mission of the university. Moreover, it will help to remind everyone (those involved in the project and those who read the results of your work) that you are trying to create a good living and learning environment on campus. It will underscore that your work is intended to educate those who do not understand what it means to be part of an academic community. The code is intended to help those who misbehave, those who are the victims of misconduct, and everyone else—students and employees alike—who is part of the community. This project may take you only one afternoon, or it may take several meetings. If you can discuss it thoughtfully, however, experience indicates that it will help you immensely as you proceed.

Attend a Hearing

Most of the people who serve on your working committee already will have attended a campus student conduct code hearing. If someone in your working group has not, however, each person who has not should do so. The person can sit quietly in the back, and what he or she learns by actually observing a hearing will make the person a much more effective member of your working group.

Similarly, be sure that at least two members of your working group have attended a meeting of your appeal process so that its workings are understood correctly.

Identify Areas of Concern

There are two obvious sources for identifying subject matter areas for your working group's attention: your campus and other campuses.

On your own campus, you may have identified areas of concern during the resource-gathering process. For example, do students not use your process for stalking cases or sexual conduct cases? If that is the case, is it because you need either to redraft your code or to reeducate those who administer in these issues? Does your underage alcohol or drug policy need to be revised? Does your process take too long? Do you use inappropriate sanctions because they are set by diverse hearing boards rather than by student affairs professionals? Are appellate reviewers substituting their judgment on credibility for that of the people who were actually in the hearing? Is the process too much like a junior court of law? You will recognize these issues when you see them. Indeed, your SSAO probably already has a list of them in his or her top drawer.

Other campuses are also good resources. You can learn a lot by seeing student conduct codes of other campuses. Try to pick schools with a profile similar to yours (public versus private, size, number of residence halls and students who live on campus).

Consider how you deal with academic dishonesty. An excellent practice is for faculty to "own" the primary responsibility for this, as it falls naturally in the academic area. Many schools, however, deal with it in their conduct code, either because faculty prefer that avenue or as a supplement to the academic process. In any event, if such violations are treated by two processes, make sure the "second" process considers any sanction imposed in the "first." There is no "right" answer to where to handle academic offenses; simply be sure that your processes state accurately your campus's preference.

In addition, it is important to identify issues that events on other campuses have raised. Three examples follow.

The tragic events at Virginia Tech contain many issues for review. One of many is that we must focus on how we handle stalking cases. Research how a stalking case is handled on your campus. What do you do to educate students about what stalking is, and what can you do to help students who believe they have been stalked? Are students aware how posting personal information on Internet sites can help to make them victims of a stalker? If a student is found to have violated your rule on stalking but violates your "no contact" sanction, is the student offender removed from campus? Investigate whether you impose serious sanctions for this serious violation. There is, of course, no suggestion that a student code approach can guarantee there will be no recurrence of the tragedy at Virginia Tech, but it is a good idea to see what lessons we can learn.

The matter at Duke University in 2006 involving members of the lacrosse team who were accused of sexually assaulting a local woman was not a student conduct code case, either. Yet, even possibly incorrect versions of what happened there suggest a number of points for you to consider. Do you separate students from campus with no campus process merely because they have been indicted? How do you deal with alleged underage alcohol violations when combined with alleged sexual conduct violations? Are student athletes treated the same as (or more leniently or more harshly than) student nonathletes? Do your athletics coaches understand, respect, and promote the values set forth in the student conduct code? How do you interact with local law enforcement and the local district attorney? What do you do if the media and/or your faculty demand action even before hearing from an alleged victim? Do you use and value the work of campus security with alleged victims? Based on what you have heard about a case like Duke's, it is helpful to discuss how you would handle the issues they faced if such an event occurred on your campus. If there had been a campus conduct code hearing based on what you knew about that scenario, how would you have handled it under your code?

A good hypothetical run-through of a scenario like the one attributed to Duke is often very valuable in the code revision process—even if our knowledge of what happened on someone else's campus is based not on objective reality but on what some television commentator speculated might have happened there.

A third example is to take a look at the most current high-tech violations. Students are very creative. Usually, this creativity is a good thing, but students today may demonstrate bad judgment and bad behavior when using modern technology. Make sure your code addresses the latest "fad" in technology offenses, such as using small or concealed cameras to take pictures of people in showers or when they are engaged in other private (they thought) conduct. Try to make your conduct code keep up with the spirit of insubordination of our always innovative students.

Check Your Product Against Standard Goals

When you think you have finished your effort, it is worthwhile to check your product against your goals. Here are some common ones:

- Is your student conduct code written in simple English that entering first-year students, parents, journalists, and others can understand?

- Is it in chronological order, enabling the reader to follow how a typical code matter would be handled?
- Does your student conduct code establish a system that meets your original objectives and mission statement?
- Is your student conduct code friendly to students who come before a hearing panel, not requiring them to pretend they are junior lawyers, just enabling them to tell what happened in an educational, not confrontational setting? Keep it mind that some students who come before hearing panels are really victims of another student's actions; you do not want your process to revictimize them.
- Will your student conduct code enable you to handle a difficult and high-profile case, such as one involving sexual conduct, as well as possible? To answer this, carefully work a hypothetical sexual misconduct case through the steps involved in your code.
- Will your student conduct code enable you to handle matters promptly?
- Does the appeal process allow reviewers to respect the credibility determinations made by those who serve on a hearing panel?
- Does your student conduct code enable you to apply sanctions that are as consistent as possible (allowing, of course, for the fact that each student's conduct and record may be different)?
- Can you follow the code even in a difficult case? (This is critical to allowing your attorney to successfully defend the conclusion you have reached.) Does the attorney who will defend your actions approve of and support your new/revised code?
- Have you avoided using legal jargon in your student conduct code, and have you avoided calling your process a "judicial" one? If not, get out your red pencil!

Educate Your Community

Now that you have a marvelous new student conduct code, take a moment to focus on how you tell your campus community about it.

First, make sure it is part of new student orientation that includes time to discuss campus expectations about particularly common and troublesome behaviors (such as sexual misconduct, stalking, underage alcohol use, and drug use). Put your conduct code in a written pamphlet or handbook and make it available on your campus website.

Second, make sure every person who volunteers time to serve in a student code capacity is properly educated about his or her role and what is expected. This should include every person who serves on a hearing or appeals panel. Every year, every participant should attend your training, and include the attorney who advises and defends you in the training—as a trainee or presenter or both.

Last, make sure that your president and board understand your process. When a difficult case arises, you will be glad these people already understand and support your student conduct code.

Enjoy the process. It is a very key part of establishing a good living and learning environment on campus. Moreover, a lot of current student personnel professionals got their first exposure to this career by serving on a student conduct hearing or a student code revision committee.

Note

1. Jefferson's letter of November 2, 1822, was to Thomas Cooper, second president of South Carolina College (now called the University of South Carolina). (1884). *The Works of Thomas Jefferson*, Vol. VII, 268.

References

Pavela, G. (2000). Applying the power of association on campus: A model code of student conduct. *Synthesis* (11), 817.

Stoner, E. N., II. (2000). *Reviewing your student discipline policy: A project worth the investment*. Retrieved October 1, 2007, from www.edstoner.com

Stoner, E. N., II, & Lowery, J. W. (2004). Navigating past the "spirit of insubordination": A twenty-first century model student conduct code with a model hearing script. *Journal of College and University Law, 31*.

A Twenty-First Century Model Student Conduct Code

Article I: Definitions

1. The term [College] [University] means [name of institution].

2. The term "student" includes all persons taking courses at the [College] [University], either full-time or part-time, pursuing undergraduate, graduate, or professional studies. Persons who withdraw after allegedly violating the Student Code, who are not officially enrolled for a particular term but who have a continuing relationship with the [College] [University] or who have been notified of their acceptance for admission are considered "students" as are persons who are living in [College] [University] residence halls, although not enrolled in this institution. This Student Code [does] [does not] apply at all locations of the [College] [University], including the campus in [e.g., a foreign country or another state].

3. The term "faculty member" means any person hired by the [College] [University] to conduct classroom or teaching activities or who is otherwise considered by the [College] [University] to be a member of its faculty.

4. The term "[College] [University] official" includes any person employed by the [College] [University], performing assigned administrative or professional responsibilities.

5. The term "member of the [College] [University] community" includes any person who is a student, faculty member, [College] [University] official or any other person employed by the [College] [University]. A person's status in a particular situation shall be determined by [title of appropriate college or university administrator].

6. The term "[College] [University] premises" includes all land, buildings, facilities, and other property in the possession of or owned, used, or controlled by the [College] [University] (including adjacent streets and sidewalks).

7. The term "organization" means any number of persons who have complied with the formal requirements for [College] [University] [recognition/registration].

8. The term "Student Conduct Board" means any person or persons authorized by the [title of administrator identified in Article I, number 13] to determine whether a student has violated the Student Code and to recommend sanctions that may be imposed when a rules violation has been committed.

9. The term "Student Conduct Administrator" means a [College] [University] official authorized on a case-by-case basis by the [title of administrator identified in Article I, number 13] to impose sanctions upon any student(s) found to have violated the Student Code. The [title of administrator identified in Article I, number 13] may authorize a Student Conduct Administrator to serve simultaneously as a Student Conduct Administrator and the sole member or one of the members of the Student Conduct Board. The [title of administrator identified in Article I, number 13] may authorize the same Student Conduct Administrator to impose sanctions in all cases.

10. The term "Appellate Board" means any person or persons authorized by the [title of administrator identified in Article I, number 13] to consider an appeal from a Student Conduct Board's determination as to whether a student has violated the Student Code or from the sanctions imposed by the Student Conduct Administrator.

11. The term "shall" is used in the imperative sense.

12. The term "may" is used in the permissive sense.

13. The [title of appropriate administrator] is that person designated by the [College] [University] President to be responsible for the administration of the Student Code.

14. The term "policy" means the written regulations of the [College] [University] as found in, but not limited to, the Student Code, Residence Life Handbook, the [College] [University] web page and computer use policy, and Graduate/Undergraduate Catalogs.

15. The term "cheating" includes, but is not limited to: (1) use of any unauthorized assistance in taking quizzes, tests, or examinations; (2) use of sources beyond those authorized by the instructor in writing papers, preparing reports, solving problems, or carrying out other assignments; (3) the acquisition, without permission, of tests or other academic material belonging to a member of the [College] [University] faculty or staff; (4) engaging in any behavior specifically prohibited by a faculty member in the course syllabus or class discussion.

16. The term "plagiarism" includes, but is not limited to, the use, by paraphrase or direct quotation, of the published or unpublished work of another person without full and clear acknowledgment. It also includes the unacknowledged use of materials prepared by another person or agency engaged in the selling of term papers or other academic materials.

17. The term "Complainant" means any person who submits a charge alleging that a student violated this Student Code. When a student believes that s/he has been a victim of another student's misconduct, the student who believes s/he has been a victim will have the same rights under this Student Code as are provided to the Complainant, even if another member of the [College] [University] community submitted the charge itself.

18. The term "Accused Student" means any student accused of violating this Student Code.

Article II: Student Code Authority

1. The Student Conduct Administrator shall determine the composition of Student Conduct Boards and Appellate Boards and determine which Student Conduct Board, Student Conduct Administrator and Appellate Board shall be authorized to hear each matter.

2. The [title of appropriate administrator] shall develop policies for the administration of the student conduct system and procedural rules for the conduct of Student Conduct Board Hearings that are not inconsistent with provisions of the Student Code.

3. Decisions made by a Student Conduct Board and/or Student Conduct Administrator shall be final, pending the normal appeal process.

Article III: Proscribed Conduct

A. Jurisdiction of the [College] [University] Student Code
B. Conduct Rules and Regulations
   Any student found to have committed or to have attempted to commit the following misconduct is subject to the disciplinary sanctions outlined in Article IV:
   1. Acts of dishonesty, including but not limited to the following:
      a. Cheating, plagiarism, or other forms of academic dishonesty.

    b. Furnishing false information to any [College] [University] official, faculty member, or office.

    c. Forgery, alteration, or misuse of any [College] [University] document, record, or instrument of identification.

2. Disruption or obstruction of teaching, research, administration, disciplinary proceedings, other [College] [University] activities, including its public service functions on or off campus, or of other authorized non-[College] [University] activities when the conduct occurs on [College] [University] premises.

3. Physical abuse, verbal abuse, threats, intimidation, harassment, coercion, and/or other conduct which threatens or endangers the health or safety of any person.

4. Attempted or actual theft of and/or damage to property of the [College] [University] or property of a member of the [College] [University] community or other personal or public property, on or off campus.

5. Hazing, defined as an act which endangers the mental or physical health or safety of a student, or which destroys or removes public or private property, for the purpose of initiation, admission into, affiliation with, or as a condition for continued membership in, a group or organization. The express or implied consent of the victim will not be a defense. Apathy or acquiescence in the presence of hazing are not neutral acts; they are violations of this rule.

6. Failure to comply with directions of [College] [University] officials or law enforcement officers acting in performance of their duties and/or failure to identify oneself to these persons when requested to do so.

7. Unauthorized possession, duplication or use of keys to any [College] [University] premises or unauthorized entry to or use of [College] [University] premises.

8. Violation of any [College] [University] policy, rule, or regulation published in hard copy or available electronically on the [College] [University] website.

9. Violation of any federal, state or local law.

10. Use, possession, manufacturing, or distribution of marijuana, heroin, narcotics, or other controlled substances except as expressly permitted by law.

11. Use, possession, manufacturing, or distribution of alcoholic beverages (except as expressly permitted by [College] [University] regulations), or public intoxication. Alcoholic beverages may not, in any circumstance, be used by, possessed by or distributed to any person under twenty-one (21) years of age.

12. Illegal or unauthorized possession of firearms, explosives, other weapons, or dangerous chemicals on [College] [University] premises or use of any such item, even if legally possessed, in a manner that harms, threatens or causes fear to others.

13. Participating in an on-campus or off-campus demonstration, riot or activity that disrupts the normal operations of the [College] [University] and/or infringes on the rights of other members of the [College] [University] community; leading or inciting others to disrupt scheduled and/or normal activities within any campus building or area.

14. Obstruction of the free flow of pedestrian or vehicular traffic on [College] [University] premises or at [College] [University] sponsored or supervised functions.

15. Conduct that is disorderly, lewd, or indecent; breach of peace; or aiding, abetting, or procuring another person to breach the peace on [College] [University] premises or at functions sponsored by, or participated in by, the [College] [University] or members of the academic community. Disorderly Conduct includes but is not limited to: Any unauthorized use of electronic or other devices to make an audio or video record of any person while on [College] [University] premises without his/her prior knowledge, or without his/her effective consent when such a recording is likely to cause injury or distress. This includes, but is not limited to, surreptitiously taking pictures of another person in a gym, locker room, or restroom.

16. Theft or other abuse of computer facilities and resources, including but not limited to:
    a. Unauthorized entry into a file, to use, read, or change the contents, or for any other purpose.
    b. Unauthorized transfer of a file.
    c. Use of another individual's identification and/or password.
    d. Use of computing facilities and resources to interfere with the work of another student, faculty member or [College] [University] Official.

e. Use of computing facilities and resources to send obscene or abusive messages.

f. Use of computing facilities and resources to interfere with normal operation of the [College] [University] computing system.

g. Use of computing facilities and resources in violation of copyright laws.

h. Any violation of the [College] [University] Computer Use Policy.

17. Abuse of the Student Conduct System, including but not limited to:

a. Failure to obey the notice from a Student Conduct Board or [College] [University] official to appear for a meeting or hearing as part of the Student Conduct System.

b. Falsification, distortion, or misrepresentation of information before a Student Conduct Board.

c. Disruption or interference with the orderly conduct of a Student Conduct Board proceeding.

d. Institution of a student conduct code proceeding in bad faith.

e. Attempting to discourage an individual's proper participating in, or use of, the student conduct system.

f. Attempting to influence the impartiality of a member of a Student Conduct Board prior to, and/or during the course of, the Student Conduct Board proceeding.

g. Harassment (verbal or physical) and/or intimidation of a member of a Student Conduct Board prior to, during, and/or after a student conduct code proceeding.

h. Failure to comply with the sanction(s) imposed under the Student Code.

i. Influencing or attempting to influence another person to commit an abuse of the student conduct code system.

18. Students are required to engage in responsible social conduct that reflects credit upon the [College] [University] community and to model good citizenship in any community.

C. Violation of Law and [College] [University] Discipline

1. [Alternative A]

[College] [University] disciplinary proceedings may be instituted against a student charged with conduct that potentially violates both the criminal law and this Student Code (that is, if both possible violations result from the same factual situation) without regard to the pendency of civil or criminal litigation in court or criminal arrest and prosecution. Proceedings under this Student Code may be carried out prior to, simultaneously with, or following civil or criminal proceedings off campus at the discretion of [the person identified in Article 1(13)]. Determinations made or sanctions imposed under this Student Code shall not be subject to change because criminal charges arising out of the same facts giving rise to violation of University rules were dismissed, reduced, or resolved in favor of or against the criminal law defendant.

[Alternative B]

If a violation of law which also would be a violation of this Student Code is alleged, proceedings under this Student Code may go forward against an Accused Student who has been subjected to criminal prosecution only if the [College] [University] determines that its interest is clearly distinct from that of the community outside the [College] [University]. Ordinarily, the [College] [University] should not impose sanctions if public prosecution of a student is anticipated or until law enforcement officials have disposed of the case.

2. When a student is charged by federal, state, or local authorities with a violation of law, the [College] [University] will not request or agree to special consideration for that individual because of his or her status as a student. If the alleged offense is also being processed under the Student Code, the [College] [University] may advise off-campus authorities of the existence of the Student Code and of how such matters are typically handled within the [College] [University] community. The [College] [University] will attempt to cooperate with law enforcement and other agencies in the enforcement of criminal law on campus and in the conditions imposed by criminal courts for the rehabilitation of student violators (provided that the conditions do not conflict with campus rules or sanctions). Individual students and other members of the [College] [University] community, acting in their personal capacities, remain free to interact with governmental representatives as they deem appropriate.

Article IV: Student Conduct Code Procedures

A. Charges and Student Conduct Board Hearings
   1. Any member of the [College] [University] community may file charges against a student for violations of the Student Code. A

charge shall be prepared in writing and directed to the Student Conduct Administrator. Any charge should be submitted as soon as possible after the event takes place, preferably within [specify time period].

2. The Student Conduct Administrator may conduct an investigation to determine if the charges have merit and/or if they can be disposed of administratively by mutual consent of the parties involved on a basis acceptable to the Student Conduct Administrator. Such disposition shall be final and there shall be no subsequent proceedings. If the charges are not admitted and/or cannot be disposed of by mutual consent, the Student Conduct Administrator may later serve in the same matter as the Student Conduct Board or a member thereof. If the student admits violating institutional rules, but sanctions are not agreed to, subsequent process, including a hearing if necessary, shall be limited to determining the appropriate sanction(s).

3. All charges shall be presented to the Accused Student in written form. A time shall be set for a Student Conduct Board Hearing, not less than five nor more than fifteen calendar days after the student has been notified. Maximum time limits for scheduling of Student Conduct Board Hearings may be extended at the discretion of the Student Conduct Administrator.

4. Student Conduct Board Hearings shall be conducted by a Student Conduct Board according to the following guidelines except as provided by article IV(A)(7) below:

   a. Student Conduct Board Hearings normally shall be conducted in private.

   b. The Complainant, Accused Student and their advisors, if any, shall be allowed to attend the entire portion of the Student Conduct Board Hearing at which information is received (excluding deliberations). Admission of any other person to the Student Conduct Board Hearing shall be at the discretion of the Student Conduct Board and/or its Student Conduct Administrator.

   c. In Student Conduct Board Hearings involving more than one Accused Student, the Student Conduct Administrator, in his or her discretion, may permit the Student Conduct Board Hearings concerning each student to be conducted either separately or jointly.

d. The Complainant and the Accused Student have the right to be assisted by an advisor they choose, at their own expense. The advisor must be a member of the [College] [University] community and may not be an attorney. The Complainant and/or the Accused Student is responsible for presenting his or her own information and, therefore, advisors are not permitted to speak or to participate directly in any Student Conduct Board Hearing before a Student Conduct Board. A student should select as an advisor a person whose schedule allows attendance at the scheduled date and time for the Student Conduct Board Hearing because delays will not normally be allowed due to the scheduling conflicts of an advisor.

e. The Complainant, the Accused Student and the Student Conduct Board may arrange for witnesses to present pertinent information to the Student Conduct Board. The [College] [University] will try to arrange the attendance of possible witnesses who are members of the [College] [University] community, if reasonably possible, and who are identified by the Complainant and/or Accused Student at least two weekdays prior to the Student Conduct Board Hearing. Witnesses will provide information to and answer questions from the Student Conduct Board. Questions may be suggested by the Accused Student and/or Complainant to be answered by each other or by other witnesses. This will be conducted by the Student Conduct Board with such questions directed to the chairperson, rather than to the witness directly. This method is used to preserve the educational tone of the hearing and to avoid creation of an adversarial environment. Questions of whether potential information will be received shall be resolved in the discretion of the chairperson of the Student Conduct Board.

f. Pertinent records, exhibits, and written statements (including Student Impact Statements) may be accepted as information for consideration by a Student Conduct Board at the discretion of the chairperson.

g. All procedural questions are subject to the final decision of the chairperson of the Student Conduct Board.

h. After the portion of the Student Conduct Board Hearing concludes in which all pertinent information has been received, the Student Conduct Board shall determine (by majority vote if the Student Conduct Board consists of more than one person) whether the Accused Student has violated each section of the Student Code which the student is charged with violating. The Student Conduct Board's determination shall be made on the basis of whether it is more likely than not that the Accused Student violated the Student Code.

i. Formal rules of process, procedure, and/or technical rules of evidence, such as are applied in criminal or civil court, are not used in Student Code proceedings.

5. There shall be a single verbatim record, such as a tape recording, of all Student Conduct Board Hearings before a Student Conduct Board (not including deliberations). Deliberations shall not be recorded. The record shall be the property of the [College] [University].

6. If an Accused Student, with notice, does not appear before a Student Conduct Board Hearing, the information in support of the charges shall be presented and considered even if the Accused Student is not present.

7. The Student Conduct Board may accommodate concerns for the personal safety, well-being, and/or fears of confrontation of the Complainant, Accused Student, and/or other witness during the hearing by providing separate facilities, by using a visual screen, and/or by permitting participation by telephone, videophone, closed circuit television, video conferencing, videotape, audio tape, written statement, or other means, where and as determined in the sole judgment of [title of administrator identified in Article I, number 13] to be appropriate.

B. Sanctions

1. The following sanctions may be imposed upon any student found to have violated the Student Code:

a. Warning—A notice in writing to the student that the student is violating or has violated institutional regulations.

b. Probation—A written reprimand for violation of specified regulations. Probation is for a designated period of time and includes the probability of more severe disciplinary sanctions if the student is found to violate any institutional regulation(s) during the probationary period.

c. Loss of Privileges—Denial of specified privileges for a designated period of time.

d. Fines—Previously established and published fines may be imposed.

e. Restitution—Compensation for loss, damage, or injury. This may take the form of appropriate service and/or monetary or material replacement.

f. Discretionary Sanctions—Work assignments, essays, service to the [College] [University], or other related discretionary assignments.

g. Residence Hall Suspension—Separation of the student from the residence halls for a definite period of time, after which the student is eligible to return. Conditions for readmission may be specified.

h. Residence Hall Expulsion—Permanent separation of the student from the residence halls.

i. [College] [University] Suspension—Separation of the student from the [College] [University] for a definite period of time, after which the student is eligible to return. Conditions for readmission may be specified.

j. [College] [University] Expulsion—Permanent separation of the student from the [College] [University].

k. Revocation of Admission and/or Degree—Admission to or a degree awarded from the [College] [University] may be revoked for fraud, misrepresentation, or other violation of [College] [University] standards in obtaining the degree, or for other serious violations committed by a student prior to graduation.

l. Withholding Degree—The [College] [University] may withhold awarding a degree otherwise earned until the completion of the process set forth in this Student Conduct Code, including the completion of all sanctions imposed, if any.

2. More than one of the sanctions listed above may be imposed for any single violation.

3. (a) Other than [College] [University] expulsion or revocation or withholding of a degree, disciplinary sanctions shall not be made part of the student's permanent academic record, but shall become part of the student's disciplinary record. Upon graduation, the student's disciplinary record may be expunged of disciplinary actions other than residence hall expulsion, [College] [University] suspension, [College] [University] expulsion, or revocation or withholding of a degree, upon application to the Student Conduct Administrator. Cases involving the imposition of sanctions other than residence hall expulsion, [College] [University] suspension, [College] [University] expulsion or revocation or withholding of a degree shall be expunged from the student's confidential record [insert preferred number] years after final disposition of the case. (b) In situations involving both an Accused Student(s) (or group or organization) and a student(s) claiming to be the victim of another student's conduct, the records of the process and of the sanctions imposed, if any, shall be considered to be the education records of both the Accused Student(s) and the student(s) claiming to be the victim because the educational career and chances of success in the academic community of each may be impacted.

4. The following sanctions maybe imposed upon groups or organizations:

   a. Those sanctions listed above in article IV(B)(l)(a)–(e).

   b. Loss of selected rights and privileges for a specified period of time.

   c. Deactivation. Loss of all privileges, including [College] [University] recognition, for a specified period of time.

5. In each case in which a Student Conduct Board determines that a student and/or group or organization has violated the Student Code, the sanction(s) shall be determined and imposed by the Student Conduct Administrator. In cases in which persons other than, or in addition to, the Student Conduct Administrator have been authorized to serve as the Student Conduct Board, the recommendation of the Student Conduct Board shall be considered by the

Student Conduct Administrator in determining and imposing sanctions. The Student Conduct Administrator is not limited to sanctions recommended by members of the Student Conduct Board. Following the Student Conduct Board Hearing, the Student Conduct Board and the Student Conduct Administrator shall advise the Accused Student, group and/or organization (and a complaining student who believes s/he was the victim of another student's conduct) in writing of its determination and of the sanction(s) imposed, if any.

C. Interim Suspension

1. Interim suspension may be imposed only: 1) to ensure the safety and well-being of members of the [College] [University] community or preservation of [College] [University] property; b) to ensure the student's own physical or emotional safety and well-being; or c) if the student poses an ongoing threat of disruption of, or interference with, the normal operations of the [College] [University].

2. During the interim suspension, a student shall be denied access to the residence halls and/or to the campus (including classes) and/or all other [College] [University] activities or privileges for which the student might otherwise be eligible, as the [title of administrator identified in Article I, number 13] or the Student Conduct Administrator may determine to be appropriate.

3. The interim suspension does not replace the regular process, which shall proceed on the normal schedule, up to and through a Student Conduct Board Hearing, if required.

D. Appeals

1. A decision reached by the Student Conduct Board or a sanction imposed by the Student Conduct Administrator may be appealed by the Accused Student(s) or Complainant(s) to an Appellate Board within five (5) school days of the decision. Such appeals shall be in writing and shall be delivered to the Student Conduct Administrator or his or her designee.

2. Except as required to explain the basis of new information, an appeal shall be limited to a review of the verbatim record of the Student Conduct Board Hearing and supporting documents for one or more of the following purposes:

    a. To determine whether the Student Conduct Board Hearing was conducted fairly in light of the charges and information presented, and in conformity with prescribed procedures giving the complaining party a reasonable opportunity to prepare and to present information that the Student Code was violated, and giving the Accused Student a reasonable opportunity to prepare and to present a response to those allegations. Deviations from designated procedures will not be a basis for sustaining an appeal unless significant prejudice results.

    b. To determine whether the decision reached regarding the Accused Student was based on substantial information, that is, whether there were facts in the case that, if believed by the fact finder, were sufficient to establish that a violation of the Student Code occurred.

    c. To determine whether the sanction(s) imposed were appropriate for the violation of the Student Code which the student was found to have committed.

    d. To consider new information, sufficient to alter a decision, or other relevant facts not brought out in the original hearing, because such information and/or facts were not known to the person appealing at the time of the original Student Conduct Board Hearing.

3. If an appeal is upheld by the Appellate Board, the matter shall be returned to the original Student Conduct Board and Student Conduct Administrator for re-opening of Student Conduct Board Hearing to allow reconsideration of the original determination and/or sanction(s). If an appeal is not upheld, the matter shall be considered final and binding upon all involved.

Article V: Interpretation and Revision

A. Any question of interpretation or application of the Student Code shall be referred to the [title of administrator identified in Article I, number 13] or his or her designee for final determination.

B. The Student Code shall be reviewed every [_____] years under the direction of the Student Conduct Administrator.

5

LAWS, POLICIES,
AND MANDATES

John W. Lowery

F
ew college students recognize that most of the rights they are afforded
through the campus conduct system are largely a result of court decisions handed down before they were born. The courts first meaning-
fully addressed the rights enjoyed by public college students under the U.S.
Constitution in *Dixon v. Alabama State Board of Education* (1961). The students in *Dixon* were expelled from Alabama State College for Negroes (now
Alabama State University) in Montgomery as a result of their participation
in civil rights demonstrations in February and March 1960. However, the
students only learned that they were facing disciplinary action when they
were notified they had been suspended or expelled. Supported by the
NAACP Legal Defense and Education Fund, including Thurgood Marshall
and Jack Greenberg, a group of the expelled students brought suit in federal
court against the Alabama State Board of Education claiming that their constitutional rights had been violated. After the district court sided with the
Board of Education, the students appealed the decision to the U.S. Court of
Appeals for the Fifth Circuit. That court ruled that "due process requires
notice and some opportunity for [a] hearing before students at a tax-sup-
ported college are expelled for misconduct" (*Dixon*, p. 151). The court
concluded:

> In the disciplining of college students there are no considerations of imme-
> diate danger to the public, or of peril to the national security, which should
> prevent the Board from exercising at least the fundamental principles of

fairness by giving the accused students notice of the charges and an opportunity to be heard in their own defense. (*Dixon*, p. 157)

This decision stood in stark contrast to earlier cases concerning challenges to the student conduct process in which the courts consistently sided
with the institution (e.g., *Anthony v. Syracuse*, 1928; *Gott v. Berea*, 1913).
While the U.S. Supreme Court declined to hear the case when the Alabama
State Board of Education appealed the decision, the Court later referred to
this ruling as a "landmark decision" (*Goss v. Lopez*, 1975, p. 576).

Elements of Due Process at Public Universities

As the court in *Dixon* (1961) noted, the U.S. Constitution defines the legal
relationship between a public institution and its students. Under the Fifth
Amendment, which applies to public institutions through the Fourteenth
Amendment, students at public colleges and universities may not "be de-
prived of life, liberty, or property, without due process of law." In suspension
or expulsion cases, both liberty and property interests are at stake for the
student. However, the courts have not delineated the exact standards of due
process that must be met (Kaplin & Lee, 2006; Silverglate & Gewolb, 2003,
Wood, 2004). Considering the general question of due process, the Supreme
Court noted, "Due process is an elusive concept. Its exact boundaries are
indefinable, and its content varies according to specific factual contexts"
(*Hannah v. Larche*, 1960, p. 442). The Supreme Court built on this ruling in
Goss v. Lopez (1975) by requiring only that students "be given *some* kind of
notice and afforded *some* kind of hearing" (p. 579). Although the *Goss* case
involved K–12 students, the principles apply to higher education as well.

While procedural due process focuses on the process, substantive due
process focuses on the nature of the institution's rules and the need to avoid
the problems of vagueness and overbreadth. Kaplin and Lee (2006) noted
that many of these cases have involved claims related to violations of students' rights under the First Amendment. The relationship between the campus conduct system and the First Amendment is discussed in a later chapter.

In *Connally v. General Construction Co.* (1926), the Supreme Court addressed the standards applied to avoid the problem of unconstitutionally
vague rules:

[The rule] must be sufficiently explicit to inform those who are subject to it what conduct on their part will render them liable to its penalties, is a well-recognized requirement, consonant alike with ordinary notions of fair play and the settled rules of law. And a statute [or rule] which either forbids or requires the doing of an act in terms so vague that men of common intelligence must necessarily guess at its meaning and differ as to its application, violates the first essential of due process of law. (p. 391)

However, Kaplin and Lee (2006) noted that the courts have seldom invalidated college rules for vagueness, citing *Soglin v. Kauffman* (1969) as one of the few cases to reach this result. In *Soglin*, the University of Wisconsin's rules simply prohibited "misconduct" (p. 167) without further elaboration. The U.S. Court of Appeals for the Seventh Circuit concluded,

The inadequacy of the rule is apparent on its face. It contains no clues which could assist a student, an administrator or a reviewing judge in determining whether conduct not transgressing statutes is susceptible to punishment by the University as "misconduct." We do not require university codes of conduct to satisfy the same rigorous standards as criminal statutes. We only hold that expulsion and prolonged suspension may not be imposed on students by a university simply on the basis of allegations of "misconduct" without reference to any preexisting rule which supplies an adequate guide. The possibility of the sweeping application of the standard of "misconduct" to protected activities does not comport with the guarantees of the First and Fourteenth Amendments. The desired end must be more narrowly achieved. (pp. 167–168)

In *Esteban v. Central Missouri State College* (1968/1969), the U.S. Court of Appeals for the Eighth Circuit reached a similar conclusion even while upholding an institutional rule and warned, "We do not hold that any college regulation, however loosely framed, is necessarily valid" (p. 1089). Silverglate and Gewolb (2003), citing *Woodis v. Westark Community College* (1998) as illustrative, note that the more obvious it would be to the average person that one's behavior was prohibited, the less likely the court would be to void a rule for vagueness. Beyond the First Amendment issues discussed in later chapters, the issues of vagueness and overbreadth are most likely to arise in the context of rules that are unique to the college campus.

After ensuring that the institution's rules are drafted with an appropriate degree of specificity, public colleges and universities must also provide for a campus conduct system that affords students procedural due process. In seeking to determine the content of the due process required in a particular case, the courts seek to balance the rights of the individual and the legitimate interests of the state (Wood, 2004). In *Osteen v. Henley* (1993), the U.S. Court of Appeals for the Seventh Circuit cited the Supreme Court's "canonical test" (p. 226) from *Mathews v. Eldridge* (1976) for determining the process due which requires consideration of:

1. the cost of the additional procedure sought,
2. the risk of error if it is withheld, and
3. the consequences of error to the person seeking the procedure. (p. 226)

The courts have largely addressed the process required in cases in which students face suspension or expulsion; however, the courts have not carefully outlined the process required in less serious cases. In fact, the courts have even suggested that some cases are so minor as to require "very little or no process" (Silverglate & Gewolb, 2003, p. 22).

Due Process Before the Hearing

Since *Dixon* (1961), the courts have expected that students be provided notice of their alleged conduct and which institutional rules or policies they are alleged to have violated. The courts have left institutions considerable leeway in determining how specific the notice must be. The U.S. Court of Appeals for the Fifth Circuit built on its *Dixon* ruling regarding the notice required, but did not mandate the same degree of specificity required in the criminal court system. The court required that the notice be "in sufficient detail to fairly enable them [the accused students] to present a defense" (*Jenkins v. Louisiana State Board of Education*, 1975, p. 1000).

The notice students receive should also include information regarding the evidence to be presented against them; however, the information provided need only be general. The Supreme Court in *Goss v. Lopez* (1975) was more specific regarding the notice, "The student [must] first be told what he is accused of doing and what the basis of the accusation is" (p. 582). While the court in *Dixon* (1961) required that a student be given the "names of the witnesses against him and an oral or written report on the facts to which each witness testifies" (p. 159), it is important to understand that the *Dixon* court was establishing requirements for notice in cases in which witnesses did not present information in the presence of the accused student. Silverglate and Gewolb (2003) warned students, "While committed to appropriate notice in theory, the courts, in practice, unfortunately find almost all notice appropriate" (p. 55). However, in at least some cases, the courts have required new hearings when the notice was insufficient, including when students were found responsible for violations not included in the notice (*Fellheimer v. Middlebury Coll.*, 1994) or when evidence was presented of which they were not made aware (*Weidemann v. SUNY College at Cortland*, 1992).

The courts have not consistently held that the Constitution required a specific number of days before the hearing the notice must be provided—only that the notice be provided in advance (Kaplin & Lee, 2006; Stoner & Cerminara, 1990; Stoner & Lowery, 2004). The notice requirement has varied from as few as two days (*Jones v. State Board of Education*, 1968/1969; *Nash v. Auburn University*, 1987) to as long as ten days (*Esteban*, 1969). Kaplin and Lee (2000) noted that most courts have identified some period of time between these outer limits, but have also required institutions to comply with their policies regarding the timing of this notice. In *Goss v. Lopez* (1975), the Supreme Court held in K–12 cases, "There need be no delay between the time 'notice' is given and the time of the hearing. In the great majority of cases the disciplinarian may informally discuss the alleged misconduct with the student minutes after it has occurred" (p. 582). This approach is most likely to be defensible in higher education for less serious offenses in which suspension or expulsion is not a possible consequence. Silverglate and Gewolb (2003) noted regarding higher education, "In the case of less serious misconduct, notice may be oral and may be given immediately before the informal give-and-take between the student and administrator that fulfills the minimal constitutional requirement for a hearing" (p. 54).

Due Process During the Hearing

The fundamental right that public colleges and universities must provide for during the hearing is [a]n opportunity to speak in their own defense and explain their side of the story. . . . [C]ourts usually will accord the right to hear evidence against them and to present oral testimony or, at minimum, written statements from witness. Formal rules of evidence need not be followed" (Kaplin & Lee, 2006, pp. 978–979).

Beyond the opportunity to be heard, students have raised other legal concerns and courts have reached varying conclusions regarding specific aspects of the hearing, including allegations of bias by board members, a right to consult counsel, and a right to cross-examine witnesses and complainants.

Students have also claimed that their due process rights were violated by public institutions of higher education when members of the hearing body were allegedly biased against them. The courts have been generally unreceptive to these claims, however. In *Gorman v. University of Rhode Island* (1988), the U.S. Court of Appeals for the First Circuit noted, "Generally, in examining administrative proceedings, the presumption [regarding bias] favors the administrators, and the burden is upon the party [the student] challenging the action to produce evidence sufficient to rebut this presumption" (p. 15). The court noted that merely having prior knowledge of a case or working in a particular office did not give rise to bias, observing, "In the intimate setting of a college or university, prior contact between the participants is likely, and does not *per se* indicate bias or partiality" (p. 15). An associated claim students have often raised relates to the multiple roles played by university administrators. Courts have repeatedly rejected this claim (*Gorman*, 1988; *Nash*, 1987; *Osteen*, 1993). In *Nash*, a student board member had knowledge of the case in question, but absent specific evidence of bias, the court did not find the board member's participation in the hearing violated the accused student's rights). In either case, the burden rests with the student to demonstrate the existence of bias as "The disciplinary committee, which included a student representative, is entitled to a presumption of honesty and integrity, absent a showing of actual bias, such as animosity, prejudice, or a personal or financial stake in the outcome" (*Holert v. University of Chicago*, 1990, p. 1301; see also *Hill v. Board of Trustees of Mich. State Univ.*, 2001).

A more complicated question is the circumstances under which a student may have a right to consult with an attorney during the hearing and what role the attorney may play. The courts have "never recognized any absolute right to counsel in school disciplinary proceedings" (*Donohue v. Baker*, 1997, p. 146); however, the courts have recognized limited circumstances in which students might have a right to consult an attorney. In *Gabrilowitz v. Newman* (1978), the U.S. Court of Appeals for the First Circuit recognized the right to consult counsel when the student was facing criminal charges resulting from the same set of facts. However, the accused student was only entitled to receive advice, but not the active representation, of counsel regarding his pending criminal case during the disciplinary hearing. In *Osteen v. Henley* (1993), the U.S. Court of Appeals for the Seventh Circuit concluded on reviewing these issues that

> [t]he most interesting question is whether there is a right to counsel, some-how derived from the due process clause of the Fourteenth Amendment, in student disciplinary proceedings. An oldish case (by the standards of constitutional law at any rate) says yes, *Black Coalition v. Portland School District No. 1,* 484 F.2d 1040 (9th Cir. 1973), but the newer cases say no, at most the student has a right to get the advice of a lawyer; the lawyer need not be allowed to participate in the proceeding in the usual way of trial counsel, as by examining and cross-examining witnesses and addressing the tribunal. Especially when the student faces potential criminal charges (Osteen was charged with two counts of aggravated battery; the record is silent on the disposition of the charges), it is at least arguable that the due process clause entitles him to consult a lawyer, who might for example advise him to take the Fifth Amendment. (p. 225)

The court in *Osteen* concluded that a requirement that the student's attorney be allowed to play an active role in the disciplinary hearing could be detrimental. Most recently, in *Holmes v. Poskanzer* (2007), the court concluded, "due process does not require that Plaintiffs be represented by counsel to perform the traditional function of a trial lawyer and convert the proceedings into the mold of adversary litigation" (p. 22) (see also *Nguyen v. University of Louisville,* 2006). The other two situations in which any court found an affirmative right for a student to be accompanied by his or her attorney was when the university was represented by an attorney or a senior law student only months before graduating from law school, as in the case of *French v. Bashful* (1969) or "the hearing [was] subject to complex rules of evidence or procedure" (*Jaska v. University of Michigan,* 1984/1986, p. 1252).

The last major issue regarding due process during the hearing relates to the cross-examination of witnesses, especially those witnesses presenting information that is adverse to the accused student's case. Kaplin and Lee (2006) note that the right of cross-examination is not generally acknowledged as a constitutional requirement (see also *Dixon,* 1961; *Winnick v. Manning,* 1972). In *Donohue v. Baker* (1997), the court noted that while generally "the right to cross-examine witnesses has not been considered an essential requirement of due process in school disciplinary proceedings. . . . If a case is essentially one of credibility, the cross-examination of witnesses might [be] essential to a fair hearing." (p. 147). The U.S. Court of Appeals for the Eleventh Circuit concluded, "There was no denial of appellants' constitutional rights to due process by their inability to question the adverse witnesses in the usual, adversarial manner" (*Nash*, 1987, p. 664; see also *Jaska*, 1984/1986). In systems that allow for some limited form of cross examination, some commentators (Stoner & Cerminara, 1990; Stoner & Lowery, 2004) have recommended an indirect form of questioning during which questions by the accused student are directed through the judicial board. In *Donohue v. Baker*, the court specifically accepted this limited form of cross-examination, concluding:

> At the very least, in light of the disputed nature of the facts and the importance of witness credibility in this case, due process required that the panel permit the plaintiff to hear all evidence against him and to direct questions to his accuser through the panel. (p. 147)

Related to the issue of cross-examination of witnesses is the use of a visual barrier between the accused student and a witness. These barriers are used most commonly in sexual assault cases and are used to prevent direct visual contact, rather than shield the identity of the witness (Stoner & Lowery, 2004). The court in *Cloud v. Boston Univ.* (1983) specifically approved the use of visual barriers as adequately providing for a student's due process rights, and the court in *Gomes v. Univ. of Maine Sys.* (2004) seemed generally accepting of some use of screens in sexual assault cases.

Due Process After the Hearing

After the conduct of the hearing itself, additional due process considerations must be considered. In determining whether the student violated the code of student conduct, the decision must be based on the information presented during the hearing and must rise to the level of the standard of proof established by the institution. The courts have not imposed any specific standard of proof that colleges and universities must use in student conduct systems. The most commonly used standard of proof in campus student conduct system is a preponderance of the evidence or a more likely than not standard.

The courts do not generally rehear cases when students bring lawsuits challenging the outcome of the campus judicial system. Instead, the courts require that the decision be supported by substantial evidence, which is an even lower standard (*Papachristou v. Univ. of Tenn.*, 2000; Silverglate & Gewolb, 2003; Stoner & Cerminara, 1990; Stoner & Lowery, 2004).

Once a decision has been reached in the case, the courts require that the institution notify the student in writing, at least in serious cases, of its decision. The courts have not generally required a specific content beyond some brief explanation of the reasons for its decision (*Jaska*, 1984); however, the *Jaska* court noted that the written decision did not require the degree of detail required under the Federal Code of Civil Procedure (see also *Herman v. University of South Carolina*, 1971/1972). In *Jaska*, the student also claimed the failure to create a transcript of the hearing had violated his due process rights, an argument that was soundly rejected by that court and many others (see also *Due v. Florida A&M Univ.*, 1961; *Gorman*, 1988; *Schaer v. Brandeis Univ.*, 2000; *Trahms v. Columbia Univ.*, 1997). In *Jaska*, the court noted, "While this case illustrates the wisdom of recording such hearings, it is clear that the Constitution does not impose such a requirement" (p. 1252). A final posthearing consideration is the question of the right to appeal. Most commentators (Kaplin & Lee, 2006; Silverglate & Gewolb, 2003, Stoner & Cerminara, 1990; Stoner & Lowery, 2004; Wood, 2004) agree that students have no constitutional right to an appeal, but an institution may create such a right (see also *Nash v. Auburn*, 1987; *Winnick v. Manning*, 1972). Stoner and Lowery further encouraged institutions to establish an appeal process to promote "an image of fairness" (p. 60).

Institutional Promises

Beyond those minimal due process requirements established by the courts, public institutions are also expected to meet those contractual promises made through its student handbook or other documents. In fact, many institutions have gone far beyond these minimal procedural due process requirements and created systems that more closely mirror the criminal courts (Dannells, 1977, 1990, 1991, 1997; Dannells & Lowery, 2004). Writing in 1987, Travelstead described the impact of *Dixon* (1961) and the cases that followed on the practice of student conduct:

The courts have intervened when the constitutional rights of students have been abridged or ignored. This is only to be expected. Much of the complaining about excessive proceduralism and legalism is hollow. The excessive proceduralism, where it exists, has largely been caused by the institutions themselves. (p. 15)

Gehring (2001) argued that many institutions have "unnecessarily formalized their procedures" (p. 477). These institutions seem to have forgotten the important advice offered by Justice Harry Blackmun in *Esteban v. Central Missouri State University* (1968/1969), who wrote, "it is not sound to draw an analogy between student discipline and criminal procedure" (p. 1088). Stoner (2000) advised, "This unfortunate situation is often compounded by misunderstandings about criminal law and why criminal principles are the wrong perspective from which to understand a college's efforts to deal with student misconduct" (p. 7). Regarding the impact of this trend, Dannells (1997) concluded, "This trend—often called 'creeping legalism' or proceduralism—undermined the informal and uniquely educational element of college student discipline" (p. 69). This is not to suggest that all provisions for student rights not required by the courts are inappropriate or ill-advised, but rather to caution institutions to bear in mind the fundamental educational purpose of the student conduct system.

The Process Due at Private Institutions

Private institutions are not legally required to provide students the rights required at public colleges and universities by the Constitution unless the institutions are engaged in state action. In the absence of a legal relationship between the state and a private institution to administer a public program (*Powe v. Miles*, 1968), the courts have rejected students' claims regarding state action by private institutions and the student conduct system (e.g., *Albert v. Carovano*, 1988; *Cummings v. Virginia School of Cosmetology*, 1979; *Grossner v. Trustees of Columbia*, 1968). The courts instead consider the contractual relationship to determine what procedural rights must be afforded the private college student. Stoner and Lowery (2004) described the courts' expectations for the private colleges and universities:

Although twenty-first century courts no longer merely rubber-stamp college or university decisions, as they once may have done under the doctrine of *in loco parentis*, courts continue to afford institutions of higher education a great deal of discretion. Nevertheless, when colleges and universities do specify the process they will follow for student discipline, courts expect them to follow the process they select. (p. 10)

A New York court limited its scrutiny of the disciplinary actions of a private college to "determining whether the university substantially adhered to its own published rules and guidelines for disciplinary proceedings so as to ascertain whether its actions were arbitrary or capricious" (*In re Rensselaer Soc. of Eng. v. Rensselaer Poly. Inst.*, 1999, p. 295; see also *Boehm v. University of Pa. Sch. of Veterinary Med.*, 1990; *Holert v. University of Chicago*, 1990; *Nguyen v. University of Louisville*, 2006; *Slaughter v. Brigham Young University*, 1975). Furthermore, the courts have noted that these deviations from published rules must be substantial before the courts will intervene on behalf of students. Silverglate and Gewolb (2003) warned students considering lawsuits against institutions for failing to follow their own rules that, "[the courts] tend to give universities a certain leeway if they have followed their rules in a general way, even if not to the letter" (p. 37).

Private institutions are not required by the U.S. Constitution to provide the basic requirements of due process that public colleges and universities must offer. However, various authors (Kaplin & Lee, 2006; Pavela, 2000; Stoner & Cerminara, 1990; Stoner & Lowery, 2004) have argued that private institutions would be well advised to provide these basic rights, including:

- the right to have your case heard under regular procedures used for all similar cases;
- the right to receive notice of the charges against you;
- the right to hear a description of the university's evidence against you; and
- the right to present your side of the story to an impartial panel (Silverglate & Gewolb, 2003, p. 6).

Stoner and Lowery (2004) noted that private institutions should avoid using phrases such as due process or fundamental fairness, suggesting instead that "[a] better practice is to state exactly what process is provided without using such platitudes" (p. 11). In several cases (*Ackerman v. College of the Holy Cross*, 2003; *Fellheimer v. Middlebury Coll.*, 1994; *Goodman v. Bowdoin*

College, 2001), the courts have overturned campus disciplinary action by private institutions that promised to afford students fundamental fairness, but failed to define that term effectively, after concluding that the institutions failed to meet the courts' expectations for fundamental fairness.

Federal Laws and Student Conduct

Unlike constitutional requirements, which apply only to public institutions, compliance with federal laws that affect the practice of student conduct apply with equal force to both public and private higher education institutions. Civil rights laws such as Title IX of the Educational Amendments of 1972 require compliance of all institutions of higher education that receive federal financial assistance. This includes both direct financial support from the federal government to the institution of higher education and indirect support in the form of federal financial aid for students (*Bob Jones University v. Johnson*, 1974/1975; *Grove City v. Bell*, 1984). Compliance with such laws as the Family Educational Rights and Privacy Act of 1974 (FERPA) and the Campus Security Act is required of all institutions of higher education that participate in Title IV programs of the Higher Education Act, which includes the various federal student aid programs. While Hunter and Gehring (2005) identified more than 185 federal laws that affect higher education institutions, this chapter focuses on a select group of federal laws that most directly affect the practice of student conduct, including FERPA, the Jeanne Clery Disclosure of Campus Security Policy and Campus Crime Statistics Act, Title IX of the Educational Amendments of 1972, and the Drug-Free Schools and Communities Act.

Family Educational Rights and Privacy Act (FERPA)

The Family Educational Rights and Privacy Act was passed in 1974 as part of the larger Educational Amendments of 1974. Under FERPA, education records are defined as "those records, files, documents, and other materials which contain information directly related to a student; and are maintained by an educational agency or institution or by a person acting for such agency or institution." FERPA created three primary rights for parents and eligible students:

1. Right to Inspect and Review/Right to Access Education Records
2. Right to Challenge the Content of Education Records
3. Right to Consent to the Disclosure of Education Records

It is important to recognize that there are numerous exceptions within the regulations to allow release of a student's education records without consent. These include releases to school officials with legitimate educational interest, releases to parents of dependent students, and releases in compliance with subpoenas. Since 1974, FERPA has been amended numerous times, and many of the recent amendments are directly related to student disciplinary records (Family Policy Compliance Office, 2004).

The first major amendment to FERPA related to student conduct came in 1990 when Congress passed the Student Right-to-Know and Campus Security Act. The legislation amended FERPA to clearly allow colleges and universities to share the final results of a campus disciplinary proceeding to the victim of an alleged crime of violence or nonforcible sex offenses (Lowery, 1998, 2000, 2004). Congress again amended FERPA in 1992 to exclude campus law enforcement unit records from the definition of education records. Some groups argued that this change excluded student disciplinary records from the definitional education records as well. In issuing regulations, the U.S. Department of Education clearly stated that disciplinary records were not excluded from the definition of education records.

Congress again made significant changes to FERPA in the Higher Education Amendments of 1998. The first of these changes allowed colleges and universities to release information to the parents of a student under age 21 when the institution determined that the student had violated any local, state, or federal laws or campus policy governing the use of alcohol or other drugs (Lowery, 2005). In the years following this change, many institutions revised their policies to allow for parental notification, and this remains an area needing further research (Lowery, Palmer, & Gehring, 2005; Palmer, Lohman, Gehring, Carlson, & Garrett, 2001; Palmer, Lowery, Wilson, & Gehring, 2003). The second, and much broader, change allowed public release of the final results of a student disciplinary proceeding if the accused student was found responsible for a violation that was a "crime of violence." The regulations define final results as "a decision or determination, made by an honor court or council, committee, commission, or other entity authorized to resolve disciplinary matters within the institution. The disclosure of final results must include only the name of the student, the violation committed, and any sanction imposed by the institution against the student." While this amendment did not require the release, public institutions in many states could be compelled to release the information under open records laws (Lowery, 2000; also see *Board of Governors of Southwest Missouri State University v. Patrick M. Nolan*, 1999).

In the 1990s, lawsuits were brought in several state courts seeking access to student disciplinary records under state open records laws. In *John Doe v. Red & Black Publishing, Inc.* (1993) and *State ex rel The Miami Student v. Miami University* (1997), the Georgia and Ohio supreme courts ordered the release of student disciplinary records under those states' open record laws. However, courts in Louisiana (*Shreveport Professional Chapter of the Society of Professional Journalists and Michelle Millhollon v. Louisiana State University*, 1994), North Carolina (*DTH v. University of North Carolina at Chapel Hill*, 1998), and Vermont (*The Burlington Free Press v. University of Vermont*, 2001) refused to grant access under those states' open records laws. These issues moved to federal court in 1998 when the U.S. Department of Justice brought suit against Miami and Ohio State universities to block those institutions from complying with the Ohio Supreme Court's decision from the previous year. Ultimately, the U.S. Court of Appeals for the Sixth Circuit determined:

- FERPA prohibits the release of education records.
- Disciplinary records are education records.
- There is no First Amendment right of access to student disciplinary records.
- Student disciplinary records are not criminal in nature.
- Public access might be harmful to the disciplinary process.
- The public interest in crime prevention does not require open records (*United States v. Miami Univ.*, 2002).

The court also noted that the fundamental purpose of the campus conduct system was educational, and public access would not support that goal. The court observed, "We find that public access will not aid in the functioning of traditionally closed student disciplinary proceedings" (p. 823).

Jeanne Clery Disclosure of Campus Security Policy and Campus Crime Statistics Act

In 1990, Congress passed the Crime Awareness and Campus Security Act. In 1998, the legislation was renamed the Jeanne Clery Disclosure of Campus

Security Policy and Campus Crime Statistics Act, in memory of Jeanne Clery, who was murdered in her Lehigh University residence hall room by another student in 1986. After her death, her parents, Howard and Connie Clery, formed Security on Campus and pushed for campus safety legislation at the state and federal level. Full consideration of the requirements of the Clery Act is beyond the scope of this chapter, and readers interested in learning more about all of the law's requirements are encouraged to review *The Handbook for Campus Crime Reporting* (U.S. Department of Education, 2005). This chapter considers only those requirements of the law that have the greatest relevance to campus conduct practice.

One of the core requirements of the Clery Act is publication of the Annual Security Report, which is distributed to all current students and employees and a summary of which is provided to prospective students and employees. The Annual Security Report contains summaries of a host of institutional policies relating to campus security, including information regarding who on campus students should report crimes to. Institutions must provide specific information regarding sexual assault, including:

- Notification to students that the institution *will* change a victim's academic and living situations after an alleged sex offense, and the options for those changes if those changes are requested by the victim and are reasonably available (U.S. Department of Education, 2005, p. 104).
- Procedures for campus disciplinary action in cases of an alleged sex offense, *including a clear statement that*:
  - The accuser and the accused are entitled to the same opportunities to have others present during a disciplinary proceeding.
  - Both the accuser and the accused must be informed of the outcome of any institutional disciplinary proceeding that is brought alleging a sex offense. Compliance with this paragraph does not constitute a violation of FERPA. For the purpose of this paragraph, the outcome of a disciplinary proceeding means only the institution's final determination with respect to the alleged sex offense and any sanction that is imposed against the accused (U.S. Department of Education, 2005, p. 105).
- Sanctions the institution may impose following a final determination of an institutional disciplinary proceeding regarding rape, acquaintance rape, or other forcible or nonforcible sex offenses. (Note that

this does not require that you simply state that sanctions may be imposed; you are required to list the sanctions as well) (U.S. Department of Education, 2005, p. 105).

These requirements demand that institutions ensure that their codes of conduct and practices reflect these expectations.

Beyond the policy statements, the Annual Security Report must include statistical information regarding crimes on campus for the preceding three calendar years in the following geographic areas: on-campus, residence halls, noncampus buildings and property, and public property. The statistics must include reports made to campus security authorities of murder/non-negligent manslaughter; negligent manslaughter; forcible sex offenses; non-forcible sex offenses (statutory rape and incest); robbery; aggravated assault; burglary; motor vehicle theft; and arson. Student conduct administrators are all considered campus security authorities as "[a]n official of an institution who has significant responsibility for student and campus activities, including, but not limited to, student housing, student discipline and campus judicial proceeding" (pp. 49–50). Statistical information is also included regarding arrests and referrals for disciplinary action (not resulting in arrests) for violations of liquor laws, drug laws, and illegal weapons possession (U.S. Department of Education, 2005).

Institutions are required to maintain records to demonstrate their compliance with the Clery Act for a period of three years after compliance. Because statistics are included in the next three years' Annual Security Report, this effectively means that records to support the statistics must be maintained for seven years (U.S. Department of Education, 2005). It is important that the student conduct office have a system in place for maintaining records to support the statistics originating through the conduct system included in the Annual Security Report.

Title IX of the Educational Amendments of 1972

Under Title IX of the Educational Amendments of 1972, institutions of higher education cannot exclude any person "from participating in, be[ing] denied the benefits of, or subjected to discrimination under any educational program or activity receiving federal financial assistance." The Supreme Court has ruled that sexual harassment is a form of discrimination under

Title IX in several cases (*Davis v. Monroe County Board of Education*, 1999; *Franklin v. Gwinnett County Public Schools*, 1992; *Gebser v. Lago Vista Independent School District*, 1998). In *Davis*, the U.S. Supreme Court addressed the question of student-on-student sexual harassment. The Court ruled that institutions could be held legally liable for student-on-student sexual harassment when the institution has "substantial control over both the harasser and the context in which the known harassment occurs" (p. 645), and the harassment is "severe, pervasive, and objectively offensive that it effectively bars the victim's access to an educational opportunity or benefit" (p. 633). The Court further limited institutional liability by applying its standard from *Gebser*, which limited liability to those cases in which a school official who has authority to take corrective action has actual knowledge of the harassment and responds with "deliberate indifference" (p. 290). Under these standards, Kaplin and Lee (2006) warn that the law "provides scant opportunity for student victims of harassment to succeed with Title IX damages actions against educational institutions" (p. 950). However, the U.S. Department of Education has established a much lower threshold for determining whether an institution has violated Title IX. An institution can be found to have violated Title IX, "if the school knows or reasonably should know about the harassment, the school is responsible for taking immediate effective action to eliminate the hostile environment and prevent its recurrence" (U.S. Department of Education, 2001). In considering both civil liability and potential of action by the U.S. Department of Education for violations of Title IX, student conduct administrators must ensure that the institution has systems in place to appropriately address student on student sexual harassment, including sexual assault.

Drug-Free Schools and Communities Act

Under the Drug-Free Schools and Communities Act, institutions are required to distribute an annual notification to current students and employees that includes standards of conduct related to alcohol and other drugs and disciplinary sanctions for violations of those standards. These standards of conduct must "clearly prohibit, at a minimum, the unlawful possession, use, or distribution of illicit drugs and alcohol by students and employees" (U.S. Department of Education, 2006, p. 7). Institutions are also expected to state that the institution "will impose disciplinary sanctions on students and employees for violations of standards of conduct" (p. 7). In addition to annual notification, institutions are required to complete a biennial review, which, in part, considers whether the institution "enforces sanctions for violating standards of conduct consistently" (p. 13). For an institution to meets its obligations under Drug-Free Schools and Communities Act, student conduct administrators must be involved in revising the annual notification and preparing the biennial review.

Conclusion

Since the U.S. Court of Appeals for the Fifth Circuit ruled in the landmark case of *Dixon v. Alabama State Board of Education* (1961), the courts have consistently held that students at public colleges and universities are entitled to due process protections, although these protections differ greatly from those enjoyed by criminal defendants. While there are differences between the requirements mandated by the various federal courts of appeals, the general requirements are establishment of a student conduct system through which cases are adjudicated; notice to students of the charges they are facing; the right to know the evidence against them; and the opportunity to present their side of the story to an unbiased panel or hearing officer (Silverglate & Gewolb, 2003). Student conduct administrators should view these requirements as the foundation on which the student conduct system is built. When considering additional rights for students, institutions should balance student rights with the need to maintain the core educational purpose of the student conduct system and to avoid the creation of an adversarial system. The courts have noted that an adversarial system runs counter to this educational purpose (*Osteen v. Henley*, 1993). Private colleges and universities should strongly consider affording students at least the minimum rights required at public colleges and universities. Beyond these requirements, public and private colleges and universities must also make certain that all of the contractual obligations are established through the conduct code. Beyond these procedural considerations, public and private institutions must also be concerned with meeting the institution's requirements under federal laws such as FERPA, the Clery Act, Title IX, and the Drug-Free Schools and Communities Act.

References

Ackerman v. College of the Holy Cross, 16 Mass.L.Rep. 108 (Super. Ct. Mass. 2003).
Albert v. Carovano, 851 F.2d 561 (2d Cir. 1988).

Anthony v. Syracuse, 231 N.Y.S. 435 (N.Y. App. DIV. 1928).

Board of Governors of Southwest Missouri State University v. *Patrick M. Nolan*, No. 198CC4344 (Mo. Cir. Ct. Jan. 26, 1999).

Bob Jones University v. Johnson, 396 F.Supp. 597 (D.S.C. 1974), *affirmed*, 529 F.2d 514 (4th Cir. 1975).

Boehm v. University of Pa. Sch. of Veterinary Med., 573 A.2d 575 (Pa. Super. Ct. 1990).

The Burlington Free Press v. University of Vermont, 779 A.2d 60 (Vm. 2001).

Cloud v. Boston Univ., 720 F.2d 721 (1st Cir. 1983).

Connally v. General Construction Co., 269 U.S. 385 (1926).

Cummings v. Virginia School of Cosmetology, 466 F. Supp. 780 (E.D. Va. 1979).

Dannells, M. (1977). Discipline. In W. T. Packwood (Ed.), *College student personnel services* (pp. 232–278). Springfield, IL: Charles C. Thomas.

Dannells, M. (1990). Changes in disciplinary policies and practices over 10 years. *Journal of College Student Development, 31*, 408–414.

Dannells, M. (1991). Changes in student misconduct and institutional response over 10 years. *Journal of College Student Development, 32*, 166–170.

Dannells, M. (1997). *From discipline to development: Rethinking student conduct in higher education*. ASHE-ERIC Higher Education Report, *25*(2). San Francisco: Jossey-Bass.

Dannells, M., & Lowery, J. W. (2004). Discipline and judicial affairs. In F. J. D. MacKinnon & Associates (Eds.), *Student affairs functions in higher education* (3rd ed., pp. 178–217). Springfield, IL: Charles C. Thomas.

Davis v. Monroe County Board of Education, 526 U.S. 629 (1999).

Dixon v. Alabama State Board of Education, 294 F.2d 150 (5th Cir. 1961).

Donohue v. Baker, 976 F. Supp. 136 (N.D. NY 1997).

Drug-Free Schools and Communities Act, 20 U.S.C. § 1145g (1989).

DTH v. University of North Carolina at Chapel Hill, 496 S.E.2d 8 (N.C. App. 1998).

Due v. Florida A&M Univ., 233 F. Supp. 396 (N.D. Fla. 1961).

Esteban v. Central Missouri State College, 290 F. Supp. 622 (W.D. Mo. 1968), *aff'd*, 415 F.2d 1077 (8th Cir. 1969).

Family Educational Rights and Privacy Act, 20 U.S.C. §1232g (1974).

Family Policy Compliance Office (2004). *Legislative history of major FERPA provisions*. Retrieved September 5, 2007, from http://www.ed.gov/policy/gen/guid/fpco/ferpa/leg-history.html

Fellheimer v. Middlebury Coll., 869 F. Supp. 238 (D. Vt. 1994).

Franklin v. Gwinnett County Public Schools, 503 U.S. 60 (1992).

French v. Bashful, 303 F. Supp. 1333 (E.D. La. 1969).

Gabrilowitz v. Newman, 582 F.2d 100 (1st Cir. 1978).

Gebser v. Lago Vista Independent School District, 524 U.S. 274 (1998).

Gehring, D. D. (2001). The objectives of student discipline and the process that's due: Are they compatible? *NASPA Journal, 38,* 466–481.

Gomes v. Univ. of Maine Sys., 304 F. Supp. 117 (D. Me. 2004).

Goodman v. Bowdoin College, 135 F. Supp.2d 40 (D. Me. 2001).

Gorman v. University of Rhode Island, 837 F.2d 7 (1st Cir. 1988).

Goss v. Lopez, 419 U.S. 565 (1975).

Gott v. Berea, 161 S.W. 204 (Ky. 1913).

Grossner v. Trustees of Columbia, 287 F. Supp. 535 (S.D. N.Y. 1968).

Grove City v. Bell, 465 U.S. 555 (1984).

Hannah v. Larche, 363 U.S. 420 (1960).

Herman v. University of South Carolina, 341 F. Supp. 226 (D.S.C. 1971), *affd.* 457 F.2d 902 (4th Cir. 1972).

Hill v. Board of Trustees of Mich. State Univ., 182 F.Supp.2d 621 (W.D. Mich. 2001).

Holert v. University of Chicago, 751 F. Supp. 1294 (N.D. Ill. 1990).

Holmes v. Poskanzer, 2007 U.S. Dist. LEXIS 3216 (N.D. N.Y. 2007).

Hunter, B., & Gehring, G. D. (2005). The cost of federal legislation on higher education: The hidden tax on tuition. *NASPA Journal, 42,* 478–497.

In re Rensselaer Soc. of Eng. v. Rensselaer Poly. Inst., 689 N.Y.S.2d 292 (N.Y. App. Div. 1999).

Jaska v. University of Michigan, 597 F. Supp. 1245 (E.D. Mich. 1984) *aff'd* 787 F.2d 590 (6th Cir. 1986).

Jeanne Clery Disclosure of Campus Security Policy and Campus Crime Statistics Act 20 U.S.C. §1092 (1990).

Jenkins v. Louisiana State Bd. of Education, 506 F.2d 992 (5th Cir. 1975).

John Doe v. Red & Black Publishing, Inc., 437 S.E.2d 474 (Ga. 1993).

Jones v. State Board of Education, 279 F. Supp. 190 (M.D. Tenn. 1968), *aff'd,* 407 F.2d 834 (6 Cir. 1969).

Kaplin, W. A., & Lee, B. A. (2006). *The law of higher education* (4th ed.). San Francisco: Jossey-Bass.

Lowery, J. W. (1998, Fall). Balancing students' right to privacy with the public's right to know. *Synthesis: Law and Policy in Higher Education, 10,* 713–715, 730.

Lowery, J. W. (2000, Fall). FERPA and the Campus Security Act: Law and policy overview. *Synthesis: Law and Policy in Higher Education, 12,* 849–851, 864.

Lowery, J. W. (2004). Battling over Buckley: The press and access to student disciplinary records. In D. Bakst & S. Burgess (Eds.), *Student privacy review: An annual review and compendium for higher education leaders* (pp. 40–45). Palm Beach Gardens, FL: Council on Law in Higher Education.

Lowery, J. W. (2005). Legal issues regarding partnering with parents: Misunderstood federal laws and potential sources of institutional liability. In K. Keppler, R. H.

Mullendore, & A. Carey (Eds.), *Partnering with the parents of today's college students* (pp. 43–51). Washington, DC: NASPA–Student Affairs Administrators in Higher Education.

Lowery, J. W., Palmer, C., & Gehring, D. D. (2005). Policies and practices of parental notification for student alcohol violations. *NASPA Journal, 42,* 415–429.

Mathews v. Eldridge, 424 U.S. 319 (1976).

Nash v. Auburn University, 812 F.2d 655 (11th Cir. 1987).

Nguyen v. University of Louisville, 2006 U. S. Dist. LEXIS 20082 (W.D. Ky. 2006).

Office of Judges Programs, Administrative Office of the U.S. Courts. (2003). *Understanding the federal courts.* Washington, DC: Author. Available online at http://www.uscourts.gov/understand03/media/UFC03.pdf

Osteen v. Henley, 13 F.3d 221 (7th Cir. 1993).

Palmer, C. J., Lohman, G., Gehring, D. D., Carlson, S., & Garrett, O. (2001). Parental notification: A new strategy to reduce alcohol abuse on campus. *NASPA Journal, 38,* 372–385.

Palmer, C. J., Lowery, J. W., Wilson, M. E., & Gehring, D. D. (2003). Parental notification policies, practices, and impacts in 2002 and 2003. *Journal of College and University Student Housing, 31*(2), 3–6.

Papachristou v. Univ. of Tenn., 29 S.W.3d 487, 489 (Tenn. Ct. App. 2000).

Pavela, G. (2000, Spring). Applying the power of association on campus: A model code of student conduct. *Synthesis: Law and Policy in Higher Education, 11,* 817–823, 829–831.

Powe v. Miles, 407 F.2d 73 (2d Cir. 1968).

Revised Sexual Harassment Guidance: Harassment of Students by School Employees, Other Students, or Third Parties. (2001). 66 Fed. Reg. 5512. Available online at http://www.ed.gov/about/offices/list/ocr/docs/shguide.html

Schaer v. Brandeis University, 735 N.E.2d 373 (Mass. 2000).

Shreveport Professional Chapter of the Society of Professional Journalists and Michelle Millhollon v. Louisiana State University (La. Dist. Ct., March 4, 1994).

Silverglate, H. A., & Gewolb, J. (2003). *FIRE's guide to due process and fair procedure on campus.* Philadelphia: Foundation for Individual Rights in Education.

Slaughter v. Brigham Young University, 514 F.2d 622 (10th Cir. 1975).

Soglin v. Kauffman, 418 F.2d 163 (7th Cir. 1969).

State ex rel. The Miami Student v. Miami Univ., 680 N.E.2d 956 (Ohio, 1997), cert. denied 522 U.S. 1022 (1997).

Stoner, E. N. (2000). *Reviewing your student discipline policy: A project worth the investment.* Chevy Chase, MD: United Educators.

Stoner, E. N., II, & Cerminara, K. (1990). Harnessing the "spirit of insubordination:" A model student disciplinary code. *Journal of College and University Law, 17,* 89–121.

Stoner, E. N., II, & Lowery, J. W. (2004). Navigating past the "spirit of insubordination": A twenty-first century model student conduct code with a model hearing script. *Journal of College and University Law, 31*, 1–77.

Title IX of the Educational Amendments of 1972, 20 U.S.C. § 1681 et seq.

Trahms v. Columbia Univ., 245 A.D.2d 124 (N.Y. Sup. Ct. App. Div. 1997).

Travelstead, W. W. (1987). Introduction and historical context. In R. Caruso & W. W. Travelstead (Eds.), *Enhancing campus judicial systems* (New Directions for Student Services No. 39; pp. 3–16). San Francisco: Jossey-Bass.

United States v. Miami Univ., 294 F.3d 797 (6th Cir. 2002).

U.S. Department of Education, Office for Civil Rights (2001). *Revised sexual harassment guidance: Harassment of students by school employees, other students, or third parties.* Retrieved September 5, 2007, from http://www.ed.gov/about/offices/list/ocr/docs/shguide.pdf

U.S. Department of Education, Office of Postsecondary Education. (2005). *The handbook for campus crime reporting.* Washington, DC: Author. Available online at www.ed.gov/admins/lead/safety/handbook.pdf

U.S. Department of Education, Office of Safe and Drug-Free Schools, Higher Education Center for Alcohol and Other Drug Abuse and Violence Prevention. (2006). *Complying with the Drug-Free Schools and Campuses Regulations [EDGAR Part 86]: A guide for university and college administrators.* Washington, DC: Author. Available online at http://www.higheredcenter.org/pubs/dfscr.pdf

Weidemann v. SUNY College at Cortland, 592 N.Y.S.2d 99 (N.Y. App. Div. 1992).

Winnick v. Manning, 460 F.2d 545 (2d Cir. 1972).

Wood, N. L. (2004, June). *Due process in disciplinary proceedings: Classic cases and recent trends in case law.* Session presented at the ASJA Donald D. Gehring Campus Judicial Affairs Training Institute, Salt Lake City, UT.

Woodis v. Westark Community College, 160 F.3d 435 (8th Cir. 1998).

Understanding the Courts

To fully appreciate the legal principles introduced in this chapter, it is helpful to understand as well how the judicial system works in the United States at both the federal and state levels. The largest number of federal courts are the U.S. federal district courts, which serve as the trial courts in the federal system. The district courts are each part of one of the 12 regional circuits (11 numbered circuits and the DC circuit), each of which is led by a U.S. Circuit Court of Appeals. These courts hear appeals from the district courts within each circuit. For example, when the federal district court for the Middle District of Alabama ruled against the students in *Dixon* (1961), the students appealed that decision to the U.S. Court of Appeals for the Fifth Circuit (the Eleventh Circuit, in which Alabama is currently located, was not created by Congress until 1981), which overturned the district court's decision. It is important to recognize that the rulings of the particular court of appeals are only legally binding on its circuit. See the map for information on the geographic boundaries of the federal districts and circuits. Decisions of the circuit courts, as well as state supreme courts, may be appealed to the Supreme Court of the United States, which is formally referred to as applying for a writ of certiorari. Each year more than 7,000 cases are appealed to the Supreme Court, which accepts fewer than 150 cases to hear, exercising its discretionary authority to select which cases to hear. The decisions handed down by the U.S. Supreme Court are legally binding on all courts. However, the decision of the Court to deny certiorari should not be interpreted as the Court's approval of the decision being appealed. The refusal of the Supreme Court to rehear a case does not legally change and enhance the authority of the lower court's decision. The states also have court systems with similar features to the federal courts, including trial courts, an appellate system, and a state supreme court, but the names of these levels vary from state to state (Office of the Judges Program, 2003).

Key Resources for Legal and Legislative Information

There are numerous print and Internet resources to obtain legal and legislative information. This list was developed to identify those resources that are most broadly available to readers.

Geographic Boundaries

of United States Courts of Appeals and United States District Courts

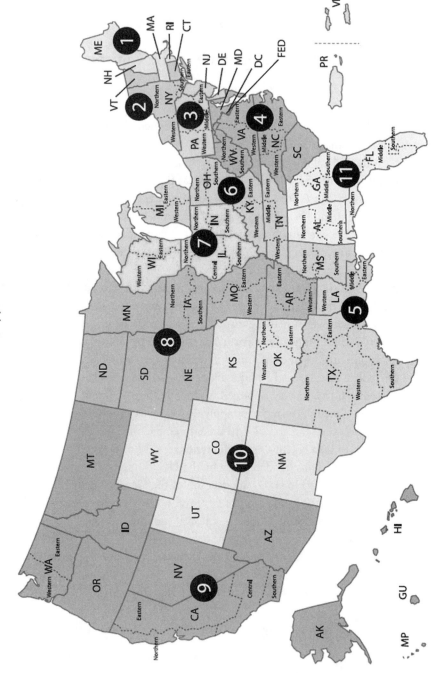

The Supreme Court of the United States' website provides useful information, including the history of the Court, published opinions, and biographies of the Justices.

http://www.supremecourtus.gov/

The Federal Judiciary's website provides information about and links to all of the aspects of the federal court system.

http://www.uscourts.gov/

The Oyez Project provides additional information about the Supreme Court of the United States and includes transcripts of oral arguments before the Supreme Court and audio recordings of selected cases.

http://www.oyez.org/

Thomas, a service of the Library of Congress, offers powerful tools for teaching for pending legislation and legislation passed by Congress since 1989. Information includes the sponsors, status, and the full text of the legislation.

http://thomas.loc.gov

The Legal Information Institute is a service of the Cornell Law School with access to various resources, including the U.S. Code, the Code of Federal Regulations, and the U.S. Constitution.

http://www.law.cornell.edu/

The Campus Legal Information Clearinghouse is a service of the Office of the General Counsel of the Catholic University of America and the American Council on Education, which offers a host of resources regarding legal issues facing colleges and universities and is organized by subject.

http://counsel.cua.edu/

The U.S. House of Representatives' website offers links to the Web pages of individual members of the House and the House committees.

http://www.house.gov

The U.S. Senate's website offers links to the Web pages of individual members of the Senate and the Senate committees.

http://www.senate.gov

The U.S. Department of Education's website provides useful information about the department's activities.

http://www.ed.gov

LexisNexis Academic is an index and database offered by LexisNexis to which many colleges and universities subscribe—even those without significant graduate programs. It offers the ability to search both federal and state judicial opinions and statutes as well as powerful news searches.

http://web.lexis-nexis.com/universe

6

FORUMS FOR RESOLUTION

Eugene L. Zdziarski and Nona L. Wood

Introduction and Philosophy

The purpose of this chapter is to introduce the reader to the forums for resolution currently in use to resolve allegations of student misconduct on college campuses in the United States. The mission of the Association for Student Judicial Affairs is "to facilitate the integration of student development concepts with principles of judicial practice in a postsecondary education setting, and to promote, encourage and support student development professionals who have responsibility for student judicial affairs" (Association for Student Judicial Affairs [ASJA], n.d., p. 1).

Contemporary practice of student judicial affairs by student conduct officers (SCOs) includes an expectation that the SCO is not merely engaging in a brief conversation to determine responsibility and assign a sanction, but is instead holistically attending to the developmental needs of the student beyond a finding of responsibility and assignment of a sanction. For this reason, the SCO must take the time necessary to learn about the student's background, the student's status within the university, and the student's goals and aspirations beyond the university community. By engaging in a conversation with the student about these personal characteristics, opportunities often arise to assist students to use campus and community resources more effectively and efficiently to help them achieve those goals and aspirations.

Basic Goals in Complaint Resolution

No matter what the form of complaint resolution, the SCO must learn the answers to several very basic questions—who, what, when, where, and in some cases, why. In many instances, the answers to these questions may appear apparent on the various complaint documents, including reports from residence life, police—both internal and external, and reports from other sources such as university staff or faculty members.

An experienced and skilled SCO, however, always keeps in mind that until the accused student is heard, all may not be as it seems on paper. Individuals' perceptions of the same event can and will vary. Witnesses may not always be truthful, and in some cases, identities may be mistaken.

Judgments concerning responsibility should be reserved until all documents have been carefully reviewed with the accused student and he or she has had the opportunity to respond fully to any other information and/or witnesses to be considered by the SCO in determining whether the student violated one or more sections of the code of student behavior.

The primary goal of any resolution process is to determine whether it is more likely than not that the student is responsible for violating one or more specific sections of the campus code of student behavior. To be truly developmental and educative, it is also critical that the student understand how his or her behavior affects others and how engaging in that behavior may affect the student's future, particularly in the context of career choice. If the student's career choice is unknown, then it is especially important to help him or her understand that without a specific career goal, maintaining a positive behavioral record on and off campus is essential to protect the student's interest for maximizing future employment and/or postgraduate opportunities.

Typical Forums for Resolution Currently in Use Across the United States

The most prevalent forms of resolution in use to process complaints concerning student behavior on college campuses include one-to-one disciplinary conferences, also called administrative hearings, and board or panel hearings. Board hearings vary greatly. They may include student-only boards, student and faculty boards, and boards that may include students, faculty, and staff to represent all campus constituencies. More and more campuses are also exploring various forms of alternative dispute resolution (ADR). These may include mediation, restorative justice, and various models of ADR.

The Disciplinary Conference

Advance preparation is key to a successful disciplinary conference. In addition to a thorough review of case documents, the SCO should learn what can be gleaned from university records about the accused student: his or her local and permanent addresses, major, classification versus terms in residence, the student's grade point average (GPA), and whether he or she is making positive progress toward degree completion.

If available, it may also be helpful to know the student's final high school GPA, and if there is a great disparity between the student's high school GPA and college GPA performance, there are several possible avenues for discussion. When the presenting issue involves substance abuse, this information provides an opening for conversation with the student concerning the degree to which time spent in alcohol- and/or drug-related social activities may have interfered with his or her ability to perform well academically. Alternatively, it also provides the opportunity to explore the possibility of undiagnosed or unattended learning disorders or anxiety, depression, or other adjustment or psychological and/or psychiatric disorders that could benefit from referral to the counseling center, academic support services, or other relevant campus resources. Although SCOs are not generally diagnosticians, experience and careful interviewing can often uncover areas of concern that warrant referral to and exploration by other appropriate professionals on or off campus.

In addition to academic standing, other areas to discuss should include career goals and how students use their time outside the classroom. Is the student employed? Is he or she working an appropriate number of hours per week in relationship to the total number of credit hours? If the student is working too many hours, the student may be unable to demonstrate his or her true academic potential.

Does the student have a defined career goal? Individuals with unclear career goals and large amounts of unstructured out-of-class time, in general, tend to drift more frequently, and in drifting, many find themselves in greater behavioral difficulties. Encouraging students to define career goals and to engage in positive extracurricular activities, particularly those related to their academic majors, can assist them in reducing the likelihood of repeating breaches of the campus code of student behavior.

Depending on the age of the student, the nature of the violation, and the type of institution, it can also be beneficial to discuss whether the student has informed his or her parents or family about the current difficulties. Parents or family can be a positive source of support in assisting their sons and daughters to make a successful recovery from difficult conduct cases. Judgment must be used, as in some cases, parents or family can be counterproductive and even enabling, refusing to believe that their offspring violated campus policies and, even if he or she did, that significant campus sanctions are warranted, particularly if separation from the campus is contemplated.

Although these issues may seem time consuming, they can be covered in the first few minutes of a disciplinary conference, especially if the SCO does careful advance preparation. Many data elements can be gleaned from university records before the disciplinary conference. An interview form can be designed so that note taking is a matter of using Xs or check marks and can be done in a relatively unobtrusive manner. Discussing these items first also helps set the stage for discussing the tougher questions to follow—the who, what, when, where, and why questions as the accused student responds to the specific allegations outlined in the previously delivered notice of charges letter. By now, having established some degree of rapport with the student, discussion of the more difficult topics should flow more easily and naturally.

From an administrative point of view, conducting this type of disciplinary conference has several advantages. First, the SCO is able to get a general overview of the student relatively quickly and to set the student at ease before entering the more difficult part of the conference. Second, the student is viewed holistically; rather than focusing only on the student's negative behavior, the SCO is focusing on how the institution can assist the student to accept responsibility for the behavior, to learn how the behavior affects others, and to learn how the behavior may affect the student's future in the context of his or her particular major.

This is a very important part of today's disciplinary conferences. More and more employers are conducting background checks on potential employees, while graduate institutions are also checking potential applicants (Liptak, 2006). Students may be unaware of these practices and may need assistance in learning how their conduct record and/or a criminal record may affect them in the context of particular majors, especially nursing, pharmacy, education, criminal justice, law, medicine, and others.

Third, this type of disciplinary conference also allows for appropriate referrals to be made, if needed, to other individuals or agencies, on or off campus. Such referrals might involve sending students to the campus career services office, the counseling center, the local rape and abuse crises center, the campus women's center, student activities, the state job service agency, the cooperative education office, and/or a host of other offices to assist the student with his or her particular interests or needs. A fourth advantage is that the student is able to see that the SCO is interested in the student as more than simply someone who has done something wrong, and, instead, is interested in seeing that individual reach his or her full potential.

A fifth advantage is that the SCO is able to bring a high degree of consistency over time, so that students in similar situations are treated in a similar manner, adjusting for their conduct records. This is particularly important so that the SCO and the office in which the SCO works is perceived as treating students fairly and consistently. Students may not always like the decisions that are reached, but having a sense of fairness is essential in maintaining the image of credibility with the institution's student body.

A final advantage is that the SCO is able to manage the work flow more efficiently and can move more cases through the office more quickly than when cases must be heard in a board format. The intimacy of this type of conversation can rarely be achieved in the context of a board hearing, especially when some or all of the board members may be one's peers.

Some students prefer an administrative hearing because it allows greater preservation of their privacy, as fewer individuals learn about their misdeeds. In addition, administrative hearings can generally be scheduled and held more quickly, thus giving students a speedier resolution, allowing them quicker relief to their anxiety, while allowing administrators a more efficient work flow.

There are some limitations to using a disciplinary conference approach. Because there is no other community involvement, the hearing officer may be vulnerable to accusations of bias and other forms of attack intended to deflect attention from the student's misconduct, especially if the conference is not recorded. In light of the need to avoid seeming adversarial, few such one-on-one disciplinary conferences are recorded.

In addition, this work can be intense and may lead to employee burnout, particularly if insufficient university resources are devoted to meeting the demand of the work flow. It is important for supervisory administrators to pay attention to ensure that adequate support is available to avoid employee burnout and to allow for timely conferences to provide for optimal educational results with each student.

The Co-Adjudication Model

During the 2001 Donald D. Gehring Campus Judicial Affairs Training Institute, Mary Beth Mackin of the University of Wisconsin-Whitewater and David Parrott, then of Western Michigan University and currently at Texas A&M University at College Station, presented information on a co-adjudication model as an alternative administrative forum. In this model, two administrative hearing officers, representing two different areas within the university, hear a case together. For example, this model might be useful in a case involving students and faculty, students in special communities, resident students, cases in which gender is an issue, and so forth.

One of the authors of this chapter used this model in a stalking case involving a male student to deflect the possibility of an accusation of gender bias. The adjudication team was composed of one male and one female. This was a good strategy, as the male student's first line of attack was one of gender bias. Having a male partner in the hearing was useful in removing gender bias as a basis for challenging the hearing's outcome.

Although this model is useful, it does not always solve the challenges it is intended to alleviate. It is, however, one more potentially beneficial strategy to consider in certain cases. Be mindful that a student may feel overwhelmed and outnumbered by this approach.

The Student Conduct Board

Student conduct boards are another common way for resolving student behavioral issues. Use of such boards is appealing because it resonates with our American sense of justice and fairness. The concept of having one's fate determined by an impartial jury of his or her peers is something we are taught as schoolchildren when we learn about the Sixth Amendment to the Constitution. Having an impartial group of people review the facts of the situation, judge those facts based on a set of community standards, and determine a reasonable and appropriate response to one's behavior is what most American's have come to expect as fair and just.

In addition to their common acceptance and inherent perceptions of fairness, student conduct boards provide significant educational benefits. Having members of the campus community judge the behavior of their peers and assign sanctions for behavior they find inappropriate is an important learning process for both the accused student and the members of the board. While a decision made by an administrator in an administrative hearing might simply be perceived as a customary institutional response, decisions made by peers in a board or panel process can be very effective in communicating community standards of acceptable behavior within the campus environment.

Types of Boards

There are many different types of student conduct boards in higher education. Boards can be used to conduct individual hearings concerning behavioral violations, academic integrity violations, or both. They can also hear organizational cases involving violations committed by student groups or clubs. Such organizational boards might hear cases involving alleged violation of university policies as well as alleged violation of organizational rules. For example, a common organizational board on many campuses is a Greek judicial board, which might address violations of university policies, such as alcohol or hazing policies and/or the policies of the campus Interfraternity Council, membership recruitment policies, or achievement standards.

Student conduct boards may also be unique to different programs within the campus community. For example, some campuses may have separate student conduct boards to address the unique needs and interests of a particular segment of the campus community. This most often involves professional programs such as medicine and law. Because of professional standards and ethics, certification and licensure requirements, or other legal requirements, the implications of some violations may be much different from those of other parts of the campus. Therefore, while these boards enforce the same code of conduct and use the same process for adjudication as other conduct boards within the campus community, how they might sanction a particular violation could be significantly different within the professional school environment.

Another type of student conduct board is an appellate board. While student conduct boards can be used as primary hearing bodies, they can also hear appeals. In some campus judicial systems, primary adjudication of student conduct cases is conducted through disciplinary conferences or administrative hearings, and appeals are heard by a board (e.g., Texas A&M University, University of Maine). On other campuses, primary adjudication is conducted through boards, and appeals are heard by an administrative official (e.g., Illinois State University, Ohio Northern University, and Seaton Hall University). On still other campuses a combination of administrative hearings and board hearings is available at both the primary and appellate levels.

The number and types of different boards used on any campus depends on the individual history and culture of each institution. At the same time, administrators should have a clear rationale and justification for the existence of each of the different boards, because when a new board is created to address the needs of one group, others will surely seek to have a board created to address their needs, and as the number of boards increases, it is more difficult to provide adequate training and maintain an appropriate level of consistency across the judicial system. Another approach to address the various needs of the campus community is through the composition of student conduct boards.

Board Composition

Much like the different types of boards, the composition of student conduct boards can take a variety of forms. Such boards can be composed entirely of students, faculty, or staff, or any combination. Again, the individual history and culture of each campus will play a role in how some boards are comprised.

As noted earlier, part of the allure of a board is the concept of having a decision made by a jury of one's peers. The primary question, however, becomes, how does one define peers? Students often define peers as other students. Student conduct boards comprised entirely of students can be very effective in adjudicating cases if they are trained properly. A former SCO, Diane Waryold (1998), notes, "students dialoguing with student in a disciplinary hearing regarding the behavioral expectations of the university community can be the best method for redirecting behavior" (p. 228). Examples of student conduct boards composed solely of students can be found throughout the country (e.g., College of William and Mary, University of Florida, University of Virginia).

Others might suggest that faculty are the primary determiners of institutional standards, so such decisions should be made by a faculty board. This is particularly true when dealing with academic honesty violations, where many faculty feel a strong sense of responsibility for maintaining the institution's academic integrity.

Fundamentally however, student conduct boards should represent the campus community, which includes students, faculty, and staff, so one might argue that all are peers and should be represented in such campus decisions. Student conduct boards should also be representative of the campus makeup. Thus, board composition should consider such things as race, gender, classification, college, etc.

While boards should be representative of the campus community and draw from a wide cross-section of the campus, we must be careful to ensure that the size of the board does not become unwieldy. Although it may be tempting for some campuses to comply with the American concept of a jury comprised of 12 members, routinely getting a group of 12 together for campus hearings can be challenging, depending on the frequency of such hearings. Further, as the size of the board grows, the longer the hearings tend to be and the more difficult it is to reach consensus. In addition, an even number of members can lead to a split decision requiring added time in deliberations to break the tie, or the case be reheard altogether. It is for these reasons that boards consisting of 5–7 members seem ideal; the number is sufficient to represent the campus community, while still making the group manageable in terms of scheduling and group processing.

Although you may require 5–7 members to conduct a hearing, you will typically want to select and train a larger group of individuals to manage your case load. Minimally, you will want to have alternate members to fill in when other members are unable to attend a particular hearing or when a member must be excused because of prior knowledge of the case or a relationship with the accused. When a large number of cases are referred to a particular student conduct board, you may wish to create multiple sub-boards to handle the volume. For example, an institution's student conduct board might consist of three sub-boards that hear the actual cases. One sub-board might consist of individuals available to hear cases on Monday afternoons, another hears cases on Tuesday mornings, and a third hears them on Wednesday evenings. With multiple sub-boards, SCOs can address the class/

work schedules of the board members, accused students, and witnesses who may need to be involved.

Another approach to managing caseload with a student conduct board is to develop a pool of individuals trained in the student conduct process from which members can be drawn for various hearings. This approach provides the greatest flexibility in both scheduling and board composition. With thoughtful recruitment and selection of members, a pool of board members can be useful in ensuring that the composition of the student conduct board represents the community in which an infraction took place, and that the members appreciate the unique needs and interests of that community. For example, it was noted earlier that because of professional standards and ethics, certification and licensure requirements, or other legal requirements, it is important to have involvement of members from a particular professional school in the hearing process. With a pool of board members, students and faculty from the particular professional school could be drawn on to participate in a hearing that involves a student from that school, and the nature of the case requires input from individuals in that particular discipline.

Recruitment and Selection of Members

The different types of boards and their and size will affect the recruitment and selection process required to fill them. Members can be elected, appointed, nominated, or apply for seats on student conduct boards.

In some cases, board members may be appointed or even elected. For example representatives from student government or the faculty senate may be elected to serve as members of a student conduct board. In other cases, board members may be appointed by the student body president or faculty senate chair. This approach to recruitment and selection of board members can provide a consistent and stable source of board members. On the other hand, when board members are elected or appointed, sometimes they can bring with them a particular agenda or issue that they may seek to achieve through membership on the board. In these cases, student conduct board training must focus on creating an understanding of the process and the need for board members to maintain their objectivity in every case.

In other cases, board members may be nominated or may apply for positions. Particularly in situations where there is an application process, the SCO has a significant level of responsibility to recruit potential members.

The campus community needs to be educated not only about the opportunity to serve on the student conduct board, but also about the benefits and advantages of doing so. It is during this recruitment phase that SCOs should give careful consideration to various constituencies within the campus community and ensure that representation is obtained from all parts of the institution.

In a process where individuals either apply or are nominated to serve on a board, there is usually some type of interview process. The primary purpose of such interviews is to ensure that the individuals who have applied or been nominated clearly understand what the time commitments will be, the training that will be required, and the types of decisions they will be asked to make. With this information, some individuals will choose to opt out on their own. The interview process also provides SCOs with an opportunity to evaluate whether potential members have hidden agendas that might be counterproductive to the student conduct process. To ensure a level of objectivity, this interview process may be conducted by one or two current board members in addition to the SCO.

An issue that sometimes arises in the selection process is whether or not a student who has previously been sanctioned for misconduct should be eligible to serve on a student conduct board. We would contend that a student should not be eliminated from the process simply because he or she has previously been sanctioned. Instead factors such as the nature of the violation, how recently the violation took place, and the attitude or demeanor of the student concerning his or her own proceeding are more appropriate indicators of whether or not a student should serve on a board. Sometimes, a student who has been through the process can be one of its best proponents.

Board Training

Regardless of the type, size, or composition of student conduct boards, proper training is essential for them to operate effectively. All board members should undergo an initial comprehensive conduct board training program before participating in a hearing. A comprehensive training program should provide board members with an understanding of the educational philosophy behind campus conduct proceedings, a basic sense of fundamental due process rights and burden of proof, clear knowledge of specific campus procedures, and exposure to group process and decision-making skills. Often conducted over the course of a couple of days or several evenings, board training programs should involve a combination of lecture-style presentations, interactive discussion, and role-plays or mock hearings. It can be useful to include experienced board members in planning and implementing the board training, particularly in facilitating mock hearings so that they are realistic and relevant. In addition to the formal training program, it may be beneficial for new board members to observe an actual student conduct hearing before serving on the board.

In conjunction with the training program, it is important that all members of the student conduct board receive a procedures manual that includes a complete copy of the student conduct code and an outline of the hearing process. A good procedures manual also provides board members with a sample script to use at various stages of the hearing process.

Depending on the frequency of student conduct board hearings and the opportunity for all members to participate regularly, it is advisable to conduct periodic in-service training programs. Such programs can focus attention on areas in which boards have experienced difficulties or can clarify aspects of the process that may be the subject of frequent questions.

Like the disciplinary conference or the co-adjudication model, student conduct board hearings are another common forum for resolving allegations of student misconduct. Student conduct boards come in many types and sizes and should include a representative sample of the campus community. However, the specific form such boards take on any one campus is influenced greatly by the history and culture of the institution.

Alternative Dispute Resolution and Other Forums for Resolution

Thus far we have addressed common forums for the adjudication of student conduct violations. But not all types of situations fall under the jurisdiction of the institution or its neatly defined codes of conduct. Sometimes disputes arise between members of the campus community that fall outside the parameters of the campus conduct process, but if they are not addressed, they may become disruptive to other members in the community or might evolve into a conduct violation that might have been avoided. In these situations, we need alternatives to the traditional forums for adjudication.

Methods of alternative dispute resolution include a variety of different processes, such as negotiation, conciliation, mediation, and arbitration, to name a few. The most common forms used in college and university settings to resolve student disputes are conciliations and mediation. Both of these forms of dispute resolution involve the use of a third party, but they differ in the role and level of involvement of this third party.

Conciliation is simply the involvement of a third party in the discussions and bargaining between other parties to assist in reaching a mutually agreeable resolution of their differences. As noted in the seminal work on campus dispute resolution, *Peaceful Persuasion: A Guide to Creating Mediation Dispute Resolution Centers on College Campuses*, the third party attempts to bring the various parties together and share information between them to facilitate dialogue and encourage resolution (Girard, Rifkin, & Townley, 1985). In conciliation, the third party is not necessarily a true neutral party and often has some interest in resolving the situation. A common example of conciliation in the college and university environment is when a resident assistant helps two students involved in a roommate conflict. While the staff member plays an important role in helping to resolve the situation, he or she has a vested interest in the resolution because continuing the dispute may cause further disruptions to other residents on the floor or might force the resident assistant to take other actions, such as relocating the residents or making a student conduct referral.

Mediation is another common form of alternative dispute resolution used in higher education, but administrators are well advised to have more specific training before implementing this approach. Like conciliation, mediation is a voluntary process that involves a third party; however, the third party is a neutral party who assists the disputing parties in satisfying their interests by guiding them through a semistructured process (Waters, 2000). This process is typically described as a series of steps or stages (e.g., see Girard, Rifkin, & Townley, 1985; Goldberg, Sander, & Rogers, 1992; Lovenheim, 1989; Waters, 2000). These stages can be summarized as (1) opening statement; (2) story-telling; (3) identification of issues; (4) generation of options; and (5) agreement (Zdziarski, 1998). Each stage of the process builds on the previous stage and helps the parties to focus on the issues central to the dispute rather than just on their positions. Ultimately, the goal of the process is to reach a mutually acceptable agreement that is a win for both parties.

This form of alternative dispute resolution is particularly advantageous in cases where individuals are reluctant to pursue the traditional forms of complaint resolution on campus. Take, for example, a relationship dispute in which a boyfriend and girlfriend break up. The ex-boyfriend repeatedly calls the ex-girlfriend, but she refuses to answer his calls. Despite being told she never wants to speak to him again, he persists. E-mail messages, cards, and flowers are sent. The ex-boyfriend's actions could be considered harassment, but the ex-girlfriend does not want him to face disciplinary action; she just wants him to leave her alone. Mediation may be an appropriate alternative in this situation.

Other instances in which mediation might be useful are in instances where there are allegations of hate speech. Bringing the parties together to engage in a form of restorative justice in which each party has the opportunity to learn about the other's perspective may be productive in helping the community to heal and in reducing the chance of subsequent confrontations.

While there are a variety of situations in which mediation provides an attractive alternative to traditional campus adjudication processes, there are some instances in which the use of mediation is not appropriate. Mediation should never be used when the situation involves violence, abusive behavior, or a serious crime (Lovenheim, 1989). In particular, the U.S. Department of Education's Office of Civil Rights (2001) has determined mediation to be inappropriate in sexual assault cases. Mediation should not be used in such cases, even if the alleged victim requests it.

In each instance it is important that the mediators undergo formal training. A good resource for training in both basic and advanced mediation is available from ASJA at the Donald D. Gehring Academy for Student Conduct Administration at the University of Utah. Information about this training program can be found at http://www.asjaonline.org.

Conclusion

A variety of forums for resolution are available today in the administration of campus conduct systems. Whether a disciplinary conference, a student conduct board, or an alternative method of dispute resolution, each of these forums has advantages and disadvantages. How these forums fit into the student conduct system and how they are applied on each campus depends on the unique history and characteristics of the institution. Yet, administrators need to be familiar with these different forums and how they might be used in administering student conduct and ethical development on college campuses.

References

Association for Student Judicial Affairs (ASJA). (n.d.). *Constitution of the Association for Student Judicial Affairs*. Retrieved June 24, 2007 from http://www.as jaonline.org/attachments/files/1/ASJAConstitution.pdf

Girard, K., Rifkin, J., & Townley, A. (1985). *Peaceful persuasion: A guide to creating mediation dispute resolution centers on college campuses*. Amherst, MA: The Mediation Project, University of Massachusetts.

Goldberg, S. B., Sander, F. E., & Rogers, N. H. (1992). *Dispute resolution: Negotiation, mediation, and other processes* (2nd ed.). Boston: Little, Brown & Co.

Liptak, A. (2006). Criminal records erased by courts live to tell tales. *New York Times*. Retrieved October 17, 2006, from http://www.nytimes.com/2006/10/17/uw/17expunge.html?th&emc = th

Lovenheim, P. (1989). *Mediate, don't litigate. How to resolve disputes quickly, privately, and inexpensively—without going to court*. New York: McGraw Hill.

U.S. Department of Education, Office of Civil Rights. (2001, January). *Revised sexual harassment guidance: Harassment of students by school employees, other students, or third parties*. Retrieved June 24, 2007, from http://www.ed.gov/about/offices/list/ocr/docs/shguide.pdf

Waryold, D. M. (1998). Increasing campus judicial board effectiveness: Are two heads truly better than one? In Brent G. Paterson & William L. Kibler (Eds.), *The administration of campus discipline: Student, organizational, and community issues*. Asheville, NC: College Administration Publications.

Waters, W. C. (2000). *Mediation in the campus community: Designing and managing effective programs*. San Francisco: Jossey-Bass.

Zdziarski, E. (1998). Alternative dispute resolution: A new look at resolving campus conflict. In Brent G. Paterson & William L. Kibler (Eds.), *The administration of campus discipline: Student, organizational, and community issues*. Asheville, NC: College Administration Publications.

7

CAN WE BE GOOD WITHOUT GOD?

Exploring Applied Ethics With Members of Student Conduct Hearing Boards

Gary Pavela

D o college disciplinary systems have an educational aim? Most conduct administrators say yes, with the caveat that a just penalty is part of the educational process. What may be overlooked is the learning that occurs when members of the student judiciary hear disciplinary cases. These students (often among the best on our campuses) are probably being tutored in good listening skills, principles of due process, and respect for ethnic diversity, among other desirable qualities. Their participation in the disciplinary process, however, is also a good way to engage them in one of the core questions in the humanities: What is the origin of applied ethics? Is what we define as good or virtuous behavior (specified, in part, in our campus disciplinary codes) a product of natural selection, cultural evolution, reason, or divine law?

It is tempting to dismiss these questions as being too esoteric or philosophical, and so they would be in a criminal courtroom. But campus conduct systems operate in the context of higher learning. The instruction that occurs outside our classrooms (and conveys status to student development administrators as educators) is more than a matter of technique. We should also encourage members of the student judiciary to think deeply and carefully about the substantive—and sometimes emotionally powerful—experiences they encounter during hearings and deliberations.

The Origin of Applied Ethics: A Religious Perspective

Human beings engage in the seemingly inexplicable practice of cross-species altruism—rescuing stranded birds, enforcing animal cruelty laws, and the like. Aside from a few stories about dolphins saving struggling swimmers, or dogs alerting their owners to a dangerous house fire, nothing like human altruism appears in the rest of the animal world. (As best we can tell, there appears to be no organized movement among whales to save humans.) If empathy is a core component of cooperation, and cooperation is the foundation of applied ethics, we should care a great deal about the origins of the altruistic personality in human beings.

From a religious perspective, the altruistic personality is grounded in a fully developed conscience. But what are the origins of conscience? Philosopher William Barrett (1986) answers this in his book, *The Death of the Soul*:

> The human animal as the moral animal is the bearer of [an] "ought"—the one creature who submits to its call. How can we explain the power and weight this call of duty . . . has over us? Kant's answer . . . [includes the] . . . religious and the spiritual: We experience this call because, however vast and indifferent the universe that surrounds us, we are creatures that are haunted by the feeling that we have some spiritual destiny beyond the material order. To put it tersely, duty—the call of conscience—is the voice of God within us. (pp. 92–93)

It's not our role (at secular institutions) to propound this view, but no intelligent discussion of the topic can be complete without it. When we invite members of the student judiciary to discuss the philosophical implications of what they do (the obvious aim of this essay), religious perspectives cannot be excluded. Research conducted through the Cooperative Institutional Research Program (CIRP), a 40-year study (1966–2006), documents a very promising trend among first-year students. Specifically, these students self-reported that helping others is very important.

The Origin of Applied Ethics: Darwin's Theory

Charles Darwin had the courage to describe both the majestic beauty of the evolutionary process (seen from afar) and misery caused by the relentless and indifferent force of natural selection. More than many realize, Darwin was also an ethical theorist—and his theory has profound implications for educators. In *The Descent of Man* (1871/1979), he wrote,

> The development of moral qualities [in man] is a[n] . . . interesting problem. The foundation lies in the social instincts, including under this term family ties. These instincts are highly complex, and in the case of the lower animals give special tendencies towards certain definite actions; but the most important elements are love, and the distinct emotion of sympathy. . . . A moral being is one who is capable of reflecting on his past actions and their motives—of approving some and disapproving of others; and the fact that man is the one being who certainly deserves this designation, is the greatest of all distinctions between him and the lower animals . . . Owing to this condition of mind, man cannot avoid looking both backwards and forwards, and comparing past impressions. Hence, after some temporary desire or passion has mastered his social instincts, he reflects and compares the now weakened expression of such past impulses with the ever-present social instincts; and he then feels that sense of dissatisfaction which all unsatisfied instincts leave behind them, he therefore resolves to act differently for the future—and this is conscience. . . . The appreciation and the bestowal of praise and blame both rest on sympathy; and this emotion, as we have seen, is one of the most important elements of the social instincts. Sympathy, though gained as an instinct, is also much strengthened by exercise or habit. . . . The moral nature of man has reached its present standard, partly through the advancement of his reasoning powers and consequently of a just public opinion, but especially from his sympathies having been rendered more tender and widely diffused through the effects of habit, example, instruction, and reflection. (pp. 200–201).

In contemporary academic parlance, Darwin's views represent a blend of Kohlberg, Gilligan, and Aristotle. For Darwin (1871/1979), our maturing cognitive capacity (what Lawrence Kohlberg would emphasize as the means to define universal justice) is stimulated by "love . . . and the distinct emotion of sympathy" (similar to Carol Gilligan's "ethic of care" or better described as "empathy"). Darwin's concluding emphasis on habit echoes the classic formulation in Aristotle's *Nicomachean Ethics* (1962):

> For the things which we have to learn before we can do them, we learn by doing: men become builders by building houses, and harpists by playing the harp. Similarly, we become just by the practice of just actions, self-controlled by exercising self-control, and courageous by performing acts of

courage. . . . [W]e must see to it that our activities are of a certain kind. . . . Hence it is no small matter whether one habit or another is inculcated in us from early childhood; on the contrary, it makes a considerable difference, or rather, all the difference. (pp. 34–35)

Contemporary debates about teaching ethics in the United States tend to focus on self-contained theoretical frameworks grounded in ethnic or gender identity theories. As the rigidity of those frameworks wanes, Darwin's synthesis of sympathy (or, better stated, empathy), reason and habituation are likely to receive greater attention, especially if supported by empirical observation.

Applied Ethics and the Sciences

Much of the direction of pertinent anthropological research (joined by interdisciplinary contributions in economics and psychology) was summarized in an article in *The New Scientist* (Buchanan, 2005), which began with a question similar to what we posed at the beginning of this essay:

Homo sapiens is [not] the only species in which individuals bestow kindness on others. Many mammals, birds, insects and even bacteria do likewise. But their largesse tends to be reserved for their genetic relatives. . . . Humans are different, for we cooperate with complete genetic strangers—workmates, neighbours, anonymous people in far-off countries. Why on earth do we do that? (Buchanan, 2005)

According to *The New Scientist*, the answer is a variation on Darwin's theme:

Over the past decade, experiments devised by Ernst Fehr of the University of Zurich in Switzerland, among others, have shown that many people will cooperate with others even when it is absolutely clear they have nothing to gain. A capacity for true altruism seems to be a part of human nature. . . . Across disciplines, researchers now agree that people often act against their own self-interest. "This is the most important empirical work on the human sense of justice in many years," says evolutionary biologist Robert Trivers of Rutgers University in New Jersey. Unless such altruism or "strong reciprocity" represents an evolutionary "maladaptation," it constitutes a significant step forward in cultural evolution. (Buchanan, 2005)

The *New Scientist* concluded with the observation that:

[Recent research] findings suggest that true altruism, far from being a mal-adaptation, may be the key to our species' success by providing the social glue that allowed our ancestors to form strong, resilient groups. It is still crucial for social cohesion in today's very different world. "Something like it had to evolve," [said economist Herbert] Gintis [of the University of Massachusetts, Amherst]. (Buchanan, 2005).

Applied ethics, in short, entails expanding empathy and reciprocity (necessary for small-group bonding) from families to clans, cities, nations, humanity, and life itself. Achieving this goal requires both emotion and reason. Emotion provides passion and commitment, while reason develops strategies to expand the human capacity for affiliation in new and increasingly complex settings. The process has the look of inevitability until one examines history (especially the wars of the last century) close up. Our students need to consider the likelihood that ethical progress is tentative and fragile; it is as easy to lose ground as it is to gain it.

Applied Ethics and the Humanities

Faculty colleagues in the humanities have pursued many blind alleys on the subject of applied ethics, disguising rehashed theories of skepticism and nihilism in the impenetrable language of contemporary literary criticism. A sense that the tide may be turning is evidenced in a renewed interest in classical (Greek and Roman) studies and in the appeal of history as a window on patterns of human fallibility. Criticism of the war in Iraq, for example, is often buttressed by historical examples of national hubris—going as far back as the Athenian invasion of Sicily. Renewed interest in the didactic study of history was the subject of Donald Kagan's 2005 Jefferson Lecture in the Humanities:

The ancient Greek historians, the earliest and still among the greatest, set the agenda, taking as their subjects large events affecting great numbers of people in dramatic and powerful ways. . . . Thucydides understood that his careful attention to factual accuracy came at a literary price. "Perhaps," he says, "the absence of the fabulous from my account will seem less pleasing to the ear." But he judges the sacrifice necessary to achieve a higher goal, a philosophic one with great practical application: "If those who wish to have a clear understanding both of the events of the past and of the ones that some day, as is the way in human things, will happen again in the future in the same or a similar way, will judge my work useful, that will be enough for me. It has been composed not as a prize-essay in a competition, to be heard for a moment, but as a possession forever . . ." The fact is that we all need to take our moral bearings all the time, as individuals and as citizens. Religion and the traditions based on it were once the chief sources for moral confidence and strength. Their influence has faded in the modern world, but the need for a sound base for moral judgments has not. If we can not look simply to moral guidance firmly founded on religious precepts it is natural and reasonable to turn to history, the record of human experience, as a necessary supplement if not a substitute. History, it seems to me, is the most useful key we have to open the mysteries of the human predicament. (Kagan, 2005)

An Opportunity for Learning

Recent studies show high levels of spiritual interest among college freshmen, although CIRP data (2006) suggest the percentage of students claiming no affiliation with an *organized* religion has increased. That doesn't mean, however, that students are unreceptive to serious discussion about the origins of applied ethics—whether from a religious, scientific, or historical perspective. A *Michigan Daily* overview of a UCLA Higher Education Research Institute freshman survey (Neuman, 2005) reported, "83 percent of students [surveyed last year] believe those who are non-religious can be just as moral as those who are." The relative tolerance and openness of college students on this subject represents an extraordinary opportunity for educators in and outside the classroom. There is a good prospect for learning if we seize the occasion. Hosting a formal lecture with a dry academic title probably will not work, but an evening discussion, perhaps facilitated by a faculty colleague in philosophy, classics, psychology, or history, is likely to be animated and productive if we start with the deceptively simple question: Can we be good without God?

References

Aristotle. (1962). *Nicomachean ethics* (Martin Ostwald, trans). New York: Macmillan.

Barrett, W. (1986). *The death of the soul.* New York: Doubleday.

Buchanan, M. (2005, March 12). Charity begins at Homo sapiens. *New Scientist.* Retrieved July 8, 2007, from http://www.newscientist.com/channel/being-human/mg 18524901.600

Cooperative Institutional Research Program (CIRP). (2006). *UCLA News: Official press release.* Retrieved July 8, 2007, from http://www.gseis.ucla.edu/heri/PDFs/PR_TRENDS_40YR.pdf

Darwin, C. (1979). *The descent of man.* New York: Norton. (Originally published 1871).

Kagan, D. (2005). *In defense of history: 2005 Jefferson lecture.* Retrieved July 8, 2007, from http://www.neh.gov/whoweare/kagan/lecture.html

Neuman, R. (2005, June 13). Poll: College students highly spiritual, religious. *Michigan Daily.* Retrieved July 8, 2007, from http://www.michigandaily.com/

8

DEVELOPMENT
AND DIVERSITY

A Social Justice Model

Matthew Lopez-Phillips and Susan P. Trageser

C onduct officers often find themselves at the intersections of power and privilege that our student development theory and preparatory programs have left us unprepared to handle. The practice of social justice offers one direction for reconciling the various injustices and inequalities that are inherent in our society. These same inequalities and injustices are present in our practice of conduct on our college campuses. Social justice involves an understanding of social identity (race, gender, religion, sexual orientation, class, mental ability, etc.), which provides a framework to further comprehend oppression. In this chapter, social identity, of both the student and the reader, is explored while suggesting a context that consists of one's institution and one's practice as a conduct officer. Our goal in this chapter is neither to provide a comprehensive review of student development theories nor to perform a comparative analysis of their use with every oppressed group. It is our hope to engage the reader in a thoughtful, self-reflective process about how one might use the principles of social justice, student development theory, and life experiences in working as a conduct officer.

Fundamental to engaging in this dialogue are a few definitions of some of the principles of social justice education. Bell writes in Adams, Bell, and Griffin (1997):

> Social justice education is both a process and a goal. The goal of social
> justice education is full and equal participation of all groups in a society

that is mutually shaped to meet their needs. Social justice includes a vision of society in which the distribution of resources is equitable and all members are physically and psychologically safe and secure. We envision a society in which individuals are both self-determining (able to develop their full capacities) and interdependent (capable of interacting democratically with others). Social justice involves social actors who have a sense of their own agency as well as a sense of social responsibility toward and with others and the society as a whole. The process of attaining the goal of social justice we believe should also be democratic and participatory, inclusive and affirming of human agency and human capacities for working collaboratively to create change. (p. 4)

What Bell has laid out in the preceding definition is not far from what some hope our institutions aspire to. Could we not agree or at least hope that our intuitions should be safe and secure as well as places where resources are shared and human agency and capacities are nurtured and developed in a participatory democratic way? We acknowledge that using social justice principles is a work in progress for all seeking to implement it. However, to achieve these lofty goals of human development, we must examine our institutions and their social actors to see how oppression operates. For purposes of this conversation, we use a definition of oppression from Goodman and Schapiro's work on sexism in Adams, Bell, and Griffin (1997): "Oppression: A systemic social phenomenon based on the perceived and real differences among social groups that involve ideological domination, institutional control, and the promulgation of the oppressor's ideology, logic system, and culture to the oppressed group. The result is the exploitation of one social group by another for the benefit of the oppressor group" (p. 118). Hardiman and Jackson in Adams and associates (1997) further refine our working definition of oppression by stating that it occurs on three levels: individual, institutional, and societal/cultural. "Individual oppression focuses on the beliefs or behaviors of an individual person. . . . Here we refer to the conscious or unconscious actions or attitudes that maintain oppression" (pp. 18–19). Institutional-level oppression can further be explained as "The application of institutional policies and procedures in an oppressive society run by individuals or groups who advocate or collude with social oppression produces oppressive consequences" (Adams, Bell, & Griffin, 1997, pp. 18–19). Finally, they provide us with the definition of societal-/cultural-level oppression as

[s]ociety's cultural norms perpetuated implicit and explicit values that bind institutions and individuals. In an oppressive society the cultural perspective of the dominant groups is imposed on the institutions by individuals and on individuals by institutions. These cultural guidelines, such as philosophies of life, definitions of good, normal, healthy, deviance, and sickness, often serve the primary functions of providing individuals and institutions with the justifications for social oppression. (pp. 18–19)

So who are the students before you today? What are their social identities? Are they from a dominant group or subordinate group? What might not be obvious? Do they identify as persons of color? Transgendered? Are they on financial aid? Do they have a learning disability, or are they temporarily able-bodied? What is their connection to the powerful people on your campus? Are their families big donors to the athletic program or are they your star athletic (name the sport) players? Do they have a team of lawyers and unlimited funds to deal with the issue at hand? Are the students working two jobs and single parents? Are they the president of your Gay, Lesbian, Bisexual, Transgender (GLBTQ) organization on campus? In what year of enrollment are they—first or fifth? What do we know from our student development theory about the challenges they face? How can we challenge them to be transformative? Before we can understand the student(s) with whom we are working, we first must examine ourselves in our roles as conduct officers.

Few individuals on the college campus have the conduct officer's positional power to significantly change a student's reality. With that power great responsibility is incurred to render "caring and just" decisions. We must be wise stewards and not use the power that our institution has given us to oppress our students' development. Each of us should examine his or her own privilege, as well as social power, with the same critical eye that we use to examine the student before us. We must be aware of our own target (subordinate; limited, or no access to some type of social power) or nontarget (dominant, greater access to some type of social power) status with regard to race, class, gender, ability, sexual orientation, religion, age, and so on. Do we consider ourselves to be part of dominant groups, and what do we know about our status in these groups? Are we subordinate to these groups, and what is our level of self-awareness? Our journey to self-awareness in such matters is a lifelong process, so it is important to acknowledge our own continuing struggle with these issues as well that of our students.

We believe that reflection is key to "caring and just" action. How can one be caring and just without thoroughly "unpacking" one's own values beliefs and paradigms of reality making? What does my office, the ring on the fourth finger of my left hand, or the pictures on the wall say to a student? What biases do I bring into the meeting with the student, and where are my learning edges (unexamined areas of social identity)? What are the things about me that might get in the way of the developmental opportunity before me? Where and how does my privilege show up? What if the student before me perceives that I am subordinate/targeted (limited or no access to social power) in all social identities except in my position of power as a conduct officer? (For example, the conduct officer is a female person of color, and the student is a white male from an affluent family.)

We start this exploration with the knowledge that in our recent past, we (higher education) have oppressed others. Several examples illustrate this point. We only educated men at one time; only recently was it decided that women could earn degrees as well. On one campus with which we are familiar, only recently were family bathrooms created where only female or male facilities were offered previously. This change acknowledged gender as a continuum, not a bimodal choice, thus recognizing transgendered persons. In our affirmative action reports on many campuses we continue to use forms that ask individuals to identify how much and in what proportion they identify with one particular race or ethnic background. We are told that this process is used to justify hiring practices and the all-important quantifiable report of people of color applying at our institution. Such examples suggest that it is time we take a deeper look as to how we might contribute or collude in acts of oppression on our campuses and, more specifically, in our roles as conduct officers. To begin this look, we need to examine our institutions, our students, and ourselves.

Any conversation about oppression, social justice, and the practice of student conduct needs a context within which to work. We ask you to reflect on some questions about the institution at which you are employed and your work as a conduct officer. It is also useful to examine what has been said about millennial generation students. This examination will yield some broad generalizations, but your own specific institutional and personal context should give these generalities discrete meaning for you.

Let us start with a few questions about your institution: How does the university at which you are working categorize itself (i.e., religious-affiliated, historically Black colleges and universities (HBCU), large state, Ivy League, research-based, tech-based, etc.)? What values, beliefs, ideologies, and paradigms does your university hold as truths, and how do they oppress certain individuals or groups of people? These questions may be difficult to answer, so consider some examples:

- Where is the closest family bathroom?
- Do all of your forms have only two choices for gender?
- Are all of your student services buildings accessible?
- Does your university offer domestic partner benefits?
- How is the current distribution of power at your institution maintained?
- What constitutes "power," who holds it, and what are their social identities?
- In your organizational structure, to what constituencies is power allocated: to deans, faculty, the provost, the vice president of finance, conduct officers, or students?

Such questions are not intended as indictments but rather as a means to clarify your institutional mindset.

These questions should provoke further examination of the concepts of power and privilege. Griffin, in Adams and associates (1997), defines power as "Access to resources that enhance one's chances of getting what one needs or influencing others in order to lead a safe, productive, fulfilling life" and privilege as "unearned access to resources (social power) only readily available to some people as a result of their social group membership" (p. 73). Now that you have begun to analyze your institution, you have a part of the context within which to examine the use of social justice principles in your practice of conduct. It is now time to examine our students and ourselves.

While traditional-age students are used for context in this chapter, it is important not to exclude nontraditional-age, graduate, or other student populations. The impact of social justice discussed pertains to all student populations. Traditional-age college students are a part of what we often refer to as the "Millennial Generation." These students were born between 1982 and 2000. We are certainly not implying that all of our students fit into a mold; however, we would like to provide you with a set of characteristics to consider. Today's students comprise the most ethnically diverse and non-White generation to date. There are many ways to characterize this generation; sheltered, confident, team-oriented and conventional, and pressured to name a few (Howe & Strauss, 2000, 2003). This generation is and has always been "connected" to their friends and to the rest of the world, via cell phones, text messaging, e-mail, and instant messaging, along with a variety of online social networking communities. Some of the events that have affected these students' lives include the terrorist attacks of September 11, 2001, the death of Princess Diana, the Bill Clinton/Monica Lewinsky scandal, the Columbine shootings, and the Virginia Tech shootings. These students are often competitive and focused on success and excellence and, as a result, experience great pressure. The Millennial Generation student also takes a more active role in decision making than students of past generations (i.e., voting, developing short- and long-term plans). It is also important to understand a little about this generation's parents, as they have been and will remain very involved in the lives of these students. Parents of this generation have assisted in the planning and supervision of their children's lives, from ballet, piano, soccer, and other extracurricular activities, to goal setting and college selection. These parents often have abundant resources and are strong and vocal advocates for their student (Howe & Strauss, 2000, 2003).

We cannot ignore the generational attitudes of the nontraditional-age students and graduate students with whom we work as well as the parents of all students (most often Baby Boomers and Generation Xers). It is important for the reader to be familiar with the characteristics of the other generations of which these students and parents are a part and their differences from the Millennial Generation not only to attempt to understand everyone with whom you interact, but also to recognize the challenges they face so you can further assist your students, and their parents, in achieving success and reaching their goals.

In this section we look at student development theory and its intersections with social justice principles. Important to this discussion are a few theories most relevant to our work as conduct officers as well as to the development of our students. For these purposes, we will focus on Kohlberg, Gilligan, Kolb, and Dewey.

Lawrence Kohlberg focused his work on moral reasoning. Moral reasoning is different from moral behavior. It is "the intellectual or reasoning ability to evaluate "goodness" or "rightness" of a course of action in a hypothetical situation" (Muuss, 1988, p. 206). "Moral behavior is the ability to resist temptation in a real life situation" (p. 206). Kohlberg considered the principle of justice to be central as moral judgment is developed, and he viewed "moral development as representing the transformations that occur in a person's form or structure of thought with regard to what is viewed as right or necessary" (Kohlberg & Hersh, 1977, p. 54, as cited by Evans, Forney, & Guido-DiBrito, 1998, p. 173).

Kohlberg's theory predicts three levels of moral development divided into six stages. Everyone processes through the stages at different rates and ages, and one stage must be completed before moving on to the next. A significant portion of moral development occurs during the college years. The majority of adolescents and adults function in level 2 (conventional or moral level), which deals with meeting social expectations, acceptance of social order, the recognition of the rights of others, and conformity. Most individuals remain somewhere between stages three and five in their moral development during their lives. However, if one is to reach level 3 (postconventional) it is most likely to occur during the college years; however, this level may not be maintained throughout life.

Table 8.1 depicts the levels and stages of moral development as described by Kohlberg (Muuss, 1988, pp. 209–213; Evans et al., 1998, pp. 173–175).

While Kohlberg's research focused on adolescent males, his theory was applied across different cultures. He learned that the stages remained consistent across the different cultures, and that the pace and age of development still varied. In less-developed societies, with fewer technological advances, adolescents advanced through the stages at a slower rate than did those in more technologically advanced regions. These patterns were consistent within different social classes as well.

Carol Gilligan's work also focused on moral development and grew out of Kohlberg's theory. Gilligan believed that Kohlberg's work was biased in regard to women. Her work focuses on the moral development of women and their differences from men. The predominant focus of her work is care orientation, which refers to attachment to others, and means "relationships with other must carry equal weight with self-care . . ." (Evans, Forney, & Guido-DiBrito, 1998, p. 191).

Gilligan's theory comprises three levels, with a transition between each. Each of Gilligan's levels correlates to one of Kohlberg's. She refers to two voices, one of justice and one of care and responsibility. Men and women

TABLE 8.1
Kohlberg's Stages of Moral Development

	Level 1: Preconventional	Level 2: Conventional	Level 3: Postconventional
Stage 1: Heteronomous Morality or Obedience and Punishment	Obeying a rule to avoid punishment		
Stage 2: Individualistic, Instumental Morality or Instumental Relativism	Needs and interests may conflict		
Stage 3: Interpersonally Normative Morality or Interpersonal Concordance		Living up to expectations; approval seeking	
Stage 4: Social System Morality or Orientation Toward Authority, Law, Duty		Upholding laws and carrying out responsibilities; belief in "law and order"	
Stage 5: Human Rights and Social Welfare Morality or Social Contract Orientation			Fundamental human rights and values; welfare of the larger community
Stage 5: Human Rights and Social Welfare Morality or Social Contract Orientation			Fundamental human rights and values; welfare of the larger community
Stage 6: Morality of Universalizable, Reversible, and Prescriptive General Ethical Principles or Universal Ethical Principles			Process is as important as fairness of procedures; "liberty and justice for all"

have both voices, but each individual generally prefers one over the other. Women most often prefer care and responsibility, with the majority of men preferring justice. The premise of care and responsibility is the one through which moral problems are seen in relation to issues or relationships and are resolved through care.

When tested across different cultures, Gilligan's theory maintained that there are gender differences in moral development. A single contradiction to this theory was found within a population of college-age Native American women, who scored considerably higher on justice than did those of other cultures. This may be attributed to tribal values and roles (power positions) within a tribe (Evans, Forney, & Guido-DiBrito, 1998).

David Kolb's theory focuses on the concept of "experiential learning." "Learning, according to Kolb [1984], is "the process whereby knowledge is created through the transformation that comes with experience" (Hamrick, Evans, & Schuh, 2002, p. 69). Kolb's theory of learning consists of four stages, often not viewed as developmental stages, but as a series of steps providing foundations for the next. Current demands, experiences, and heredity all influence the learning styles outlined by Kolb. As a result, learning is viewed as a person-environment transaction requiring flexibility in style to be adaptive rather than a balance of all styles (Evans, Forney, & Guido-DiBrito, 1998).

Student development theorist John Dewey supported the notion of education as a reflective process based on experiences and learning. To be most effective, all information taught should have a corresponding experiential component. Dewey also stated that experiences should not be ranked, but all of them should be given appropriate reflection (Hamrick, Evans, & Schuh, 2002, pp. 218, 258–259).

"Student discipline is, and always has been, an excellent opportunity for developmental efforts," states Dannells (Rentz & Saddlemire, 1988, p. 139). Many types of theories speak to a student's development: moral, identity, cognitive, ethical, and many, many more. These theories help us to understand similar developmental issues students experience in the cycle of socialization. Our goal as conduct officers is to be transformative in our work with our students and to help them develop the transformative learning skill for themselves and the world in which they live. "Transformative learning increases students' ability to think about the world, themselves, and how they think and learn" (Keeling, 2006, p. 5). Some of the major themes of the conduct experience stated by Dannells (Rentz & Saddlemire, 1988) support this idea:

> First is a commonly stated objective and a means to further growth in the individual "offender" (Dannells, 1977). Second, self-understanding or clarification of personal identity, attitudes and values, especially in relation to authority, for both the student whose behavior is in question and also for students who sit on judicial boards, is often described (Boots, 1987; Greenleaf, 1978). Third, the goals of self control, responsibility and accountability are often mentioned (Caruso, 1978; Pavela, 1985; Travelstead, 1987). Fourth, the use of ethical dialogue in confronting the impact of the individual's behavior and its moral implications and in examining the fairness of rules is receiving increasing attention (Pavela, 1985; Smith, 1978). Last, there appears to have been an extension of the scope and goals of student discipline beyond that of simple adjudication and control/rehabilitation to a broader objective of moral and ethical development as it relates to contemporary social issues such as prejudice, health and wellness, sexism, racism and human sexuality (Dalton & Healy, 1984). (p. 140)

The goal of social justice work can be seen as having many of these same objectives. If we want our students to become transformative and authentic human beings, they need a greater sense of self. Freire (1993) speaks to this process of self-knowledge in his pedagogy of the oppressed, stating, "Knowledge emerges only through invention and re-invention, through the restless, impatient, continuing, hopeful inquiry human beings peruse in the world, with the world and with each other" (p. 53). To dialogue with students in a teacher-student/student-teacher paradigm can truly be transformative for the student, the conduct officer, and the conduct process.

Harro's 1982 work on the cycle of socialization lays out for us a process by which we come to understand and try to make sense of the world around us (see Figure 8.1).

Now look at the model through the lens of student development theory. Just as we are born into the world, our lens of identity is blank; we have no information, biases, traditions, guilt etc. If you look at the arrow that connects the lens of identity to the lens of socialization and teaching, you can see the developmental challenges and where we might apply our student development theories (see Figure 8.2). Since abstract thought is possible, the adolescent begins to develop a sense of ethical and moral responsibility based on abstract principles of what is right or wrong:

FIGURE 8.1
Cycle of Socialization

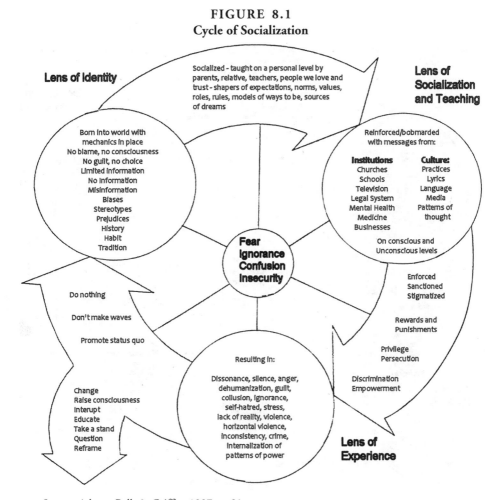

Source: Adams, Bell, & Griffin, 1997, p. 81

The same is true of the concept of social justice and of rational, aesthetic, or social ideals. As a result of the acquisition of such values, decisions, whether in opposition to or in agreement with the adult, have an altogether different significance than they do in small social groups of younger children. . . . The possibilities opened up by these new values are obvious in the adolescent, who differs from the child in that he is not only capable of forming theories but is also concerned with choosing a career that will permit him to satisfy his needs for social reform and for new ideas (Piaget and Inhelder, 1969, p. 151, as cited in Muuss, 1998, p. 208)

FIGURE 8.2
Cycle of Socialization and Student Development Theory

Lens of Identity

Socialized - taught on a personal level by parents, relative, teachers, people we love and trust - shapers of expectations, norms, values, roles, rules, models of ways to be, sources of dreams

Kohlberg - Level 1 - Preconventional
Gilligan - Level 1 - Orientation toward Self-interest

Lens of Socialization and Teaching

Born into world with mechanics in place
No blame, no consciousness
No guilt, no choice
Limited information
No information
Misinformation
Biases
Stereotypes
Prejudices
History
Habit
Tradition

Reinforced/bombarded with messages from:

Institutions	Culture:
Churches	Practices
Schools	Lyrics
Television	Language
Legal System	Media
Mental Health	Patterns of
Medicine	thought
Businesses	

On conscious and Unconscious levels

**Fear
Ignorance
Confusion
Insecurity**

Do nothing

Don't make waves

Promote status quo

Enforced
Sanctioned
Stigmatized

Rewards and Punishments

Privilege
Persecution

Discrimination
Empowerment

Kohlberg - Level 3 -
Postconventional
Gilligan - Level 3 -
Focusing on the
Dynamics between self
and others

Resulting in:

Dissonance, silence, anger, dehumanization, guilt, collusion, ignorance, self-hatred, stress, lack of reality, violence, horizontal violence, inconsistency, crime, internalization of patterns of power

Kohlberg - Level 2 -
Conventional
Gilligan - Level 2 -
Identification of
Goodness with
Responsibility for
Others

Change
Raise consciousness
Interupt
Educate
Take a stand
Question
Reframe

Lens of Experience

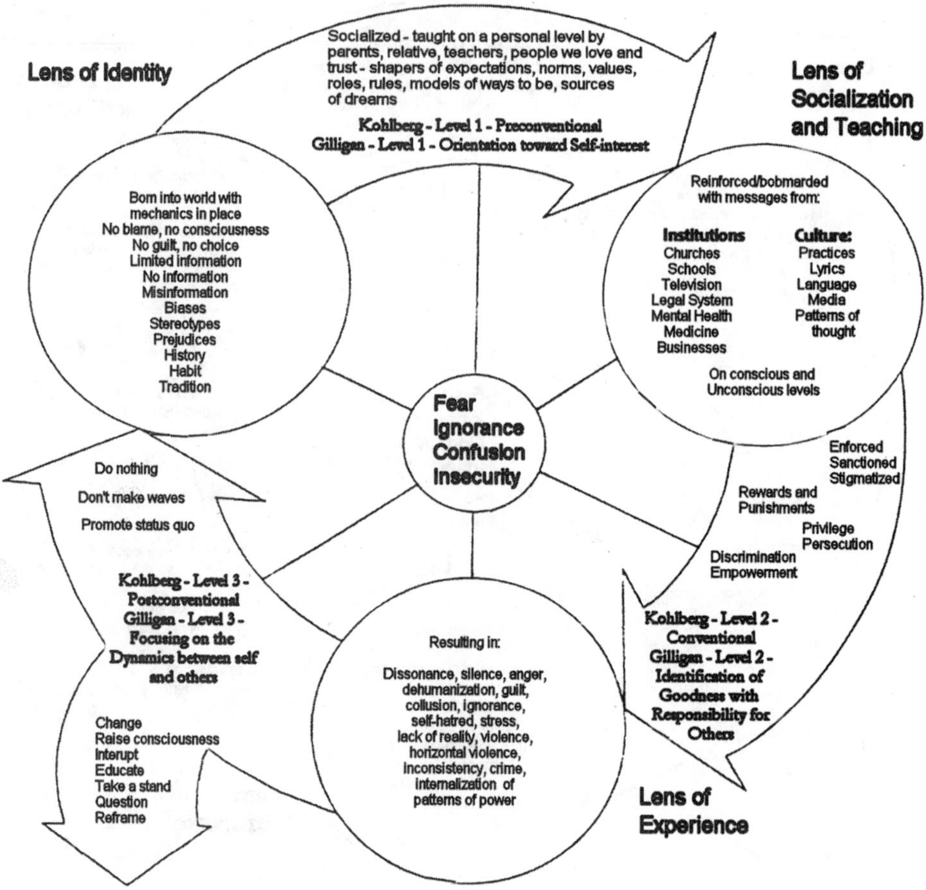

Source: Adapted from Adams, Bell & Griffin, 1997, p. 81

While we have applied the theories of Kohlberg and Gilligan to the cycle, we have not applied those of Kolb and Dewey. How do you see the concepts of experiential learning and learning through reflection work into the cycle of socialization? As you continue to consider the application of student development theory to the cycle of socialization, think of how and where the conduct process would apply and fit.

We should be cautious that our use or misuse of theory is not manipulated to further oppress our students:

[A]s this review of recent theory and research underlying student development concludes, a few remarks about the abuse of theory may be in order. Brownsword (1997) . . . provided a brief synopsis of this important topic. He reminded student affairs professionals that thorough knowledge of theory is both professionally powerful and subject to abuse. If professionals use knowledge to stereotype or limit themselves or others, then they are abusing their knowledge of theory.

"Oh he's only a Kohlberg Stage 3, we can't pick him."

"She's an ISTJ; She'd never make a career in student affairs."

　　Similarly, when a professional uses knowledge of theory as an excuse for behavior, he or she is abusing theory.

Other: "You missed our appointment again."

Self: "What can you expect, I'm a P!"

"He's a Kegan 3 and that's why he let his friends into the back gate of the concert. What else can you expect?"

Awareness, understanding, appreciation, and facilitation of the growth of developmental and typological differences are not the same as excuses, stereotypes, and preemptive limitations. Seek the former; avoid the latter. (Brownsword, as cited in Creamer & Associates, 1990, p. 73)

It is important that we be mindful of our power to name things in student affairs and the practice of student conduct, otherwise we run the risk of pounding the square peg into the round hole. In some instances, naming can be viewed as a form of oppression.

Case Studies

Two case studies follow. As you consider them, remember and apply the concepts and models discussed earlier in the context of your current setting. Questions for reflection and processing have been provided. Since each university is a unique entity, we have not provided summaries or conclusions for the case studies. Conclusions to these case studies will vary, depending on the university considered and identities of the student(s) you envision. Readers are encouraged to consider their own social identity and the social identity of the student(s) involved, coupled with your institution's values, beliefs, and paradigms.

Case 1

You receive a call from the director of the GLBTQ center asking you whether it is a violation of the student code of conduct to use the bathroom of the opposite gender. You examine the code and find it listed as a violation in the housing section; therefore, it applies only to the residence halls. However, it is also violation of state law, so it applies to other university facilities and, as such, is chargeable under the code. The center's director then recounts to you a story of a transgendered (male to female) student, Bobbie, who would like to use the recreational center on campus. She has been living as a woman for the last few years and is waiting for the final surgery that will take place some time within the year. Bobbie has asked for the GLBTQ center's support as she has just returned from a meeting with the director of the Recreation Center who has informed her that she is not allowed in the women's locker room and will have to use the men's. For safety, as well as identity reasons, Bobbie and the director feel that it is inappropriate for her to use the men's locker room. The director has called and asked for your help, as you chair the Student Affairs Diversity Committee.

- What are the issues?
- How does your own social identity play into the situation?
- What are the campus values, ethics, and policies with regard to this issue?
- Through what lenses are you viewing the student?
- What theories would you consider as you work through the multiple issues?
- How does your position as chair of the Diversity Committee and university conduct officer conflict or not conflict?

Case 2

You receive a police department report of a fraternity fight involving more than 100 individuals. No citations were issued; however, there was one arrest. Trent is a sophomore and has been seen by your office once before for an alcohol violation. He feels the police targeted him. He was arrested, placed in handcuffs, and put in the patrol car, while others were just told to break it up and go back to their house. In your meeting, Trent tells you that other fraternity members were engaged in the fight, and he was trying to break it up. He admits to throwing a few punches after he was hit several times, and he presents several witnesses from both houses who corroborate his story. Trent is very angry and wants to file a report of discrimination against the police force. Trent is the only African American member of his fraternity.

- What are the issues?
- How does your own social identity play into the situation?
- Through what lenses are you viewing the student?
- What student development theories would you use?
- How do you hold Trent accountable for his behavior and address the alleged profiling that occurred?

The complicated nature of our ever-changing world is evident every day on the college campus. For us to best serve our students and our institutions we need to be prepared to stand in the intersections of power and privilege that our positions and institutions have given us. The practice of conduct without the lens of social justice falls short of the goals of a fully democratic, participatory society where individuals are safe both physically and psychologically. If we are to transform our interactions so that they are socially just, we must model for students as well as the rest of the institution a way to address the inequalities and injustices in our society. If we are effective in engaging students in this transformative process, our hope is that they will take what they have learned into the world and transform it using these principles.

We have to carefully examine ourselves, our institutions, and our policies and procedures to ensure that we are not perpetuating an unjust system. Our challenge is to take the time to examine our own multiple identities, and when a student and/or situation occurs where we find ourselves in one of those intersections of power and privilege, whether we are the target or not, we do not use our position of power to oppress.

In closing, we would like you to do an exercise that may assist you in examining what it might be like to walk in the shoes of another and have you experience the conduct process differently. Before your next student meeting, sit in the chair your student usually sits in and write down what you see. What do you conclude about the person(s) whose office you are now in? What can you tell about the person by just looking at what is before you? Try using your knowledge of all the various student development theories to create different students. What challenges come up as you think of the students? What other challenges appear? Next, do a scan of your whole operation from start to finish. We think you might be surprised by what you learn.

Finally, consider how your office is engaged in the conversation on your campus with regard to social justice. Make social justice a part of your staff and office evaluations. Examine your policies and the code and forms you use in your day-to-day operation, and continue the transformative process of your institution, your students, and yourself. We can lead by making sure that student learning outcomes are linked to an awareness and understanding of social justice issues and sound student development theory. Show others how the conduct process can be transformative, dare to be transformative yourself. Paradigm shifts are painful, and the dominant paradigm power brokers will fight against any change. But we have to ask ourselves what the cost is to our profession, our students, and the world if we don't lead.

References

Adams, M., Bell, L. A., & Griffin, P. (Eds.). (1997). *Teachings for diversity and social justice*. London: Routledge.

Creamer, D. G., & Associates (Eds.). (1990). *College student development theory and practice for the 1990s*. Alexandria, VA: American College Personnel Association.

Evans, N. J., Forney, D. S., & Guido-DiBrito, F. (1998). *Student development in college: Theory, research, and practice*. San Francisco: Jossey-Bass.

Freire, P. (1993). *Pedagogy of the oppressed*. New York: Continuum.

Hamrick, F. A., Evans, N. J., & Schuh, J. H. (2002). *Foundations of student affairs practice: How philosophy, theory, and research strengthen educational outcomes*. San Francisco: Jossey-Bass.

Howe, N., and Strauss, W. (2000). *Millennials rising: The next great generation*. New York: Vintage Books.

Howe, N., and Strauss, W. (2003). *Millennials go to college*. Great Falls, VA: Life-Course Associates.

Keeling, R. P. (Ed.). (2006). *Learning reconsidered 2: Implementing a campus-wide focus on the student experience*. Published by ACPA, ACUHO-I, ACUI, NACADA, NACA, NASPA, and NIRSA.

Muuss, R. E. (1998). *Theories of adolescence*. New York: Random House.

Rentz, A. L., & Saddlemire, G. L. (Eds.). (1988). *Student affairs functions in higher education*. Springfield, IL: Charles C. Thomas.

9

ETHICS AND DECISION MAKING

Elizabeth Baldizan

Meaning is not something you stumble across, like the answer to a riddle or the prize in a treasure hunt. Meaning is something you build into your life. You build it out of your past, out of your affections and loyalties, out of the experiences of humankind as it is passed on to you, out of your talent and understanding, out of the things you believe in, out of the things and people you love, out of the values for which you are willing to sacrifice something. (Speech by John Gardner, "Personal Renewal," delivered November 10, 1990, to McKinsey & Company in Phoenix, Arizona)

Why Personal Values?

It is odd how values are sometimes not fully realized until they are yanked away. Aspirations quickly boil down to realizations. A death, an accident, a life-altering incident may drive home a clear value. All of a sudden . . . in the blink of an eye . . . an individual is forced to discern. In contrast, there are lives that are more reflective, day by day and moment by moment, personal action that abundantly attests to values that shape daily lifestyle, use of words, considered thoughts and chosen vocation. In both situations, there is a journey that brings clarity to what is fundamentally valued.

As professionals in a field devoted to student behavior and misbehavior within higher education, our goal and purpose is to facilitate the integration of student development with student accountability. Merging student development concepts with principles of student conduct practice in postsecondary educational settings melds together holistic development with personal responsibility (Association for Student Judicial Affairs, 1986, p. 7). Yet, our educational practice appears to have fallen prey to the pressures of contemporary society with an emphasis on information transfer without a great deal of thought given to the meaning, pertinence, or application of the information in the context of the student's life (Keeling, 2006, p. 10). Why does society value moving fast, accomplishing lots, and taking little or no time for reflection?

Higher education and the experiences it offers provide a distinctive opportunity for fostering reflection and the making of meaning. Our nation's colleges and schools have a particular responsibility to help students find their own voice as they journey through a fragmented society and are bombarded with outside expectations (Orr, 2005, p. 224). The dilemma between student development and student accountability is reflected by Dalton and colleagues (2006): "in one respect, providing a supportive environment for students to explore meaning, purpose and wholeness serves to enrich lives and deepen learning" (p. 18), but the current "seriousness of student conduct on campus including alcohol abuse, academic dishonesty, abuses in athletics, racism, sexism, and materialistic values demand[s] that colleges and universities take more accountability for guiding the ethical development of college students" (p. 2).

To facilitate students' development of a sense of understanding, meaning, and insight, it is imperative that those of us in positions that affect the lives of students have a grounding sense of personal values. "We cannot give [students] what we do not have ourselves; what we do have, we cannot keep from them" (Kaplan, 1991, p. 33). These values must be firmly grounded because of the shifting territory on university campuses caused by changing leadership, new policy, fluctuating funding, political influence, and often a demanding back-to-back caseload for conduct administrators. Reconciling between competing values rests with first knowing "self" and entering into an inner journey. If we do not take this inward journey, we are more likely to live divided lives in which our values and beliefs are at odds with our actions (Intrator, 2005, p. lv). This chapter challenges student conduct administrators to approach their work in a more intentional way and always to "begin with an end in mind."

Implications of Values in Decision Making

The conundrum exists because of a healthy angst between a commitment to lifelong learning in the context of working at an educational institution and the need for grounding, enduring values that guide action. An educational setting often implies continual change based on empirical data, trends, and integration of new findings. As a result, core values sometimes take on a lesser role, though unintentionally, yet the direction slowly turns down a different path. Knowing "self" is not necessarily a concept reflected through graduation rates, funding formulas, or donor participation. Our culture's fearful obsession with results has sometimes, ironically, led us to abandon great objectives and settle for trivial and mediocre ends (Palmer, 1990, p. 75). Beech (2005) provides the following insight:

> Ours is a society filled with noise, overflowing with information and data. We extol the virtues of decisiveness, strategic thinking, and timely solutions. We celebrate but at the same time fear change. This world view conditions our personal and vocational lives, driving us to focus primarily on the short run, to see the world as either-or, to abandon self-reflection and self-awareness in favor of self-protection; and to settle for quick fixes and sound bites rather than thoughtful, in-depth consideration that respects the complexity of our lives. (p. 82)

Situations will most certainly arise when there is disequilibrium with our perception of the world. James Rest and Lawrence Kohlberg, both cognitive development psychologists, found that a person's ability to deal with moral issues is not formed all at once. Just as there are stages of growth in physical development, the ability to think morally also develops along stages, although not necessarily sequentially. And furthermore, once moral values are solidified within the individual, it takes practice and the ability to consistently check one's own sense of awareness to act in accord with one's belief system. Not unlike daily exercise, there is a "moral muscle" that can also grow stronger through personal ethics and application.

Lawrence Kohlberg and James Rest's Theory of Moral Reasoning

Kohlberg's theory is specific to moral judgment and development, referring to reasoning, not to specific beliefs. As a result, it is claimed that this theory has cross-cultural application. Student conduct administrators can be well served by exercising sensitivity toward cultural and gender application given the globalization within today's culture and the female majority within higher education. Furthermore, Kohlberg asserted that experience is critical in the cognitive process of moral development, especially experience confronting moral issues (Kohlberg & Mayer, 1972, p. 449–496). Kohlberg's theory of moral reasoning and development identifies six stages of moral reasoning, each of which is successive and hierarchical, processed in three levels, as follows:

Level I. Preconventional Morality

Stage 1: Obedience and Punishment. This stage emphasizes the avoidance of breaking rules because punishment serves as a deterrent.

> Example: I wouldn't have cheated on the test if I had known I would get caught and receive an F for the class.

Stage 2: Relative Hedonism. This stage points out that rules can be avoided as long as one is acting in a fair way.

> Example: We all agreed to share the cheat sheet for this one exam, so we made copies of it for everyone before the test.

Level II. Conventional Morality

Stage 3: Good Boy/Good Girl Orientation. This stage emphasizes living up to what is expected by others.

> Example: I am attending this university because I received a full academic scholarship. I am a first-generation college student. I cheated on the exam so I wouldn't lose my scholarship and/or disappoint my family.

Stage 4: Maintenance of Social Order and Authority. This stage stresses the need to keep and maintain a strict social conscience.

> Example: I saw the students using the cheat sheet and reported them to the Office of Student Conduct because the professor grades on a curve, and the group that had the answers to the test would skew the grades for the entire class.

Level III. Postconventional Morality

Stage 5: Democratically Accepted Law. This stage points to a social contract of sorts as determining acceptable moral behaviors for self and others.

> Example: The professor's lectures did not cover material on the test. We (the class) have written a letter to the dean to express our concerns with the unfair grading process that would result.

Stage 6: Universal Principles. This stage pertains to "universal ethics."

> Example: The students in my chemistry class cheated on an online quiz. If they cheat on a quiz, then they may cheat and take shortcuts in other areas in life that could affect others in a negative way. Therefore, I need to report this behavior.

This concept of learning or inducing from experience was originally offered by the educational philosopher John Dewey (1921, p. 169), who believed that learning occurs through reflection on actual experiences. The role of student conduct administrators offers up a particularly powerful opportunity to integrate reflection. Students involved in a student conduct hearing, including student panels that hear the case or direct participants, are more likely to be confronted by their experience. John Zacker (1998) conducted a study that, in part, measured moral judgment of all members of a student judiciary by administering Rest's (1979) Defining Issues Test (DIT). Participants were given the DIT at the beginning of the fall semester of 1996 and at the end of one semester's service. The results concluded that members of a student judiciary demonstrated gains in moral judgment during a semester's service.

An Ethical Orientation

As professionals who advance following rules but also promoting student development, it is imperative that we establish an ethical orientation approach. Lawrence Hinman (2006, p. 3), director of the Values Institute at the University of San Diego, presents two camps of thought regarding the fundamental question of what comprises ethics. These two categories are an *act-oriented approach* (How ought I act?) and a *character-oriented approach* (What kind of person ought I to try to be?).

Student conduct administrators need to consider their role in advocating for student development *and* providing for policy compliance. Student conduct involves personal accountability on behalf of students in addressing behavior in the spirit of advancing character building and fostering citizenry. Hinman (2006, p. 4) addresses the act-oriented approach toward ethics by asking, "How should I act?" There are two results that can be helpful in the realm of the student conduct profession.

Consequentialism, the first type of act-oriented approach, looks at the consequences and chooses the action that has the best consequence. For example, within the field of student conduct, consequences can include setting a precedent and a standard. If a student is found in violation of drinking alcohol in the residence hall, you can bet that the sanction is under the watchful eye of fellow students and administrators in terms of any future similar offenses. However, consequences are far reaching as we consider the implications of action on behalf of those involved in a conduct situation. The students involved, the hearing panel, and the administrative process are subpopulations affected by different consequences. How we in the conduct profession listen to these varying consequences is directly linked to our ethics. It may be tempting to provide impressive numbers with regard to caseloads and hearings held, student contacts, classroom presentations, publications, or committee involvements as examples of consequences. The fundamental consequence of listening to students before, during, and after an experience with student conduct is an ongoing challenge for the profession.

The second type of act-oriented approach, *deontology*, considers the rules and follows them. Most admittedly, rules are needed to guide behavior and communicate standards. As described in chapter 4, conduct codes are essential to the administration of every campus community. We need policies that address sexual harassment, academic dishonesty, and violent behavior. Reliance on rules can take the emphasis away from the individual for student conduct administrators. It is important to differentiate between the assessment of the rule or policy and the individual action. Hinman (2006, p. 9) further purports that the one common denominator is that *rules trump consequences*. While policy development is imperative, it is important to be wary of an overabundance of rules. It is important that the student conduct process provide the quality of space to respond to standards and students.

The character-oriented approach speaks to personal growth and development. It addresses the kind of person we want to be and become. Consistent with the values of higher education, our institutional missions involve learning, changing, and growing. This process-driven experience can collide with the rule-oriented approach because it emphasizes flexibility of rules for new situations (Hinman, 2006, p. 11). Contemporary administration of higher education often reflects a litigious and legalistic society on a collision course with developmental approaches to college and university administration (Lancaster & Cooper, 1998, p. 95). Student conduct as a profession requires policy that addresses behavioral expectations, but it also calls for room to discuss behavior and provide a place and process in which students can experience personal growth. Awareness of these orientations can prove to be pivotal benchmarks for student conduct administrators in balancing multiple perspectives.

Rest's Four-Component Decision-Making Model

Rest (1984) developed four components for moral development, which include moral sensitivity (recognizing that a moral dilemma exists); moral reasoning (considering the choices available); moral choosing (choosing among satisfying oneself, the social order, or one's principles); and moral action (doing something) (Grace, 2001, pp. 16–17).

Component I: Moral Sensitivity (interpreting the situation as moral). This component stresses awareness of the situation's moral dimension, that is, that the welfare of another person is at stake. It recognizes how possible courses of action affect all parties involved.

> Example: My friend is cheating on an exam in the same class in which I am enrolled.

Component II: Moral Reasoning (defining the morally ideal course of action). This component looks at determining what should be done. It asserts that formulating a plan of action applies a moral standard or ideal (e.g., justice).

> Example: My friend is cheating on an exam. I need to either talk with him or someone in authority about this. It is not fair to me or to the others in the class.

Component III: Moral Choosing (deciding what to do). This component speaks to evaluating the various courses of action for how they would serve moral or nonmoral values and then deciding what to do (e.g., political sensitivity, professional aspirations).

> Example: My friend is cheating on an exam. I am first going to confront her. If she agrees to stop cheating, then I am going to trust her response. If she tells me it is none of my business, then I am going to meet with the professor and tell him myself.

Component IV: Moral Action (executing and implementing a moral plan of action). This component asserts that individuals act as one intended to act and follow through with a decision. Moral action is assisted by perseverance, resoluteness, strong character, core values, the strength of one's conviction, etc.

> Example: My friend is cheating on an exam. I am going to meet him before class today at the student union. I have made notes of the points I want to cover, because I have personal convictions about cheating that are near to my heart. I want him to seriously hear what I am saying and why I think he should stop cheating.

Student conduct administrators are strategically positioned to help students make meaning of the decisions they have made and the impact these decisions have on themselves and others. Student conduct administrators have at their fingertips tools to foster student perspectives in viewing the world. Often, it can be a temptation to rely on policy compliance and minimize the pivotal "pause" to reflect. Moreover, many of today's students are hungry for hope, which is reflected in Sharon Daloz Parks (2000) introductory words in *Big Questions Worthy Dreams*:

> A talented young man, recently graduated from an outstanding college, still trying to heal from his parents' divorce, and somewhat at a loss for next steps in his search for a meaningful place in the world of adult work, is asked by his dad and stepmom, "When you think from your deepest self, what do you most desire?" To their surprise he quietly responds: "To laugh without cynicism." (p. 1)

As John Zacker notes in chapter 10, the technology, instant communication, and round-the-clock, sound-bite communication may be reassuring in completing an exam at the last minute, staying in touch with family, and even building a network of virtual friends. The backlash has resulted in many of today's college students growing up in a world that lacks consistency and structure. . . . Technology and media create a world without boundaries. . . . The search for identity and aloneness is a stunning change (Woodard, Love, & Komives, 2001).

Choosing to flex moral muscle through the cognitive action of entering into awareness of and assessing the question at hand, considering consequences, and, ultimately, deliberating action, is prime for campus life in that students are choosing to enroll in a learning arena. Learning in college is intrinsically connected to students' inner lives of emotions, feelings, attitudes, and beliefs (Dalton, Eberhardt, Bracken, & Echols, 2006, p. 2).

Another useful model of ethical decision making and leadership can be found in Grace's (2001) work. The Four "V" Model of Ethical Leadership Development accounts for a lifelong commitment to learning that coexists with a lifelong commitment to core values. The influential, guiding power of values in leadership development is exemplified through a model developed at the Center for Ethical Leadership (Figure 9.1). Grace explains:

> "Values" is at the top of the triangle, which represents the starting place for learning the craft of ethical leadership. Ethical leadership begins with knowing our core values and developing the discipline to integrate them into our daily lives. Between Values and the second V ("Vision") lies the territory of service. When our values are tested and tried in the context of service to others, they yield the latent vision within our values. "Vision" leads to "Voice" as we seek to take public action related to our vision. When we take this public action the territory changes from service into polis, the Greek word for city. . . . As "Voice" returns to "Values" the territory changes once again from polis to renewal. (2001, pp. 18–19)

At the center of this model is "virtue," the commitment to advancing a common good. Values, voice, and vision without virtue may not lead to a common good. One example of this is Hitler, who had clear values applied through personal action leading away from a common good. But an individual who knows his or her values and acts on them through advancing a common good can clearly expand a vision and voice and create authentic community. By recognizing personal values, we can then develop our personal ethics. An often-overlooked aspect recognized within the 4-V model is *renewal*, the need to pause and reflect in assessing personal alignment of

FIGURE 9.1
The Four-"V" Model of Ethical Leadership Development

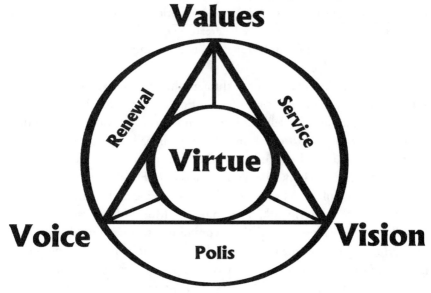

values with personal actions. The intentional exercise of reflecting on actions creates a deeper sense of meaning, a linking of "becoming" that can provide for a foundational sense of hope. Things that happen to students do not become "experience" without reflection (Woodard, Love, & Komives, 2001, p. 27). This sense of hope in aligning values creates a powerful flow, a meaningful engagement with a passion and a purpose.

Terminology has often used terms such as "morals" and "ethics" interchangeably. A useful framework for assessing a situation is identifying the difference between a *moral temptation* and an *ethical dilemma* in making value-driven decisions, as explained by Bill Grace with the Center for Ethical Leadership (2002):

Moral Temptation: A moral temptation means that there is *not* a value in each hand. Rather, there is a justification for an action that is conflicting with a value. For example, a student conduct officer may be offered prime seats at a basketball game from a coach at the conclusion of a conduct hearing that happened to end in a favorable decision for a student athlete. The student conduct officer could easily rationalize the action by thinking, "the hearing is already concluded," or "I want to maintain positive relations with the coaching staff." The temptation creates the opportunity to slide away from core values and justify, explain, or rationalize.

Ethical Dilemma: An ethical dilemma is a situation where two or more values are in conflict. Here, the values collide. Rushworth Kidder (1996, pp. 112–126) developed four categories that reflect conflicting values: justice versus mercy; truth versus loyalty; individual versus community, and short-term versus long-term. In this example, the conflicting values could be short-term versus long-term.

The reflection needed to assess the conflicting values provokes growth from moral awareness to the stage of moral reasoning. For example, a student conduct administrator may experience an ethical dilemma when upper administration overturns a hearing result (truth versus loyalty).

But the solution often rests in exercising moral courage (Grace, 2001, p. 18). Being aware of our core values and honoring them by reasoning, choosing, and acting on them in the spirit of advancing the common good allows the inner and outer selves to come together. This personal alignment of inner with outer is a refreshing point of health we call integrity, and the condition of our integrity often determines our strength and resilience in meeting the outer world with our inner world (Nepo, 2005, p. 75).

Still another tool that can aid in sorting through individual ethical dilemmas is a paradigm, called the "TCC Model" (Baldizan, 2006, p. 1; Figure 9.2). *The TCC Model: A Tool for Ethical Decisions* has at its foundation a commitment to "doing no harm," a fundamental tenet of moral intent. This underpinning bridges individual action with the desire to advance a common good.

Truth

The cornerstone characteristic of the TCC Model is *truth*, which means recognizing the reality of the situation and discerning the difference between "facts" and "feeling." For example, the truth may exist that a student participated in grievously hazing a fellow student. The emotions connected to this fact could be those of disgust or disappointment. Truth-telling looks honestly at the facts rather than the personal perception.

Courage

The second reference tool is *courage*, which involves looking at options and opportunities. It takes courage to seriously contend with personal conviction, to face the truth and consider choices. It takes courage to speak up in

FIGURE 9.2
TCC Model: A Tool for Ethical Action

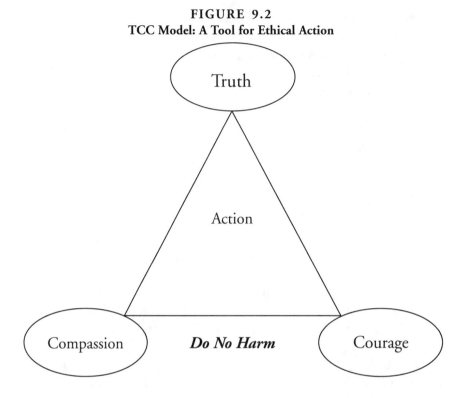

response to a sexist or racist joke or innuendo, to use chosen words in a manner that does no harm yet speaks the truth. It takes courage to face a student and address a situation that could touch both tender and tragic reality such as an evening that involved drinking too much alcohol and that culminated in an acquaintance rape.

Compassion

The third reference tool is that of *compassion*. Courage with an *equal* dose of compassion provides for nonjudgment and empathy. To learn from each other is an integral part of a commitment to community. Compassion ushers in that deep breath, leveling the field by recognizing mutual vulnerability. Conduct administrators can create a process and a space for students to face their own truth. The tone, manner, consistency, and authenticity with which conduct officers provide for the "process due" reflect an aspect of compassion.

Action

At the center of this model is the culmination of truth, courage, and compassion: *action*. Personal action is the ultimate reflection of how we respond to life occurrences, as we interpret and react to others and to ourselves. If we look at how we behave, how we use our time and our resources, our words, and our relationships, we will see our personal ethics lived out. The TCC Model for ethical action allows for an integration of values within a situation at hand and helps the individual experience greater self awareness, personal conviction, reflection, and action (Baldizan, 2006, p. 1).

Kitchener (1985), in her seminal work that defines the five principles of ethical student affairs practice, has observed that ethical principles commonly are in conflict with each other in real-life ethical dilemmas. Further, no one principle is absolute, and there are times when a higher standard of ethical conduct requires the violation of one or more principles.

Kitchener's Ethical Principles include the following five beliefs:

1. Respect Autonomy—It is assumed that individuals have the right to decide how they live their lives, as long as their actions do not interfere with the welfare of others. Therefore, student conduct administrators should encourage students to embrace self-sufficiency while assuming responsibility for self. Individual interests must be balanced with the interests and needs of the greater community.

   Example: Students are of their own free will to choose to drink alcohol. However, student behaviors and actions that result from intoxication may affect themselves and others in a negative manner and therefore are unacceptable.

2. Do No Harm—The obligation to avoid inflicting either physical or psychological harm on others may be a primary ethical principle. Therefore, student conduct administrators should encourage students to think beyond self-interest.

   Example: A student can choose to drink alcohol. However, drinking alcohol and operating a motor vehicle on campus after consuming the alcohol is unacceptable.

3. Benefit Others—There is an obligation to improve and enhance the welfare of others, even where such enhancements may inconvenience

or limit the freedom of the person offering assistance. Student conduct administrators, as educators, should always have the well-being and positive growth of students in the forefront of their thoughts.

> Example: A student has behaved in a manner that is offensive, abusive, and hateful. The student conduct officer should separate the behavior from the individual and treat the student with respect while holding the student accountable for his or her behavior.

4. Be Just—To be just in dealing with others assumes equal treatment of all, to afford each individual his or her due portion, and in general, to observe the golden rule.

> Example: A student is asking for different treatment because of mitigating circumstances beyond his or her control. The student conduct administrator should be cautious in approaching this request and might look to the golden rule to guide practice.

5. Be Faithful—One should keep promises, tell the truth, be loyal, and maintain respect and civility in human discourse. Only insofar as we sustain faithfulness can we expect to be seen as being trustworthy.

> Example: Student conduct administrators should approach their interactions with students in an honest, straightforward, and open manner. Trust is central to positive interactions with students. (1985, pp. 17–20)

Rushworth Kidder's Ethical Template is another resource in guiding practice. Kidder (1996) identified five ethical principles that provide a utilitarian tool for student conduct administrators and hearing panels in developing ethical decision making that aligns with personal values:

1. Obey the Law—How does the situation apply to the affected community? Is there a law, rule, regulation that applies to the issue at hand? For example, consider the Student Conduct Code, a Greek Life Relationship Statement, Residential Life community standard, or professional ethical reference to determine acceptable standards of conduct.

2. Front Page Test—If the choice to be made were to show up on the front page of the local or university paper, how would you feel about

the decision? For example, consider the Student Life newsletter, university home page, e-mail subject line, or a conversation between peers. Is shame involved with the anticipated shared knowledge?

3. Regard Test—If your mother, father, coach, advisor, or person held in high moral character and care were present, how would you feel about that person's knowledge and response to this decision?

4. Gut Test—Most people say that there is some sort of negative physical reaction when they are about to go against their moral grain. Sit with the decision and listen to the body.

5. Golden Rule Test—Do unto others what you would have them do unto you, also called the Reversibility Principle. If you received this decision, how would the decision be interpreted? (pp. 57–76)

Most of us recognize that human beings may or may not act in a manner that corresponds with what they say their ethics are (Parks, 2000, p. 14). The moral intent compared to personal action almost always has a gap (Grace, 2001, p. 18). Our humanness provides for a lifelong attempt to close this gap between the ideal and the real. It does not mean the effort is any less worthy, but rather, that effort exists. The profession of student conduct plays a vital role within higher education, in an environment dedicated to fostering knowledge and advancing a common good. We honor values infused within the disciplinary process itself, and we are challenged to listen to those values being represented through the voices and actions of students, whether we sit across the table at a conduct hearing or next to a student at commencement. We are mutual partners as we adhere to our own journey. As Palmer said (1990), the greatest risk in action is the risk of self-revelation, and that is also action's greatest joy (p. 22).

References

Association for Student Judicial Affairs (ASJA). (1986). *Constitution*. Retrieved October 31, 2007 from www.asjaonline.org

Baldizan, E. M. (2006). The TCC model: Ethics in action. *Student Affairs Law & Policy Weekly*, 4(8) Council on law in higher education. Retrieved January 9, 2007, from www.clhe.org/clhe/

Beech, T. (2005). The courage to learn. In S. M. Intrator (Ed.), *Living the questions: Essays inspired by the work and life of Parker J. Palmer* (pp. 81–87). San Francisco: Jossey-Bass.

Dalton, J. C., Eberhardt, D., Bracken, J., & Echols, K. (2006). Inward journeys: Forms and patterns of college student spirituality. *Journal of College & Character*, 7(8), 1–21.

Dewey, J. (1921). *Democracy and education*. New York: Macmillan.

Grace, B. (2001). *Ethical leadership: In pursuit of the common good*. Seattle: Center for Ethical Leadership. Retrieved July 20, 2007, from www.ethicalleadership.org/

Grace, B. (2002, October). *Ethical Leadership Institute training material*. Seattle: Center for Ethical Leadership.

Hinman, L. (2006, September 12). *Ethical theories: A very brief overview*. Retrieved July 14, 2007, from http://ethics.sandiego.edu/presentations/theory/brief_over view/index.asp

Intrator, S. (Ed.). (2005). A journey of questions: The life and work of Parker J. Palmer. In S. Intrator (Ed.), *Living the questions: Essays inspired by the work and life of Parker J. Palmer* (pp. xvii–lix). San Francisco: Jossey-Bass.

Jackson, M., & Jackson, R. (2005). The threads we follow. In S. M. Intrator (Ed.), *Living the questions: Essays inspired by the work and life of Parker J. Palmer* (pp. 181–195). San Francisco: Jossey-Bass.

Kaplan, A. (1991). Moral values in higher education. In D. L. Thompson (Ed.), *Moral values and higher education: A notion at risk* (pp. 11–45). New York: New York Press.

Keeling, R. P. (Ed.). (2006). *Learning reconsidered 2: Implementing a campus-wide focus on the student experience*. Published by ACPA, ACUHO-I, ACUI, NACADA, NACA, NASPA, and NIRSA.

Kidder, R. (1996). *How good people make tough choices: Resolving dilemmas of ethical living*. New York: Fireside.

Kitchener, K. S. (1985). Ethical principles and decisions in student affairs. In H. J. Canon & R. D. Brown (Eds.), *Applied ethics in student services* (pp. 17–20). San Francisco: Jossey Bass.

Kohlberg, L., & Mayer, R. (1972). Development as the aim of education. *Harvard Educational Review*, 42(4), 449–496.

Lancaster, J., & Cooper, D. (1998). Standing at the intersection: Reconsidering the balance in administration. *New Directions for Student Services, 1998* (82), 95–106.

Nepo, M. (2005). Because of my not knowing. In S. M. Intrator (Ed.), *Living the questions: Essays inspired by the work and life of Parker J. Palmer* (pp. 73–80). San Francisco: Jossey-Bass.

Orr, D. (2005). A journey of the heart: Seeking the questions worth living. In S. M. Intrator (Ed.), *Living the questions: Essays inspired by the work and life of Parker J. Palmer* (pp. 219–226). San Francisco: Jossey-Bass.

Palmer, P. (1990). *The active life: A spirituality of work, creativity and caring* (rev. ed.). San Francisco: Jossey-Bass.

Parks, S. (2000). *Big questions worthy dreams: Mentoring young adults in their search for meaning, purpose, and faith.* San Francisco: Jossey-Bass.

Rest, J. (1979). *Development in judging moral issues.* Minneapolis: University of Minnesota Press.

Rest, J. (1984). The major components of morality. In W. Kurtines & J. Gewirtz (Eds.), *Morality, moral behavior and moral development.* New York: Wiley.

Rest, J. (1986). *Moral development advances in research and theory.* Westport, CT: Praeger.

Woodard, D., Love, P., & Komives, S. (2001). *Leadership and management: Issues for a new century.* San Francisco: Jossey-Bass.

Zacker, J. (1998, February). *Moral judgment and student judiciary involvement: Effects of a reflection seminar.* Paper presented at the Association for Student Judicial Affairs International Conference, Clearwater, Florida.

10

INFORMATION TECHNOLOGY IN STUDENT CONDUCT ADMINISTRATION

John Zacker

Introduction

Picture an office of student conduct 5 to 10 years from now. Reports of misconduct will be sent electronically through a secure website and downloaded onto the office database. Office record keeping will be completely paperless—contents of files will be optically scanned into a database for immediate access and retrieval. All correspondence will be sent through electronic mail. In response to a violation of campus rules, a student will be instructed to enter a virtual reality simulation in which he or she will choose an "avatar" and navigate a series of ethical issues based on the current "Second Life." In this adventure students will have the opportunity to experience ethical decision making and the effects such decisions have on themselves and others.

But first, what is IT? Well, when looking for answers to such questions, one only has to click away on an Internet search engine to find *Wikipedia*, the "free encyclopedia that anyone can edit!" According to *Wikipedia*, information technology "defined by the Information Technology Association of America (ITAA) is: 'the study, design, development, implementation, support or management of computer-based information systems, particularly software applications and computer hardware.' In short, IT deals with the use of electronic computers and computer software to convert, store, protect, process, transmit and retrieve information, securely" (retrieved June 3,

2007). The important aspect of this definition is that IT is a tool for managing information—much the way a budget is a tool for managing finances. IT is a means to an end, not an end in itself. Often, however, we view technology as the end and are attracted by new technology without considering how it will improve the delivery of products or services. Larry Moneta (2005) observes that "[t]echnology is seductive. . . . The pressure to succumb to the latest and greatest technology can be overwhelming—and expensive!" (p. 13).

EDUCAUSE, reporting the top 10 IT issues of 2007, found that IT funding tops the list as it has since 2000 (Camp & DeBlois, 2007). "Escalating costs for IT service delivery and maintenance in the face of funding pressures at the institutional level leave little flexibility in many IT budgets. Along with these institutional pressures come broader external pressures . . . for improved accountability and productivity" (p. 16). Rounding out the top 10 in order are (2) security; (3) administrative/ERP (enterprise resource planning)/information systems; (4) identity/access management; (5) disaster recovery/business continuity; (6) faculty development, support, and training; (7) infrastructure; (8) strategic planning; (9) course/learning management systems; and (10) governance, organization, and leadership for IT. Although this list is generated from EDUCAUSE member institution chief information officers (CIOs), we can certainly ascertain institutional priorities in the years ahead by considering this list, and we might actually agree that this list represents the critical IT issues offices of student conduct must address, depending on the size and scope of the office.

Information technology has not been a topic in the student conduct administration literature, but it is now becoming increasingly integral to our work—in the administration of our offices *and* in many of the cases referred to our offices for adjudication. As society relies more on information technology for many aspects of our daily lives, such as online bill paying, Internet commerce, interactive Web-based services, and various forms of electronic communication, higher education institutions will be subject to greater expectations. Current and future generations of students will expect from our offices a level of IT beyond merely maintaining an adequate website or an occasional e-mail. This chapter provides a foundation for applying information technology to the administration of student conduct and for meeting the demands from productivity tools and database management that lie ahead to student conduct resulting from the use of technology.

Productivity Tools

In *The World Is Flat*, Thomas Friedman provides a detailed look at how technology and communication has "flattened" the world—in essence the forces that have enhanced globalization. "[T]he Windows-enabled PC gave everyone in the office the ability to create and manipulate digital content—words, data, pictures—at their fingertips on their desktops, which was a great leap forward from paper and typewriters" (2006, p. 79). Imagine typing letters on a typewriter or using carbon paper for duplicate copies of letters—yes, many of us remember such days! As desktop computers proliferated in the workplace and software programs were developed, we began to enjoy greater efficiency and productivity. It is interesting, however, that we report being busier now than ever before. There may be fewer telephone calls during each day, but the electronic mail alert "beeps" constantly letting us know of an incoming e-mail. And if the computer network goes down, there is a complete work stoppage since we now rely almost exclusively on computers to perform even the simplest of functions.

Information technology is intended to make life easier—to allow administrators to be more productive. Thus, rather than referring to such technology as e-mail, instant messenger, websites, and calendaring programs as IT, we refer to them as "productivity tools." IT tools such as these should be used to meet an office or department goal or to allow greater productivity, not just simply because they are "cool." A careful cost/benefit analysis should be conducted before implementing IT tools to be certain there will be some efficiency, productivity, and ultimate goal achievement.

Electronic Mail

E-mail has become the correspondence mode of choice not only for professional offices but for personal correspondence as well. While earlier generations of administrators may have avoided this tool, it is now ubiquitous. No longer do we spend time preparing and sending "memos" to campus colleagues. Such correspondence is now conducted almost exclusively by e-mail. This technology allows for efficient correspondence, readily accessible "address books," and "cc" (carbon copy) capability as well as correspondence filing, sorting, and retrieval. Since e-mail is sent and received in a matter of minutes rather than days, an immediate response is expected, particularly from our students. We hear, "I e-mailed you three times yesterday, and I haven't received a response yet!" E-mail is rapidly placing substantial burdens on us all.

In a recent *Washington Post* article, Mike Musgrove (2007) describes the phenomenon of people declaring "e-mail bankruptcy." Musgrove reports the following:

> Stanford University technology professor Lawrence Lessig publicly declared e-mail bankruptcy a few years ago after being deluged by thousands of e-mails. "I eventually got to be so far behind that I was either going to spend all my time answering e-mails or I was going to do my job," he said.
>
> Thereafter, Lessig's correspondents received e-mail equivalents of Dear John letters: "Dear person who sent me a yet-unanswered e-mail," he wrote, "I apologize, but I am declaring e-mail bankruptcy," he said, adding an apology for his lack of "cyber decency."
>
> He eliminated about 90 percent of his e-mail traffic, but said he can't quite abandon it entirely. "The easiest strategy is just to ignore e-mail, but I just can't psychologically do that," Lessig said in an interview.

The sheer volume of e-mail received every day makes it impossible to feel a sense of accomplishment by the end of the day. When a stack of telephone messages was disposed of by the close of business, we felt satisfaction—okay, and relief. But with e-mail, it never goes away! As you are locking the door, driving home, eating dinner, and sleeping, your e-mail inbox is filling. The first hour of each day is spent reading and responding to e-mail received since leaving the previous day. Yes, it is efficient . . . yes, it enhances productivity . . . and yes, it enhances connectedness in ways never before realized (think of the last e-mail you received from a long-lost friend), but it is becoming overwhelming. Personal management and self-discipline are essential to survive the barrage of e-mail without declaring bankruptcy.

Applying e-mail technology to student conduct administration has the potential for more efficient and arguably reliable forms of communication with students. Increasingly, colleges and universities require students to have an e-mail address, even if not through the institution, and require that all official campus correspondence be sent through this technology. Students are very sophisticated with technology and certainly with e-mail. One would expect that such a "mandatory" change might elicit outrage from them, but much of their concern is focused on which e-mail address of the several they possess to use! Once such a requirement is made of students and a secure format selected, conduct administrators may use this tool to send official notices, attach documents, send reminders for sanction completion, or even attach digital hearing recordings.[1] The e-mail may then be saved in the student's "folder," which is maintained electronically on a shared computer drive for other staff members to access. A word of caution—do not hit the "send" button until the e-mail is re-read and the lines of recipients are carefully reviewed. Too often we send e-mail in haste only to discover errors in either the content or the list of recipients.

As student conduct administrators, we must be cautiously suspicious when using e-mail. Anyone can obtain an e-mail address from hundreds of providers with no identity verification. Often the sender's e-mail address may have no relation to the actual person (e.g., xyz2243@gmail.com). Consequently, it may be necessary to obtain verification by either asking several questions the answers to which are available through existing institutional records (e.g., date of birth, zip code for permanent residence). Absent institutionally obtained or issued e-mail addresses, it is best, however, to obtain a valid e-mail address from the student when he or she appears for an initial meeting.

Instant Messaging

One of the challenging office management questions is whether to allow instant messaging from office computers. Some fear that too much personal time will be spent on instant messaging, resulting in lower productivity. Others argue that it is a tool to increase productivity and enhance customer service. One thing is certain—our students use it through a variety of devices! According to EDUCAUSE (2005), "[l]arge and growing numbers of teens—today's and tomorrow's college students—are regular users of IM, both as a personal communication tool and, in some cases, for educational initiatives in high school. As IM matures into an accepted means of communication, and as ever-larger numbers of students arrive on campus as seasoned IM users, colleges and universities are adding IM to campus functions . . ." (p. 1).

The application of IM to student conduct administration may be worth the possible arguments to the contrary. Our "customers" increasingly expect immediate service 24 hours a day, 7 days a week, and IM only makes such service all too convenient—after all, it is *instant* messaging and assumes an *instant* response. Should busy college or university administrators succumb to this technology or fight it? If the latter approach is taken, our students and other constituents, including staff, will seek to communicate with us through other means—phone, e-mail, or letter. The fact remains that they have a question, concern, or issue that needs be addressed. It would be more developmentally beneficial for us to meet with every student in person, of course, but that may be impractical, particularly on larger campuses. By using IM we may actually increase our contact with students, particularly for whom IM is a less intimidating form of communication. Certainly several concerns should be addressed. This form of technology "might encourage some . . . to engage in offensive, disruptive, or other behavior that, in different contexts, they would see as inappropriate" (EDUCAUSE, 2005, p. 2). The EDUCAUSE Learning Initiative offers several additional downsides to the use of this technology:

- IM can lead to misunderstanding about what is being said.
- IM is always on and can lead to expectations of an immediate response.
- IM pop-ups may be a significant source of distraction.
- IM may increase security risks (2005, p. 2).

While there are obvious risks in using IM as a tool, the advantages may outweigh the disadvantages. Exchanges among staff members may be enhanced by using IM as a form of interoffice communication. Then when staff are confident with this form of communication, they can give their IM usernames to students and see how they respond. Eventually, IM could be used as a central office tool to field general office or procedure questions. Referring to the conversation with a fictional student on page 160 demonstrates the potential utility of IM.

Website Development and Management

The sheer magnitude and speed with which the Internet is expanding boggles the mind. Information is no longer measured in megabytes or gigabytes, but in terabytes. A current estimation of the size of the World Wide Web is at least 14 billion terabytes (Tilberg University, 2006). Searching the Web becomes increasingly more difficult the more information is maintained there—and sorting through what is valuable has become a time-consuming process. In 1999, the late Howard Strauss, former manager of academic outreach for Princeton University and EDUCAUSE contributor, predicted, "the Web is in its infancy and has yet to show us what it will do when it matures. . . . Tomorrow, common intelligent devices that will number in the billions will routinely use the Web, with little intervention from us" (2007, p. 34). Fortunately, as student conduct administrators, all we need to do is create and manage our own websites!

It would probably seem unacceptable not to have an office website managed centrally by the college or university or locally within the office. Once a website has been established and a procedure for updating information is established, it is a matter of keeping it current. This is no small feat—a staff member should be given responsibility for website management of content. While much of the information may be considered generic, when presenting specific information regarding disciplinary processes and procedures, such information should be tailored to the constituent groups—students, faculty/staff, parents, attorneys; consider who will be visiting the site and for what purposes. A list of the minimal material recommended for student conduct websites follows:

- Mission and vision statements
- Staff information
- Codes of conduct
- Other applicable institutional policies
- Procedures for resolving allegations of misconduct
- Procedures and forms to report misconduct
- Programs and initiatives (i.e., speakers series)
- Student judiciary
- Other resources

It is critical that information maintained electronically mirror printed material, particularly policies and procedures. We can no longer direct students and others to a printed code of conduct—the sole source for conduct policies and procedures. Now we must maintain printed and electronic forms of such material. When a policy or procedure is changed, the material must be updated. Mistakes are frequent because current electronic versions are not updated and outdated material is not removed. A regular Web search may lead to such incorrect material that may be viewed as official.

The Web may provide tremendous opportunities for increasing efficiency and enhancing customer service. With an online incident reporting system, complaining parties could use a secure website to enter required information regarding an alleged incident. This website could also be linked to the student discipline database so the information entered would appear in the database as well, thus eliminating repetitive data entry. Another example may be evaluation or assessment tools. With access to a secure website, persons may complete an online evaluation of the process, thus providing important feedback to the office staff. Students and others expect online forms, not documents to be downloaded, filled in, and printed out. As processes are created or evaluated, student conduct administrators would be wise to ask if the process could be enhanced through the use of a Web application.

The Web is also a tremendous tool for creating new programs and initiatives. University of Maryland staff members are creating an online ethics and integrity seminar, called "E-thos!" A series of developmentally appropriate "modules" will be presented to students, taking each one through an introduction, reflection, character, integrity, ethics activities, and, finally, a culminating activity. There will be a series of readings as well as other media (e.g., short film clip) to augment the material. The use of online chat may also be integrated to allow for interactive exchange with staff members. Rutgers University libraries have created a website to provide policies, information, and instruction regarding plagiarism. The site uses multiple media methods to attract attention from students, but, ultimately, to help students understand plagiarism (see http://library.camden.rutgers.edu/EducationalModule/Plagiarism/real-lifeexamples.html).

Customer Service

Our students arrive each year with greater expectations for immediate "24/7" response and to be able to communicate with our offices in the manner to which they are accustomed (i.e., electronic mail, instant messaging). Larry Moneta observes, however, that "their patience with the pace of technology change in higher education will be low" (2005, p. 11). And while students expect to rely on current technology for delivery of services, parents, attorneys, and other constituents also expect technologically sophisticated service.

Increasingly, when a customer contacts a service provider, an identification number or name is requested. Obviously, on the other end of the telephone line, a database is being accessed so that service is prompt and knowledgeable, possibly even anticipating the reason for the call. Such proto-col can be adapted easily to student conduct administration, limited only by privacy issues. By asking the student calling the office for an identification number and asking a verification question or two, administrative staff should be able to "guide" a telephone call like this:

Staff: Good morning, Office of Student Conduct. How may I help you?

Student: Hi. I got this e-mail notice yesterday telling me that I'm sup-posed to arrange an interview.

Staff: To better assist you, may I ask for your student ID number please?

Student: Sure. It's 123094567.

Staff: One moment please. . . . Thank you. And this is John?

Student: Yes, it is.

Staff: May I ask your date of birth please?

Student: Yes. It's December 1, 1980.

Staff: Okay. You were sent the e-mail notice yesterday and must ar-range an interview regarding an allegation of academic dishon-esty filed with our office. I can look at our staff calendars for a convenient time, but are you aware you can schedule the appointment yourself through the university's portal and our online calendaring system?

Student: No. Oh, I just noticed the instructions in the e-mail. That's cool. I'll do that.

Staff: Is there anything else I can help you with?

Student: Well, I guess my questions can wait until I speak with someone.

Staff: You may refer to our e-mail as well for procedures to chat with a staff member online or send e-mail for a prompt response. Or you may certainly call during normal business hours to speak with a staff member.

Student: Thanks!

Staff: You're welcome. Thank you for calling.

This fictional conversation highlights several IT tools that enhance cus-tomer service—database, electronic calendaring, electronic mail, instant messaging, portal, and, of course, the good, old-fashioned telephone. Some of these tools may not be applicable or even necessary at smaller institutions where there is more direct personal contact with students—and may certainly be preferable to the scenario on page 160. But even at smaller institutions, students come to our campuses expecting the type of service delivery to which they are accustomed. We will all need to carefully consider IT applications whether small or large.

Data Management

Arguably, the most critical application of information technology in student conduct administration is data management. Hundreds if not thousands of disciplinary records must be maintained in accordance with campus, state, and federal privacy laws. But they also must be searched efficiently for such federal reporting requirements for alcohol and drug use and campus safety and security (Jeanne Clery Disclosure of Campus Security Policy and Campus Crime Statistics Act). There are increased expectations that data be immediately accessible and accurate.

Consequently, it is essential that disciplinary records be maintained through a computerized database. Yet annually, at our professional conferences, training sessions, and through discussion lists, colleagues inquire about how to create a database or which proprietary product they should consider or what to consider when purchasing a product. While student conduct offices at larger institutions with greater financial and human resources may already have data management tools, many other campuses continue to struggle to meet this technological necessity. Even those institutions with existing databases are rarely satisfied and seek additional report writing or letter composition functions. We continue to search for the "holy grail" of student disciplinary databases—but does one really exist?

The choice of a student conduct data management system is divided into at least three categories—develop your own, hire a consultant to deliver a product, or purchase an "off-the-shelf" product. Developing a database is a time-consuming project for which we generally lack the needed technological skill. For many years, "homegrown" databases were developed by colleagues (or, more often, students) who possessed the necessary skill, interest, energy, and desire. Once the author of the program moved on, however, the office was left to manage a database about which no one knew anything, particularly if its creator had integrated sophisticated, cutting-edge programming. Hiring a consultant may be a suitable option, but there are rarely sufficient financial resources to do so.

Increasingly, and particularly at larger campuses, such student conduct databases are stand-alone systems not managed by the institution. While this allows for greater autonomy, it requires a level of technical skill and knowledge that might not be readily accessible within the office staff. Careful consideration must be given to "who" will manage the database once it is created and installed—it cannot manage itself. Without a clear plan for data management, a database should not be considered.

Student conduct administrators must have adequate technological knowledge about databases, not to create them, but to ask the "right" questions about how to use them. Research, read, consult with colleagues, and visit other offices to observe how a good database can improve overall efficiency. Questions to consider when looking at this prospect include:

1. Does the office currently have adequate hardware on which to run a database, and, if not, what additional hardware will be required?
2. How much will it cost to create, install, and maintain?
3. What methods for data backup, security, and recovery will be instituted?
4. Who will manage and maintain the database?
5. Who will input the data?
6. How much training will be required for data input and data reporting, and who will conduct it?
7. What "features" will be sought?
8. Will the database integrate with other existing databases (e.g., resident life or campus police) or applications (e.g., campus student data or calendaring system)?

Since most student conduct offices are small units, it is unlikely that a committed IT staff member will be available to create and maintain a database. A collaborative effort between another office or department that may have an existing IT support structure is an excellent option. Even collaborating with several small units may generate sufficient IT support functions to warrant at least a part-time employee.

A student conduct database should be considered in the context of a shared resource across the office or department itself and potentially with other units (e.g., resident life). There are data elements that must be inserted to maintain the integrity of the data. These elements must be considered carefully as one looks at the successful interface of different units. No longer does data entry fall to administrative or support staff, who generally maintain physical files. It may be more efficient if the staff member who is designated the "case manager" inputs a certain amount of the data elements rather than writing all of the instructions on a piece of paper for someone else to enter. For example, on completing a disciplinary meeting with a student, the staff member conducting the meeting immediately turns to the computer and types up the notes, summarizing the meeting in the "notes" section of the database. The staff member then inputs the necessary data elements, such as charges, findings, sanctions, etc. Ultimately, we should be seeking an efficiency of scale and streamlining processes by eliminating either time consumption or human resources while entering the most accurate data.

In terms of record retention and privacy issues, an electronic record is considered no different from a physical record and should be maintained as such. Staff members should be mindful that data entered into a database may be subpoenaed, just as the physical file might be. A protocol should be established that mirrors the physical record for the eventual destruction of files, if permitted under campus policies. Databases are invaluable for longitudinal research efforts, but once the file is destroyed, the data may no longer be retrieved. A procedure may be created to remove personally identifiable information from the data record and to move such files into a "research archive." The archive data may then be included when conducting longitudinal research.

And, finally, optical scanning may be considered to reduce the volume of files maintained in the office. Much the same as admissions office procedures, on receipt of a written complaint, all documents may be scanned into storage and associated with a data record. While this may be a time-consuming process to initiate, it can yield substantial benefits once it is implemented completely. Such digitally stored documents are easily accessible and are deemed a satisfactory facsimile of the original. Practical decisions must be made regarding the digital storing of minor offenses, but major offenses for which a student is dismissed from campus could be optically scanned and maintained indefinitely.

Conduct Issues

While much of the information presented thus far is intended for management of student conduct offices, all of the technology addressed may be used by our students as well to engage in misconduct. We have bright, capable, intelligent, clever young people with powerful technology tools and some spare time. Some may simply explore "possibilities" of the technology—testing the boundaries. Unfortunately, others may use the technology to engage in intentional acts of deception, express threats or hatred, or steal others' written works.

Plagiarism

Technology has made plagiarism much easier than ever before, and it has reached the highest levels of respected professions, including corporate executives, city officials, and even college professors and presidents. But when a journalist commits plagiarism, it cuts at the core of integrity in reporting the news. Such was the case of Jayson Blair, a University of Maryland journalism graduate who worked as a reporter for the *New York Times*. During his tenure with the *Times*, Blair engaged in a pattern of deception, fraud, and plagiarism in reporting on events. According to CNN's reporting of the events, "[t]o create the illusion that he was on the scene, the *Times* alleged, Blair peppered his stories with details obtained from photographs of the events and material from other news organizations. . . . He used his cell phone and computer to communicate with editors, pretending to be on assignment in another city" ("New York Times Reporter . . . ," 2003). This was obviously a case of much more than simple plagiarism, but it illustrates the ease with which plagiarism may be committed, even in the trusted profession of journalism.

Technology is a tremendous tool for writing—eliminating lengthy note taking and note cards. Research material may be organized easily and, ultimately, result in high-quality research and writing. But students under the pressure of a deadline or succumbing to procrastination may now simply cut and paste material from an Internet source directly into a research paper or take an entire paper written by a student at another institution. A simple Google search of the assigned topic will yield hundreds if not thousands of "hits." Not only can the material be transferred directly onto the screen, it can then be revised even to reflect the student's writing style.

While sophisticated software has been created to detect plagiarism (i.e., Plagiarism.org), Internet search engines may be equally effective. A phrase that seems to be written at a higher level than the suspected student is capable of may be entered into the search engine for possible "hits." The troublesome part of this "cat and mouse" game is that bright students can paste portions of material into a paper and then reword the material to sound like their own. It may be possible in the near future to create technology that would embed a code or link into the copied material so that detection is easily accomplished or at least provides substantial deterrence. But in the meantime, student conduct administrators overseeing academic integrity must work with faculty to encourage unique writing assignments that may not be readily available on the Internet. Ultimately, however, we should not rely on either the technology or the assignment as a solution to deterring plagiarism or detecting it. Instead, we should rely on establishing academic integrity standards and, more important, relationships with students that demonstrate a commitment to academic integrity and trust.

Cheating

Cell phones and personal digital assistants (PDAs) have replaced programmable calculators for cheating. Students with such technology may set up an elaborate plot to cheat by having a person outside the classroom text message the answers to an exam. Recently, at the University of Maryland, a faculty member teaching a large class observed during an exam that multiple cell phones or PDAs went off. She consulted with her teaching assistants who advised her that these students might be using the technology to cheat. Eventually it was discovered that students outside the classroom were text messaging answers to students in the classroom. Only diligent faculty members who are aware of rapidly changing technology can deter such conduct. Often, students assume faculty members are ignorant about the technology, so they take advantage of the faculty by exploiting lax proctoring. A simple notice before an exam can ban the use of unauthorized electrical items during the exam, and students will have to turn them off.

Expression

The conduct cases arising out of e-mail and instant messaging has ballooned. Students seem to be more willing to express themselves inappropriately or offensively through this technology in ways they would not do in person.

Nuances in communication that are readily apparent when talking with someone in person are not so apparent through e-mail or instant messaging. "Smiley faces" and abbreviations (i.e., LOL means "laugh out loud") provide some degree of "facial" or emotional reaction, but misinterpretations abound. Conduct administrators are challenged to evaluate such communication in light of free speech standards, but still to maintain standards of conduct when not using technology. There should certainly not be separate and distinct rules for electronic communication. Students must be held to the same standards whether using electronic or personal communication. The larger issue, however, is civility, whether in electronic communication or in person. Our role in student conduct administration and in education as a whole is to teach students to treat each other with respect and to engage in civil discourse. Technology is still a tool—we must teach students to use this tool effectively and to learn from their mistakes. We are frequently presented with e-mails or instant/text messages that appear on their surface to carry a threat. When the offending student is confronted, often he or she apologizes profusely, stating that was not what was intended.

Copyright Infringement

A wide array of conduct issues is facilitated or perpetrated through the use of technology. One of the more contentious issues is that of copyright infringement on the recording and entertainment industry carried out through the use of "file sharing" or "P2P" (peer to peer). Again, according to *Wikipedia*, "[f]ile sharing is the practice of making files available for other users to download over the internet and smaller networks. Usually file sharing follows the peer-to-peer (P2P) model, where the files are stored on and served by personal computers of the users. Most people who engage in file sharing are also downloading files that other users share" (File Sharing, 2007).

Over the past several years, the Recording Industry Association of America (RIAA) has "targeted more than 1,600 individual students . . . [in a four-month period alone] demanding that each pay $3,000 for file-sharing transgressions or face a federal lawsuit" (von Lohmann, 2007). Over the past three years, the RIAA has aggressively sought to curtail the practice of peer-to-peer file sharing of copyrighted material. During this time, colleges and universities have received volumes of complaints lodged by the RIAA seeking to identify the offending Internet provider (IP) address and then inform the student possessing that address of the illegal file sharing, ultimately to punish them.

> Throughout its war on suspected file-sharers, the RIAA has used John Doe lawsuits to get the names and addresses of users of IP addresses flagged by MediaSentry. Once it gets identifying information, a settlement letter is sent. The RIAA's practices have come under scrutiny in the past, with a US Federal Court of Appeals judge reining in its former practice of serving subpoenas on ISPs without judicial involvement. The current system of John Doe lawsuits enables the RIAA to obtain ID data without the subject of the lawsuit ever knowing about it and has been the object of heavy criticism by some in the legal community. (Bangeman, 2007)

The University of Wisconsin recently decided to reject the RIAA's request to send the "settlement letters" without a court order. "While the school's administration has sent out a campus-wide e-mail to reiterate the school's 'appropriate use guidelines,' that communication will mark the limit of the school's cooperation with the RIAA" (Bangeman, 2007). But most profound is a recent *Washington Post* editorial by Fred von Lohmann, a senior staff attorney for the Electronic Frontier Foundation, which represents some of the defendants in peer-to-peer file sharing lawsuits. He first reports that House oversight committees for education and copyright "wrote a joint letter . . . scolding the presidents of 19 major American universities, demanding that each school respond to a six-page questionnaire detailing steps it has taken to curtail illegal music and movie file-sharing on campus. One of the questions—'Does your institution expel violating students'—shows just how out-of-control the futile battle against campus downloading has become" (von Lohmann, 2007). von Lohmann accurately defines this battle as "a fight about money, not about morality."

One could create an analogous scenario comparing colleges and universities as Internet service providers with the U.S. Postal Service. Higher education institutions provide the "conduit" to receive and send information much the same way the Postal Service provides a mailing address. The Postal Service processes and handles the mail, but no one expects it to inspect the size or weight of a package, other than to determine the cost of mailing, and certainly not the contents of the package. Yet in the current climate, there is increased pressure for institutions to "inspect" the contents of material being sent and received through the Internet Service Provider (ISP) or Internet post office and to close the "pipeline" for illegal downloading of copyrighted material by using antipiracy software. The pressure from the recording industry is substantial as the House Committee on Science and Technology questions "whether colleges should use tools that can monitor their networks for copyright infringements and disconnect students who commit violations" (Read, 2007; von Lohmann, 2007). But again, do we expect the U.S. Postal Service (or FedEx or United Parcel Service [UPS]) to monitor the contents of packages to determine if any criminal misconduct is occurring through their "mail conduit"?

It is essential that colleges and universities enforce campus rules and appropriately punish students found to be in possession of stolen property, especially copyrighted material. But as with any disciplinary matter, they should do so after carefully evaluating both the mitigating and aggravating factors in each individual case and imposing a proportionate disciplinary response. Certainly, students engaging in a large-scale operation of selling copyrighted material should be punished more severely than a student in possession of a downloaded song. As professionals, student conduct administrators should not succumb to the pressures of the RIAA or other outside entities to dictate the response of higher education institutions to such conduct.

Social Networking

A recent phenomenon has swept college campuses and high schools as well: social networking through such providers as MySpace.com and Facebook .com. These sites allow users to connect with other students and even faculty or staff. A variety of tools is available, such as instant messaging, e-mail, posting of pictures, and a "bulletin board" on which to post notes to a "friend." Students have the unique opportunity to meet one another virtually or to keep in touch. Faculty and staff may use this tool to correspond with current students or to remain connected with alumni. This technology presents beneficial possibilities to enhance or maintain relationships.

Student conduct administrators are challenged with this technology on two fronts. First are the obvious possibilities for expressive speech that might violate campus policies. Students may post offensive pictures either publicly viewable or for specific individuals. They may also post notes on a bulletin board or a comment space that could be perceived as offensive or, worse, threatening. Great care must be taken to avoid creating an unwritten speech code seeking to punish students for anything less than free speech standards on the campus. Expression through the use of technology should be evaluated in the same manner as written or verbal speech. Our responses to such expression need not always be disciplinary, but they can be developmental through the use of an intentional conversation with the student.

The second front on which we are challenged is whether to use this technology either for investigation purposes or even to target certain students. Students have become very free about posting pictures or written accounts on their Facebook or MySpace pages that portray activities, travel, family, and significant others. Unfortunately, these portrayals also may depict them and their friends in compromising situations—pictures of parties, drug and alcohol use, even sexual activity. Some student conduct administrators may see this technology as an ideal opportunity to "troll" for misconduct, viewing students' pages to find material that could be used as evidence. Others may use Facebook or MySpace after allegations of misconduct have been filed to obtain a "fuller" picture of the accused student.

This technology is still relatively new. In a short period students will become increasingly aware of the public nature of these sites, but in the meantime, student conduct administrators should exercise professional ethics, judicial restraint, and careful evaluation of procedural fairness. While the lure of looking into students' lives in this manner may be appealing, there should be a defensible reason for "looking." Certainly a student suspected of drug use by other students who claim that the student posts pictures of drug use on his or her Facebook page could be a wise use of the technology. But from an evidentiary standpoint one must evaluate whether such pictures surpass the institution's standard of evidence[2] and warrant disciplinary charges.

Conclusion

Database management, e-mail, instant messenger—regardless of the specific aspect of technology presented here, IT is constantly changing making any "conclusion" mere folly. There really can be no conclusion for a chapter on technology in student conduct administration, only a few words of wisdom:

- Stay abreast of changing information technology by reading about the latest innovations in periodicals within and outside of higher education.

- When confronted with administrative issues, consider how using information technology may enhance productivity and efficiency.
- Talk with your students about how they are using or misusing information technology.
- And, finally, take time to think about what potential information technology holds for student conduct administration in the very near future!

References

Bangeman, Eric. (2007, March 20). University of Wisconsin decides not to pass along RIAA settlement letters. *ars technica*. Retrieved June 6, 2007, from http://arstechnica.com/news.ars/post/20070320-university-of-wisconsin-decides-not-to-pass-along-riaa-settlement-letters.html

Camp, John S., & DeBlois, Peter B. (2007). Top 10 IT issues 2007. *EDUCAUSE Review, 42*(3), 12–32.

EDUCAUSE. (2005). *7 Things you should know about . . . instant messaging*. Retrieved June 6, 2007, from http://www.educause.edu/ir/library/pdf/ELI7008.pdf

File sharing. (2007, June 5). *Wikipedia, The Free Encyclopedia*. Retrieved June 6, 2007, from http://en.wikipedia.org/wiki/File_sharing

Friedman, Thomas L. (2006). *The world is flat: A brief history of the twenty-first century*. New York: Farrar, Straus, and Giroux.

Moneta, Larry. (2005). Technology and student affairs: Redux. *New Directions for Student Services, 2005* (112), 3–14.

Musgrove, Mike. (2007, May 25). Email reply to all: "Leave me alone,'" *Washington Post*. Retrieved June 4, 2007, from http://www.washingtonpost.com/wpdyn/content/article/2007/06/01/AR200706010 2671 .html.

New York Times: Reporter routinely faked articles. (2003, May 11). CNN.com. Retrieved June 9, 2007, from http://www.cnn.com/2003/US/Northeast/05/10/ny.times.reporter/index.html.

Read, Brock. (2007, June 15). Lawmakers encourage colleges to use technology to curtail campus piracy. *Chronicle of Higher Education*, A-34.

Tilberg University. (2006). *World Wide Web has at least 14 billion pages*. Retrieved June 6, 2007, from http://ilk.uvt.nl/events/dekunder.html

Strauss, Howard. (2007). The future of the Web, intelligent devices, and education. *EDUCAUSE Review, 42*(1), 32–46.

von Lohmann, Fred. (2007, June 6). Copyright silliness on campus. *Washington Post*. Retrieved June 6, 2007, from http://www.washingtonpost.com/wpdyn/content/article/2007/06/05/AR200706050 1761 _pf.html.

Endnotes

1. Sending official material defined as an "educational record" under FERPA through e-mail should be reviewed by legal counsel on individual campuses. This practice may be acceptable on some campuses and not on others.

2. Campuses that operate with a "preponderance of the evidence" or "more likely than not" may conclude that pictures posted on websites are sufficient evidence to conclude a violation has indeed occurred. Campuses that use a "clear and convincing" standard may be hard pressed to come to the same conclusion.

PART TWO

CURRENT ISSUES

II

INCIVILITY ON COLLEGE CAMPUSES

Brent G. Paterson and William L. Kibler

The *Oxford English Dictionary* (AskOxford, 2007) defines incivility as "rude or unsociable speech or behaviour." *Wikipedia* (2007) offers a more useful definition, "Incivility is a general term for social behaviour lacking in civility or good manners, on a scale from rudeness or lack of respect for elders, to vandalism and hooliganism, through public drunkenness and threatening behavior." As Edwin J. Feulner (2004), president of the Heritage Foundation stated, "Incivility is not a social blunder to be compared to using the wrong fork. . . . Incivility is dangerous graffiti, regardless of whether it is spray-painted on a subway car or embossed on the title page of a book." Although all behaviors and speech in this range are important issues on college campuses, this chapter focuses on those behaviors and speech that disrupt the academic environment and the lives of college students.

Judging by media stories, one would think that incivility is rampant in society and on campuses at levels never seen before. Some writers suggest that incivility can be viewed as a barometer of societal decay (Moffat, 2001). Yankelovich and Furth (2005) suggest that while the "cultural revolution" of the 1960s and 1970s had many positive results, there were unintended consequences that led to a "decline in our social morality" (p. 46). Writers on incivility point to newspaper and magazine articles on workplace rudeness and violence, road rage, "dirty" politics, shouting matches on news talk shows, fights at sporting events, and even talking loudly on cell phones during a movie as examples of incivility in today's society. On college campuses, incivility is often cited in roommate conflicts, sexual misconduct, classroom behavior, and vandalism, to cite a few examples. There is little doubt that civil discourse and behavior appear less often on college campuses and in society.

Yet, acts of incivility are not new to college campuses. During the Scottish Enlightenment, the University of Edinburgh sought to counter religious intolerance by establishing "civilized discourse and due regard for an opponent's point of view" (Nordin, 1991, p. 17). A violent town and gown riot at Oxford University in the 14th century resulted in the death of 63 students at the hands of the town residents (Cowley & Waller, 1994, p. 28). Uprisings occurred on American college campuses beginning in the colonial period and continue today. During the colonial period, campus uprisings were in response to oppressive rules and bad food. Violent protests at American colleges in the early 19th century ranged from "destruction of property at Princeton University to the death of a professor at the University of Virginia" (Magolda & Magolda, 1988, p. 7). The 1960s were a tumultuous time on college campuses as protests became a daily occurrence, and Woodstock-type concerts (sex, drugs, and rock and roll) were common. Campus protests turned violent, culminating in the shooting and killing of four students and the wounding of nine others by National Guardsmen at Kent State University in May 1970, and 10 days later, the killing of two students by police at Jackson State College (Biemiller, 1995). As Ernest Boyer (1987) wrote, "Teenagers then, as now, were inclined to test the limits of tolerance" (p. 177).

What is different about incivility on college campuses today? Perhaps we are seeing a different type of student. Much has been written about millennials, Generation X students, and Generation NeXT students. Regardless of the label, students today are different from ever before.

The so-called Generation NeXT, those born between 1982 and 1994, are products of a time when greater value has been placed on consumer interest and less on value formation (Taylor, 2007). The traditional values of higher education are in direct conflict with the beliefs of Generation NeXT about education. As Nason (1981) states, "In the broadest sense of the term education is the process by which older members of society seek to fashion the younger members into useful citizens" (p. 256). Yet, today's college students and their parents view higher education as a product that provides customer service and the students as customers (Taylor, 2006). Even U.S. Secretary of Education Margaret Spellings has called for a higher education information system that "provide[s] transparency and ease when students and families shop for colleges" (Spellings, 2006). Students today expect to be able to make choices about their education, feel a sense of entitlement about being a college student, and want to negotiate everything, from alcohol and drug policies to grades on tests and assignments. It is not uncommon to hear a student or a parent say, "I'm paying big money for tuition and I expect [fill in the blank]."

Adding to the consumer mentality is a sense of being value-free. According to Taylor (2006), "Today's young people might be tolerant of everything except people who believe that their model is superior." Students believe that everyone has the right to his or her own opinion. They also believe that no greater value should be placed on another person's opinion, regardless of that person's study of or experience with the topic. Faculty and administrators view this belief as an act of disrespect. Students often use "irony and parody to minimize the importance of anything" (Taylor, 2006). Combined with students' belief that their own efforts have less impact than fate or coincidence on their lives, it is easy to understand their frustration with traditional education and the frustration educators experience in attempting to teach this generation.

Another factor affecting higher education today is the litigious society. Generation NeXTers and their parents are more likely than were previous generations to seek legal remedy when disappointed with some aspect of higher education. The consumerism of higher education has made its way into the courts. Moffat (2001) posits that there has been an "explosion of rights" accompanied by a "growth of litigiousness in our society." As Bickel and Lake (1999) point out, the courts have begun to "enforce business-like responsibilities and rights" on colleges and universities (p. 105). While the courts remain sensitive to the unique nature of American higher education, they have applied traditional negligence and duty roles to colleges and universities. Students and their parents may not feel a shared responsibility for a student's actions. Rather, they are more likely to feel they have been wronged by the college, and if the students and/or the parents do/don't get the expected result, they may threaten, if not file, a lawsuit. Today's college students' lack of conflict resolution skills has made this situation even more difficult. Instead of students attempting to resolve a conflict themselves, they call their parents. Then, the parents demand that some administrator resolve the conflict to the parents' satisfaction immediately, even when college processes exist to resolve such conflicts.

Acts of incivility are real on college campuses today. While there is no excuse for uncivil behavior that hurts another person or damages another person's property, understanding today's college student provides insight into their behavior. Are students intending to be uncivil in their communications and actions? Perhaps not. Perhaps they are simply products of their upbringing and society. However, if education has a role in developing the values of a younger generation, then higher education needs to address incivility and provide direction to assist this generation of college students in becoming useful citizens.

The next section of this chapter examines common examples of incivility on college campuses. The authors explore causes for the behavior and share college and university best practices to address such behaviors.

Free Speech and Student Protest

While Schuster, Bird, and Mackin address these issues in chapter 12, the authors believe it is important to briefly examine the relationship between incivility and the First Amendment. The legal dimension of the university-student relationship is no more evident than in the First Amendments rights of free speech, free press, and protest issues involving students. The free expression of ideas is a foundational value of the U.S. Constitution that has been upheld and protected consistently through the years by the U.S. Supreme Court. As Justice Hugo Black stated in the *Communist Party v. SACB* (1961) decision, "the freedoms of speech, press, petition, and assembly guaranteed by the First Amendment must be accorded to the ideas we hate or sooner or later they will be denied to the ideas we cherish."

Before the 1960s there was a general public misperception and expectation that university administrators could and should control student speech, the student press, and student protests. This public misperception was grounded in the belief that college students did not have constitutional rights. The case law that helped define the right to free expression at public institutions came into being largely as a result of the court cases related to the student protests, unrest, and incivility of the 1960s. Two landmark Supreme Court cases (*Tinker v. DesMoines Independent School District* and *Healy v. James*) clarified these questions. In *Tinker v. DesMoines* (1969), the

U.S. Supreme Court ruled, "It can hardly be argued that either students or teachers shed their constitutional rights to freedom of speech or expression at the schoolhouse gate." The Court reinforced the constitutional rights of students by ruling in *Healy v. James* (1972), "State colleges and universities are not enclaves immune from the sweep of the First Amendment . . ." The Court further defined the college environment as a "marketplace of ideas."

The 1980s and 1990s saw the establishment of so-called speech codes as colleges and universities attempted to provide a welcoming environment for students of different ethnicities, races, and cultures. According to Pavela (2006a), "Speech codes . . . may serve the primary purpose of diverting attention from more substantive issues of inclusion and civility, allowing administrators to focus on cosmetic approaches unlikely to produce any lasting change in campus cultures." The courts have consistently struck down speech codes, often citing the U.S. Supreme Court ruling in *Papish v. Board of Curators of the University of Missouri* (1973). The Court stated that "the mere dissemination of ideas—no matter how offensive to good taste—on a state university campus may not be shut off in the name alone of 'conventions of decency.'"

These legal concepts continue to influence how free speech is viewed in the college setting. University administrators should walk a path that protects student rights to free speech, free press, and student protest while simultaneously exercising the free speech rights, free press rights, and the authority of their position to speak in opposition to offensive free speech, offensive free press, and offensive student protests. Students often engage in free expression that is not offensive. The exercise of free expression that has offensive content can be most powerfully engaged through the use of opposing free speech. This protects the free expression rights of students, uses the power and authority of the university administration, and models effective citizenship skills for students.

Celebratory Riots

As the authors indicated earlier, rioting has been occurring on college campuses for centuries. In fact, the primary duty of the provost, when such positions were created in the Middle Ages, was to control rioting by students that affected residents in nearby neighborhoods (Hall, 2003, p. 3). According to McCarthy and McPhail (as cited in Hacker, 2005), disorderly college student gatherings historically come in waves. They identified themes for these gatherings—panty raids of the 1950s, war protests of the 1960s, streaking of the 1970s, antiapartheid demonstrations of the 1980s, and celebratory riots of the 1990s and early years of the 21st century (Hacker, 2005).

A celebratory riot has been defined as "a large gathering of students who have consumed alcohol and who spontaneously engage in destructive, antisocial behavior" (The Ohio State University Task Force, 2003, p. 7). Celebratory riots have common characteristics that distinguish them from other types of disorderly conduct:

- Riot is prompted by athletic event, campus tradition, or other triggering event.
- Riot occurs late at night and extends into early morning hours.
- Participants most commonly are young white males.
- Degree of homogeneity of participants stimulates feeling of anonymity and support from group.
- Lack of respect for police causes participants to "push until there is a response."
- Participants include those from other universities and some participants who are not college students.
- Participants are often intoxicated (Andrews, 2003, pp. 22–23; Madensen & Eck, 2006).

It is not surprising that researchers found a correlation between identifying with a team and inappropriate actions during and after sporting events. Participants who engaged in more inappropriate behavior at the sporting event were found to be more active at future events. Researchers also found that participants who consumed more alcohol were more likely to participate in inappropriate behavior (Wann, 2003, p. 19).

In 2003, close to 150 athletic representatives, higher education administrators, and representatives of key constituents attended a summit on sportsmanship and fan behavior organized by the National Collegiate Athletic Association (NCAA). Following the summit, a report was issued highlighting the significant findings. The report cites 12 incidents of significant spectator aggression during and after NCAA sporting events between 1999 and 2003. These incidents include the 1999 Men's Final Four basketball game between Michigan State University and Duke University. Michigan State fans rioted in East Lansing, Michigan, resulting in 132 arrests for overturned vehicles, burned furniture, and other behavior. Also listed were the riots in Minnesota and New Hampshire following the 2003 Frozen Four (NCAA Men's Division I Ice Hockey Championship). In these riots an estimated $100,000 in damage occurred when rioters threw rocks through windows, set fire to vehicles, including a TV news van, and looted businesses (NCAA, 2003, p. 3).

The summit report commends Ohio State University and the Columbus, Ohio, community for their preparations and response to fan behavior before, during, and after the 2002 Ohio State-Michigan football game in Columbus. The best practice initiatives of Ohio State University included:

1. educational materials;
2. general appeals for calm;
3. alternative activities for celebration;
4. university/community coordination;
5. police presence and liquor control;
6. appeals for parental support;
7. partnership with property managers;
8. direct contact with students;
9. environmental changes; and
10. enforcement (NCAA, 2003, p. 5)

The University of Florida has successfully addressed fan behavior on campus and in the community of Gainesville following repeated national championships in men's basketball and a national championship in football, all within two years. According to Dean of Students Gene Zdziarski (personal communication with Brent Paterson, April 3, 2007), the key is communication and collaboration. The university has an established process to address fan behavior for major sporting events that is "ramped up" for national championships. The university response includes communication plans, use of the O'Connell Center (campus arena) to gather fans during the championship game away from alcohol, prerecorded messages from the head coach promoting appropriate fan behavior, closing key streets to permit crowd movement without other traffic, communication and support from key student organizations and student leaders, and police presence. The University Police coordinate their efforts with Gainesville Police, Alachua

County Sheriff's Office, and the Florida State Police. Pre- and postgame plans and emergency procedures are developed, communicated, and coordinated on the day/night of the event. Appendix 11A contains an agenda from the 2007 Men's Basketball Championship Game Meeting.

Other universities have experienced celebratory rioting following World Series games (University of Massachusetts and Illinois State University), sporting events with key traditional rivals, and traditional campus events. The warning factors are the same—too much alcohol, white male students urged on by a crowd of onlookers, a sense of anonymity by participants and a belief that there are no consequences for actions, and a police response that is viewed as not responsive by some and too harsh by others. These acts of incivility are not likely to disappear from college campuses in the near future. In fact, a celebratory riot in one community acts as an impetus for students in other college communities to riot following key sporting events and other traditional campus events (Van Slyke, 2005). Campuses need to be prepared to handle such situations when they might occur; reacting to the event without planning beforehand is likely to lead to disaster.

Hazing

The history of hazing parallels the history of education. Plato seems to describe hazing-like behaviors when he describes the "savagery of young boys." An increase in hazing correlates with the rise of universities in the 1400s (Nuwer, 2004, p. xxv). The first recorded act of hazing in the American colonies was in 1657 at Harvard (p. xxv). In 1874 Congress passed legislation making hazing a criminal offense for hazing acts at the U.S. Naval Academy (Paterson, , 2006).

In the United States, hazing is viewed as the norm for initiation into an organization. Traditionally, hazing is considered a problem for fraternities and sororities, yet research suggests that hazing is also prevalent in high schools and in intercollegiate athletics. A study on hazing in American high schools found that 48% of high school students reported participating in acts that would be considered hazing (Hoover & Pollard, 2000). In another study 79% of NCAA student athletes indicated they participated in acts that could be considered hazing (Hoover & Pollard, 1999). Anecdotal data suggest that hazing is common in academic student organizations, religious student organizations, residence halls, and almost any group with which a student might associate. The authors suggest that hazing behavior is learned very early in life. Students experienced hazing activities on youth sport teams, in church youth groups, and at camp. As children, they watched slime wars on Nickelodeon and as young teens have identified with shows such as *Fear Factor* and *Survivor*. It is no wonder that hazing is alive and well on college campuses.

Today, 43 states have laws prohibiting hazing. While each state's law defines hazing in different terms, the intent is similar. A working definition of hazing is "Conduct which causes or threatens to cause serious physical or psychological injury to another as a condition of joining a team, student organization, or social group" (Fierberg, 2006). Hazing activities may take many forms. Some activities seem innocuous, such as scavenger hunts or carrying an item with you at all times, but other activities have the potential for serious bodily harm or even death. Such practices include binge drinking, drug use, branding, sleep deprivation, physical punishment, consuming unacceptable foods, and consuming excessive amounts of water (Association for Student Judicial Affairs [ASJA] & Association of Fraternity Advisors [AFA], 2006).

In hazing incidents, typically, no one intends to seriously harm or kill another person; however, the actions, and sometimes the inaction, of an individual or a group may lead to such consequences. Researchers have suggested groupthink, cultural beliefs about what it means to be a "real" man (or woman), sociopathology, cycles of abuse, identification with the aggressor, rites of passage, need for esteem, expression of power, need for intimacy, misperceived norms, and perceived lack of alternatives as causes for hazing (Esther, 2006).

The Alfred University study (Hoover, 1999) of NCAA student athletes found some remarkable results:

- Over 75% of college athletes experienced some form of hazing to join a collegiate athletic team.
- Fifty percent of these athletes were required to participate in drinking contests or alcohol-related hazing.
- Sixty-six percent of the athletes were subjected to humiliating hazing.
- Hazing of female athletes was more likely to include alcohol-related hazing than were other forms of hazing.
- Football players are the athletes who are most at risk for dangerous hazing.

Colleges need to promote an institutional culture that opposes hazing by instituting social change. According to Campo, Poulos, and Sipple (2005), "A multifaceted approach to intervention involves targeting on various levels to promote behavior change" (p. 148). VanDeventer Iverson and Allen (2004) suggest that eradicating hazing in an organization requires reshaping some important aspects of the culture in the organization and, perhaps, the institution. More specifically, attractive elements of the culture need to be replicated in positive ways. To accomplish this change requires "heroes" to serve as "role models and provide a powerful moral example" (p. 258). It is not necessarily important who the "hero" is; he or she may be a former member of the organization, a person in a leadership position in the organization, or an external person with considerable influence on the organization or its leadership.

Novak (2006) has suggested that colleges draw on the environmental management strategy for reducing alcohol and other drug use on college campuses as a model for addressing hazing on campus. Adapting the environmental management strategy to hazing requires institutions to focus their efforts on campus social norms and expectations, campus policies and procedures, enforcement of regulations and law, education and communication on expectations, policies and penalties, commitment to collaboration, developing solutions to problems, and seeking the collective good.

Hoover and Pollard (2000) recommended these strategies to prevent hazing:

- Send a clear antihazing message in policy, education, and enforcement.
- Expect responsibility, integrity, and civility on the part of athletes, team captains, coaches, and administrators.
- Offer team-building initiation rites facilitated by trained coaches or other adults (p. 6).

It is unlikely that hazing will be eradicated from college campuses in the near future, but colleges and universities must take deliberate steps to reduce hazing and its impact on students and the community. It will take a conscientious collaborative effort by all members of the college community to reduce hazing and prevent the resulting serious injuries and tragic deaths.

Campus Violence

The term "campus violence" is defined in numerous ways. Commonly campus violence is thought to include assault, sexual assault, damage and destruction of property, and shootings. Assaults, sexual assaults, and damage or destruction to property often are a product of alcohol and/or other drug use. Students' abuse of alcohol and drugs is a major problem on college campuses throughout the United States. Despite designating significant resources to fight alcohol and drug abuse over the past 20 years, in dollars and staff, colleges have continued to see high rates of abuse and the myriad affects of abuse on college students' lives. Alcohol abuse is not unique to college campuses; it is a societal problem. Alcohol and drug abuse by professional athletes, elected officials, and even university administrators are in the headlines regularly. Parents often do not consider their student's use of alcohol or drugs such as marijuana to be a problem until the student is arrested or removed from the university. Colleges need to address alcohol and drug abuse.

Those who work in mental health on campuses have warned us about a troubled generation of students and the increasing pathology being seen in college counseling centers (Carlson, 2007; Federman, 2007; Pavela, 2006b; also see chapter 13). At times, students with mental health issues act out in a manner inconsistent with college expectations. Many of us have had to respond to a faculty or staff member who has encountered a rude, abusive, and/or threatening student. Faculty or staff members' expectation may be characterized as "I do not want to have to deal with the student any more." They may want the student to be restricted from their office and from having any contact with them. As Maggie Olona, director of student counseling at Texas A&M University, stated in responding to questions from a reporter about the Virginia Tech tragedy, "Writing scary stories is not against the law. Odd behavior is not a crime. Not talking to people is not a crime. . . . You have to wait for someone to do something, and sometimes the first step can be murder" (Carlson, 2007). From a student conduct perspective, you cannot take formal action unless the code of student conduct is violated.

Since the Virginia Tech tragedy, the media have projected an image of unsafe campuses governed by administrators who fail to address warning signs. While any student death on campus is one too many, the murder rate on college campuses was 0.28 per 100,000 people, compared with 5.5 per 100,000 nationally (Kingsbury, 2007). U.S. Secret Service and U.S. Department of Education (2002) research found that profiling is not an accurate or useful means to identify students engaged in school violence (p. 20). *Threat Assessment in Schools: A Guide to Managing Threatening Situations and to Creating Safe School Climates* (U.S. Secret Service and U.S. Department of Education, 2002) provides five principles for a threat assessment process:

- Targeted violence is the end result of an understandable and often discernible process of thinking and behavior.
- Target violence stems from an interaction among the individual, the situation, the setting, and the target.
- An investigative, skeptical, inquisitive mindset is critical to successful threat assessment.
- Effective threat assessment is based on facts, not on characteristics or "traits."
- An "integrated systems approach" should guide threat assessment inquiries and investigations (pp. 30–33).

The central question in a threat assessment inquiry or investigation is whether a student poses a threat, not whether the student has made a threat (Pavela, 2007). Many institutions have informal committees that meet regularly to discuss students who are "hitting the radar" because of their behavior. For example, the University of South Carolina has a Behavioral Intervention Team "to determine if a distressed person, whether a student or other individual, is a danger to himself or others, so that appropriate treatment, including hospitalization in extreme cases, may be necessary" (Sorensen, 2007). The student's behavior may not have been addressed in the student conduct system because it has not reached the level of an alleged violation of the code of student conduct. By sharing information, the committee learns whether a student is acting out in various parts of the university (hitting the radar). A "watch list" of students is developed, and, if concern reaches a predetermined level, a comprehensive intervention may be developed and used. Interventions may take many forms and are dependent on the situation.

When a university considers removing a student because that student is perceived as a danger to him or herself or others, administrators should consider the guidance from the Office for Civil Rights (OCR) to Bluffton University (2004). OCR clearly indicates that universities can address "direct threats" to the health or safety of self or others posed by individuals, even when such individuals have a disability. OCR defines a "direct threat" as having a "high probability of substantial harm and not just slightly increased, speculative, or remote risk" (p. 4). In evaluating such situations, OCR recommends that the university assess the "nature, duration, and severity of risk; the probability that potentially threatening injury will actually occur; and whether reasonable modifications of policies, practices, or procedures will significantly mitigate the risk" (p. 4). The university may take interim action against a student in such situations with minimal due process (notice and opportunity to respond to evidence). If the action taken by the university extends beyond an interim separation from the university, a student is entitled to full due process permitted in a student conduct process to include a hearing and an appeal mechanism (pp. 4–5).

Not all campus violence is the result of mental health issues or alcohol or drug abuse. Sometimes youthful exuberance, jealousy, and pressures for success in all aspects of one's life cause students to act out in inappropriate ways. It is the role of student affairs administrators to be on the lookout for students who may be exhibiting "strange behaviors," who may be threatening to others, or who may be a threat to harm self or others. Further, student affairs administrators need to provide leadership in monitoring these students, conducting threat assessments, and taking appropriate action.

Classroom Incivility

Nowhere on our campuses is the breakdown of civility more troublesome, particularly to the faculty, than in the classroom. Classroom incivility may be defined as "any action that interferes with a harmonious and cooperative learning atmosphere in the classroom (Feldmann, 2001, p. 137). Feldmann identifies four categories of uncivil classroom behavior—annoyances, classroom terrorism, intimidation, and threats or acts of violence against an individual. Annoyances include ringing cell phones and pagers, reading a newspaper or searching the Web on a laptop, talking to friends, or wearing inappropriate clothing. Classroom terrorism describes acts such as a student attempting to dominate discussion or interfere with instruction by expressing intolerant ideas and opinions intended to hurt others and discussing a topic that is not relevant to course material for that day. Intimidation refers to students threatening instructors that they will go to the dean, provost, or president to complain about the instructor's teaching or grading. It may also include taping and posting to a website unflattering scenarios involving the instructor. Acts of violence or threats to commit acts of violence against property or a person are very serious and demand immediate attention.

Colleges and faculty are challenged to balance the claims of freedom of expression and responsibility in and outside the classroom. Ernest Boyer's description of college students in 1987 is still true today, but it is made more complex for reasons discussed earlier. But the question Boyer (1987) poses is still very relevant:

> Consider the students. Today's undergraduates are, by every measure, more mature than the teenagers who enrolled a century or two ago. They bring sophistication and a determined independence to the campus. But . . . increasingly, many students come to college with personal problems that can work against their full participation in college life. And administrators are now asking: Is it possible for colleges to intervene constructively in the lives of students whose special needs and personal lifestyles are already well established? (Boyer, 1987, p. 3)

To address classroom misbehavior effectively, faculty members must assume an authority role that some find very uncomfortable. Faculty must understand the balance between an individual student's freedom of expression and the right of the instructor to teach and of the other students in the classroom to learn. "Professors who model respect for their students and open-mindedness toward alternative points of view will promote respect and tolerance among their students" (Baldwin, 1998). As in the case of other sample policies, the sample policy in appendix 11B hinges on the behavior of the student, not on the content of the student's expression.

Parental Notification

The Higher Education Reauthorization Act of 1998 amended the Family Educational Rights and Privacy Act of 1974 (FERPA) to allow, but not require, colleges and universities to notify parents or guardians of students under the age of 21 who violate institutional alcohol and drug policies. Congress's original intent was to create full disclosure by colleges and universities to parents about the alcohol- and drug-related activities in which their underage student(s) were engaged. Pressure from advocacy and lobbying groups that were concerned that colleges and universities were not forthcoming about disclosing crimes on their campuses was, in part, impetus for the change. The amendment changed FERPA provisions from prohibiting disclosure of disciplinary records to parents without the student's consent to a permissive law that allowed, but did not require, such disclosure.

Institutions have responded in a variety of ways, and it is apparent that there is no "one size fits all" approach to parental notification. A review of some institutional policies indicates that there is a continuum that starts at "not notifying parents at all" and ends with "notifying parents in almost every case of a violation." It also appears that some responses fall in between those two approaches, including notifying parents after the first offense and notification based on the level of severity of the offense. Further, notification seems to be triggered at different points in the process, depending on the institution. This variation includes notifying parents/guardians whenever an underage student is charged with an alcohol or drug violation, notifying as part of the sanctioning process, and notifying when the outcome of a case is final and the sanctions are in effect.

Many institutions are finding that parental notification is viewed positively by parents, and, as a result, alcohol violations are reduced. In a 2000 national survey of student judicial officers, it was reported by the respondents that approximately 72% of parents notified of alcohol violations were very supportive of the notification policies (Palmer, Lohman, Gehring, Carlson, & Garrett, 2001, p. 382). The same survey further noted that in the opinion of the participating judicial officers who had such policies in effect, "The policies have had more favorable than unfavorable effects on the number of alcohol violations on campus" (p. 382). Some respondents "emphasized that the greatest reduction was in the number of repeat offenses on the part of students whose parents have been notified" (p. 383).

Institutions are responding to the changing role of parents. Parents are much more involved with their students now than they were a generation ago. A 2006 College Parents of America (CPA) survey revealed that 74% of college parents communicate at least "two to three times a week" with their students, and 34% communicate with them at least daily. Advances in technology have made frequent communication easier, but this generation of parents is also "showing up" more. Ninety percent of the parents responding to the CPA survey reported that they attended orientation with their students, 75% report visiting campus once or twice a semester, and 17% say they visit once a month or more. Three-quarters of the respondents also report that they are "more involved" or "much more involved" than their parents were (CPA, 2006).

It is not surprising that "health and safety" is listed as a topic of greater concern by parents than by students. Twelve percent of parents in the CPA survey cited health and safety as a concern, behind only academics and finances. Yet, only 5% of the parents reported health and safety as an area of concern by their students (CPA, 2006). Parental notification, therefore, can serve as an opportunity to facilitate discussion between parents and students on a topic that students are unlikely to initiate.

More and more parents are claiming a right to be involved in their students' lives. Institutions are responding by initiating more communication and outreach to parents through newsletters, e-mails, and parent organizations initiated by the college. The federal government responded to this trend by modifying FERPA to allow parental notification for alcohol and drug offenses.

With this backdrop, it is interesting to note the variety of philosophical positions and creative solutions associated with parental notification. A prevalent stance views parental notification as an opportunity to partner with parents to engage students in conversations about alcohol and drugs. This solution produces many healthy and engaging side effects, including aligning the institution, the parents, and the student in a manner that can produce educational benefits for all three; bringing the knowledge and expertise of the institution, the skills of the parents, and the inherent need of the student to have a family support system to bear on the problem of underage alcohol and drug use; creating opportunities for parents to engage their student in meaningful dialogue about alcohol and drugs; and creating another channel of communication between the parent and the university that often generates goodwill for the university.

Some campuses have used a number of tools or strategies to assist parents in this regard. One popular tool is a document containing talking points to facilitate parent-student communication about alcohol and drugs. These talking point documents are shared during orientation and are mailed as an attachment to the parental notification document. Parents then have a valuable source of information and encouragement to assist them in talking with their student. An example of such a talking points document in use at Texas A&M University is included in appendix 11C.

Another strategic partnering tool involves providing parents information about drug and alcohol use on college campuses in general and on the specific campus their student has chosen. This allows parents to be informed and armed when tackling this issue, and it helps to diminish any denial within the university or the parents about students' alcohol and drug use. A third strategy is the manner in which the parents are notified. Instead of just a factual letter informing the parents of the violation and sanction, letters are crafted to engage parents in the partnering relationship, to frame the alcohol/drug issues as an opportunity to work on the critical issue, and to seek shared problem solving and a team approach to engaging the student.

The preceding paragraphs deal with how institutions can communicate with parents without the consent of the student on the important issues of alcohol and drugs. More institutions are also implementing procedures for communicating information to parents about their students with the students' permission. One area in particular is grades. There are growing demands for more information about student performance, and some institutions are implementing methods for collecting students' permission to communicate grades to parents in a "wholesale" way. Parents' desire for information seems to be particularly prevalent during the first year of a student's enrollment. Institutions are finding it valuable to seek students' permission to share their grades during new student orientation or other occasions at the very beginning of the college career. This is found to be more effective than addressing the permission issue "one parent at a time" after the first round of grades comes out.

Partnering with parents to address these issues not only opens doors for collaborative efforts, but, if done well the university-parent-student partnership can facilitate the student experience and assist the student and parent as they change their relationship from the parent-child dynamic to the adult-adult dynamic.

Institutions that choose to engage in parental notification should be clear about their reasoning, so they can explain it to students and parents. Assessment is another important component of parental notification. Institutions should use assessment to determine the perception and effectiveness of their parental notification program.

Parents can be powerful partners in the student learning and development enterprise, but the relationship must be managed carefully. Communications must be honest and straightforward and should always include justification for providing the information. Communication should also provide suggestions for response, as suggested, and should include offers for institutional assistance and follow-up. The intent should be to communicate with parents that the institution has a shared interest in and commitment to its students' health, well-being, learning, and development.

Practitioners should be aware of the degree of risk involved in polices or approaches that promote parental involvement. Some students come to college from homes with unhealthy or dysfunctional parent-child relationships. College officials should always make it clear that waiving privacy protections is voluntary. Further, in small-group settings away from parents during orientation, in residence halls, or in other settings, students should be made aware of their right to revoke waivers and of counseling and other college services that help students address their concerns. Students should also be made aware of the measures and policies in place at the college to help ensure their privacy.

Conclusion

College students have been involved in uncivil behavior throughout the history of higher education. However, the changing relationship between administrators and students has resulted in new approaches to incivility. The days of *in loco parentis*, where the dean acted in place of parents, are no longer. Today, students and their parents exhibit a consumer's mentality regarding the college experience. Students "shop" for colleges and select which one to attend based on amenities, quality, and cost. Students and their parents seek legal remedies when the product offered by the college does not meet their expectations.

Yet, we find today's students to be tolerant of behavior that others find abhorrent. Students believe they have a right to express their opinion and that their opinion is as worthy as anyone else's. This belief is troublesome to professors and administrators who place significant value on a person's knowledge and experience with an issue. Such beliefs lead to behaviors viewed as uncivil. We have highlighted some of these behaviors in this chapter—student protest, celebratory riots, hazing, campus violence, and classroom behavior, and we have offered some ways to address such behavior.

We cannot ignore the important role that parents play in the education and development of a student. We have examined this issue and suggested that a partnership should exist between the college and parents to guide students through the college experience. It is a careful balance between involving parents and creating an environment where parental over-involvement hinders student development.

Campus administrators will continue to face incivility. The authors hope that the information provided will assist those administrators in lessening the impact of incivility on their campuses.

References

Andrews, D. (2003). *Understanding violent and destructive fan and student behavior: Observations from the OSU Task Force on the prevention of celebratory riots.* Proceedings of the National Conference Addressing Issues Related to Celebratory Riots. Retrieved March 22, 2007, from http://www.higheredcenter.org/violence/riots/proceedings.pdf

AskOxford. (2007). *Definition of incivility.* AskOxford.com. Retrieved March 19, 2007, from http://www.askoxford.com/concise_oed/incivility?view = uk

Association for Student Judicial Affairs (ASJA) & Association of Fraternity Advisors (AFA). 2006 *For friends and family: Hazing—What it means for you and your student.* Retrieved April 10, 2006, from http://www.asjaonline.org/

Baldwin, R. G. (1998). *Academic civility in the classroom.* The Professional & Organizational Development Network in Higher Education. Retrieved February 5, 2007, from http://cstl.syr.edu/CSTL3/Home/Resources/Subscriptions/POD/V9/V9N8.html

Bickel, R. D., & Lake, P. F. (1999). *The rights and responsibilities of the modern university: Who assumes the risks of college life?* Durham, NC: Carolina Academic Press.

Biemiller, L. (1995, May 5). Tragic days remembered. *The Chronicle of Higher Education.* Retrieved March 19, 2007, from http://chronicle.com/che-data/articles.dir/articles-41.dir/issue-34.dir/34a00101.htm

Boyer, E. L. (1987). *College: The undergraduate experience in America.* New York: Harper & Row.

Campo, S., Poulos, B. S., & Sipple, J. W. (2005). Prevalence and profiling: Hazing among college students and points of intervention. *American Journal of Health Behavior, 29*(2), 137–149.

Carlson, S. (2007, April 19). Counselors say cases like Cho's are hard to spot as students' behavior becomes more extreme. *The Chronicle of Higher Education.* Retrieved April 19, 2007, from http://chronicle.com/free/2007/04/20070419n.htm

College Parents of America (CPA). (2006). *National parent survey reveals high level of communication.* Retrieved June 29, 2007, from http://www.collegeparents .org/cpa/resources-current-campus survey.html

Communist Party v. SACB, 367 U.S. 1 (1961).

Cowley, W. H., & Waller, W. (1994). A study of student life. In A. L. Rentz (Ed.), *Student affairs: A profession's heritage* (pp. 27–34). Washington, DC: American College Personnel Association.

Esther, J. (2006). *Hazing: Historical and current cultural information.* Proceedings of the Donald D. Gehring Student Judicial Affairs Institute. Salt Lake City, UT, June.

Federman, R. (2007, April 23). *Security on America's college campuses.* Opening statement testimony for the Committee on Homeland Security and Governmental Affairs. Washington, DC: U.S. Senate.

Feldmann, L. J. (2001). Classroom civility is another of our instructor responsibilities. *College Teaching, 49*(4), 137–140.

Feulner, E. J. (2004). *Lay your hammer down.* Commencement address to the Hillsdale College class of 2004. Retrieved March 15, 2007, from http://www.hills dale.edu/imprimis/2004/07/

Fierberg, D. E. (2006). *Representing victims of hazing and other group violence on campus.* Retrieved May 1, 2006, from http://www.hazinglaw.com/hazingvic tims.htm

Hacker, A. (2005, November 18). *Preventing civil disturbances. Experts: There isn't one-size-fits-all answer.* Inside Iowa State. Retrieved March 26, 2007, from http:// www.iastate.edu/inside/2005/1118/summit.shtml

Hall, K. (2003). *What goes around comes around when you want to get out of hell.* Proceedings of the National Conference Addressing Issues Related to Celebratory Riots. Retrieved March 22, 2007, from http://www.higheredcenter.org/violence/ riots/proceedings.pdf

Healy v. James, 408 S. Ct. 2338 (1972).

Hoover, N. C. (1999). *National survey: Initiation rites and athletics for NCAA sports teams.* Alfred University. Retrieved April 23, 2006, from http://www.alfred.edu/ sports_hazing/

Hoover, N. C., & Pollard, N. J. (2000). *Initiation rites in American high schools: A national study.* Alfred University. Retrieved from April 23, 2006, from http:// www.alfred.edu/hs_hazing/

Kingsbury, A. (2007, April 22). Toward a safer campus: The ivory tower is more secure than ever, but more safeguards may still be needed. *U.S. News and World Report.* Retrieved May 14, 2007, from http://usnews.com/usnews/news/articles/ 070422/30security.html

Madensen, T. D., & Eck, J. E. (2006). *The problem of student party riots.* Center for Problem-Oriented Policing. Retrieved March 26, 2007, from http://www.pop center.org/problems/problem-studentriots.htm

Magolda, M. B., & Magolda, P. M. (1988). Student activism: A historical overview. In K. M. Miser (Ed.), *Student affairs and campus dissent: Reflections of the past and challenges for the future* (pp. 7–22). Washington, DC: National Association of Student Personnel Administrators.

Moffat, R. C. L. (2001). Incivility as a barometer of societal decay. *Florida Philosophical Review, 1*(1). Retrieved March 15, 2007, from http://www.cah.ucf.edu/philosophy/fpr/journals/volume1/issue1/moffat.html

Nason, J. W. (1981). Presidents and governing boards. In P. G. Altbach & R. O. Berdahl (Eds.), *Higher education in American society* (pp. 253–268). Buffalo, NY: Prometheus Books.

National Collegiate Athletic Association (NCAA). (2003). *Report on the sportsmanship and fan behavior summit.* Retrieved March 22, 2007, from www.ncaa.org/sportsmanship/sportsmanshipFanBehavior/report.pdf

Nordin, V. D. (1991). *Civility on campus: Harassment codes vs. free speech.* (ERIC Document Reproduction Services No. ED 339 303).

Novak, K. (2006, June). *Shifting culture through successful partnerships.* Proceedings of the Donald D. Gehring Student Judicial Affairs Institute. Salt Lake City, UT.

Nuwer, H. (2004). A chronicle of hazing events. In H. Nuwer (Ed.), *The hazing reader* (pp. xxv–xxvii). Bloomington, IN: Indiana University Press.

Office for Civil Rights. (2004). *Letter to Bluffton University.* Retrieved from http://www.nacua.org/meetings/virtualseminars/october2005/Documents/OCRBluff tonU.pdf

The Ohio State University Task Force on Preventing Celebratory Riots. (2003). Final report. Retrieved March 26, 2007, from http://hec.osu.edu/taskforce/FinalReport.pdf

Palmer, C. J., Lohman, G., Gehring, D. D., Carlson, S., & Garrett, O. (2001). Parental notification: A new strategy to reduce alcohol abuse on campus. *NASPA Journal, 38*(3), 372–385.

Papish v. Board of Curators of the University of Missouri, 410 U.S. 667, 92 S. Ct. 1197 (1973).

Paterson, B. G. (2006, June). *Hazing: Case law at U.S. colleges and universities.* Proceedings of the Donald S. Gehring Student Judicial Affairs Institute. Salt Lake City, UT.

Pavela, G. (2006a). Only speech codes should be censored. *The Chronicle of Higher Education.* Retrieved February 5, 2007, from http://chronicle.com/weekly/v53/i5/15b01401.htm

Pavela, G. (2006b). *Questions and answers on college student suicide: A law and policy perspective.* Asheville, NC: College Administration Publications.

Pavela, G. (2007, May 3). School violence: Threat assessment, part II. *ASJA Law and Policy Report.* Retrieved May 8, 2007, from http://www.asjaonline.org/

Sorensen, A. A. (2007, April 19). *An open letter to the Carolina community regarding the tragic events on the Virginia Tech campus.* University of South Carolina News. Retrieved May 14, 2007, from http://uscnews.sc.edu/ADMN041907.html

Spellings, M. (2006). *Secretary Spellings announces plans for more affordable, accessible, accountable and consumer-friendly U.S. higher education system.* Retrieved March 23, 2007, from http://www.ed.gov/news/pressreleases/2006/09/09262006.html

Taylor, M. (2006). *Generation NeXT comes to college: Meeting the postmodern student.* Retrieved May 5, 2005, from http://www.lib.wayne.edu/or/accreditation/exam ples/documents/generationnext.pdf.

Taylor, M. (2007, February 23). *Generation NeXT comes to college: Understanding and teaching today's postmodern students.* Presentation to faculty and administrators at Illinois State University.

Texas A&M University (2007). *Alcohol and college: A parents' guide.* Retrieved June 29, 2007, from http://studentlife.tamu.edu/adep/resources/families.htm

Tinker v. Des Moines Independent School District, 393 U.S. 503, 89 S. Ct. 733 (1969).

U.S. Secret Service & U.S. Department of Education (2002). *Threat assessment in schools: A guide to managing threatening situations and to creating safe school climates.* Retrieved May 14, 2007, from http://www.secretservice.gov/ntac/ssi_ guide.pdf

VanDeventer Iverson, S., & Allen, E. J. (2004). Initiating change: Transforming a hazing culture. In H. Nuwer (Ed.), *The hazing reader* (pp. 252–274). Bloomington, IN: Indiana University Press.

Van Slyke, J. M. (2005). An analysis of issues related to celebratory riots at higher education institutions. *Proceedings of the Education Law Consortium Forum.* Retrieved March 22, 2007, from http://educationlawconsortium.org/forum/2005/ papers/VanSlyke2005.pdf

Wann, D. (2003). *Understanding fan misbehavior and rioting at sporting events.* Proceedings of the National Conference Addressing Issues Related to Celebratory Riots. Retrieved March 22, 2007, from http://www.higheredcenter.org/violence/ riots/proceedings.pdf

Wikipedia. (2007). Definition of incivility. *Wikipedia: The Free Encyclopedia.* Retrieved March 19, 2007, from http://en.wikipedia.org/wiki/Incivility

Yankelovich, D., & Furth, I. (2005). The role of colleges in an era of mistrust. *The Chronicle of Higher Education, 52*(4), 4b.

National Championship Game Meeting Agenda 3/26/07

I. **Communication Plan**
    A. Press Release
    B. University website
    C. Communication on first day of class
    D. Safety reminder to students/fans traveling to Atlanta
II. **O'Connell Center**
    A. Access restricted to Gator One ID (only)
    B. Exit and re-entry policy consistent with normal game procedures
    C. Entry restricted after half time?
    D. All four gates will be opened
    E. Info on O'Dome website
    F. T-shirt distribution (at the door or on seats/Rowdy Reptiles)
III. **University Police Department**
    A. Pre-game plan
        1. Post-game plan
        2. Parking
        3. Emergency procedures
IV. **University Athletic Association**
    A. Pre-recorded message from Coach Donovan
    B. Dazzlers, cheerleaders, mascots?
V. **UAA Marketing**
    A. Game-like atmosphere
    B. Contests, give-aways and promos
VI. **Sorority/Fraternity Affairs**
VII. **Housing**
    A. Viewing areas in all residence halls
    B. Secure loose items around buildings
VIII. **Student Government**
IX. **Reitz Union**
    A. Staff support for O'Connell Center support/crowd control
    B. No requirement for overflow seating
X. **Trauma Response Team**

APPENDIX 11B

Sample Policy Addressing Classroom Misbehavior

The University supports the principle of freedom of expression for both instructors and students. The university respects the rights of instructors to teach and students to learn. Maintenance of these rights requires classroom conditions that do not impede their exercise. Classroom behavior that seriously interferes with either (1) the instructor's ability to conduct the class or (2) the ability of other students to profit from the instructional program will not be tolerated. An individual engaging in disruptive classroom behavior may be subject to disciplinary action (see Student Conduct Code).

1. When a student's behavior in a class is so seriously disruptive as to compel immediate action, the instructor has the authority to remove a student from the class on an interim basis, pending an informal hearing on the behavior. A student who has been removed from a class on an interim basis is entitled to an informal hearing before the head of the department offering the course within three working days of the removal. The department head may either:

    1.1 Approve an agreement of expectations between the student and the instructor and reinstate the student to the class, or,

    1.2. Extend the removal of the student from the class and refer the case to Student Affairs for adjudication. A copy of all material sent to Student Affairs should be provided to the instructor's academic dean and to the student's academic dean.

2. When a student action is not so serious as to require immediate removal from the class, these steps are to be followed:

    2.1. The instructor responsible for the class or activity where the alleged disruptive behavior occurred will inform the student that his/her behavior has been inappropriate. The instructor will describe to the student specific needed changes in the student's behavior. The student will be provided an opportunity to modify his/her behavior in accordance with the changes identified. The instructor will provide the student with a written, dated summary of his/her discussion with the student, and the instructor will retain a file copy of this summary.

2.2. If a student believes the instructor's expectations are unreasonable, he/she may confer with the instructor's department head about this matter. The department head may choose to support the guidelines developed by the instructor, or he or she may work with the instructor to develop a modified set of expectations. If there are changes in the instructor's original set of expectations, a signed and dated copy will be provided by the department head to both the student and the instructor.

2.3. Should a student's behavior continue to be unacceptable, the instructor will apprise his/her (the instructor's) department head of what has occurred and will share with the department head the written summary of the discussion with the student. The department head may wish to initiate additional discussion with the instructor and/or the student. If the department head concurs with the instructor's view that the problem has not been resolved, the situation may be referred to Student Affairs. A memorandum briefly describing the student's behavior, as well as a copy of the written summary of the instructor's discussion with the student and any other related material, should be forwarded to Student Affairs for adjudication. A copy of all material sent to Student Affairs should be provided to the instructor's academic dean and to the student's academic dean.

APPENDIX 11C

Alcohol and College: A Parent's Guide

Alcohol and Drug Education Programs, Texas A&M University

For many parents, bringing up the subject of alcohol is not easy. You may be unsure of when or how to begin and your student may dodge the conversation. However, it is important for you to be aware of the risks and consequences associated with alcohol so you can help your student be aware. Impaired judgment from drinking can lead to risky behavior causing academic, legal, and personal problems. It is important to understand the risks associated with drinking.

To help start the conversation, Alcohol and Drug Education Programs has provided you with a list of eight discussion topics compiled by College Parents of America (CPA). By having this conversation before your student arrives on campus, you help educate them so they can make responsible decisions. While parents may not be able to actively monitor students away from home, they can be available to talk and listen, and that is just as important. It can do more than help shape lives; it can save lives.

- **Set clear and realistic expectations regarding academic performance.** Studies conducted nationally have demonstrated that partying may contribute as much to a student's decline in grades as the difficulty of his or her academic work. If students know their parents expect sound academic work, they are more likely to be devoted to their studies and have less time to get in trouble with alcohol.
- **Stress to students that alcohol is toxic and excessive consumption can fatally poison.** This is not a scare tactic. Students die every year from alcohol poisoning. Discourage dangerous drinking such as drinking games. Parents should ask their students to also have the courage to intervene when they see someone putting their life at risk through participation in dangerous drinking.

- **Tell students to intervene when classmates are in trouble with alcohol.** Nothing is more tragic than an unconscious student being left to die while others either fail to recognize that the student is in jeopardy or fail to call for help due to fear of getting the student in trouble.
- **Tell students to stand up for their right to a safe academic environment.** Students who do not drink can be affected by the behavior of those who do, ranging from interrupted study time to assault or unwanted sexual advances. Students can confront these problems directly by discussing them with the offender. If that fails, they should notify the Residence Hall Director, Resident Advisor or Director of Student Life.
- **Know the alcohol scene on campus and talk to students about it.** Students grossly exaggerate the use of alcohol and other drugs by their peers. A recent survey found that Texas A&M students believed 92 percent of their peers drink alcohol at least once a week, when the actual rate was 56 percent. Students are highly influenced by peers and tend to drink up to what they perceive as the norm. Confronting misperceptions about alcohol use is vital.
- **Avoid tales of drinking exploits from your own college years.** Entertaining students with stories of drinking back in "the good old days" normalizes what, even then, was abnormal behavior. It also appears to give parental approval to dangerous alcohol consumption.
- **Encourage your student to become involved in student organizations and to volunteer in community work.** In addition to structuring free time, involvement provides students with opportunities to develop leadership and job-related skills and to gain valuable experience. Helping others also gives students a broader outlook and healthier perspective on the opportunities they enjoy. Involvement on campus helps students further connect to their school, increasing the likelihood of staying in college.
- **Make it clear: underage alcohol consumption and driving after drinking are against the law.** Parents should make it clear that they do not condone breaking the law. Parents of college students should openly and clearly express disapproval of underage drinking and dangerous alcohol consumption. And, if parents themselves drink, they should present a positive role model in the responsible use of alcohol. (Texas A&M University, 2007)

12

FIRST AMENDMENT ISSUES

Saundra K. Schuster, Lee E. Bird, and Mary Beth Mackin

S ome of the most difficult and complex student and organization behavior issues that arise are those that involve the First Amendment to
the Constitution. Often, the First Amendment issues are not apparent
on initial review and do not become evident until a thorough investigation
reveals them. It is critical, therefore, to assess any incident to determine if it
involves issues of speech, religious expression, the student press, or rights of
assembly. It is also important to remember that "speech" may take many
forms and that many methods of expression are constitutionally protected.
Rapid technological advances have spawned an increasingly broad array of
venues for expression, not only on campuses but around the world as well.
Consequently, administrators must consider student expression that is beyond simply the spoken word on the campus proper.

The First Amendment to the Constitution of the United States reads,
"Congress shall make no law respecting an establishment of religion, or prohibiting the free expression thereof; or abridging the freedom of speech or of
the press; or the right of the people peaceably to assemble, and to petition
the Government for a redress of grievances."

While the law of the land may seem fairly straightforward, the reality is
that at public colleges and universities the First Amendment is often inadver-
tently or purposefully violated, and First Amendment issues remain complex,
dynamic, and vexing.

Robert M. O'Neil, founder of the Thomas Jefferson Center for the Protection of Free Expression and author of *Free Speech in the College Community* (1997), wrote,

> The starting point is that all public colleges and universities are bound by the First Amendment. That means they must tolerate much speaking and writing that may not be pleasing to many of their students, faculty, alumni, trustees, and others. Case after case has reaffirmed this principle with regard to student protest, campus newspapers, radical student groups and outspoken faculty. While private campuses are not directly governed by the Bill of Rights, many pride themselves on observing standards of expression at least as high as those their public counterparts must meet. Thus the guiding principle for virtually all institutions of higher learning is that free speech must be protected, even when the speech for which freedom is sought may be offensive or disruptive or at variance with the campus mission. (p. 15)

Administrators generally support the educational benefits of preserving the "marketplace of ideas" where students may listen and judge for themselves the credibility of the speaker and the value of the ideas expressed. However, when the proverbial "tug-of war" begins between preserving First Amendment rights and protecting widely accepted institutional values, such as civility or respect for individual differences, administrators may find themselves in a conundrum, questioning just what the right thing is to do. Legally the answer is easy—protect the First Amendment; yet, in practice, standing up for the First Amendment may create an unintended maelstrom of conflict.

The Current Climate on Campuses

Watchdog groups, such as the Foundation for Individual Rights in Education (FIRE), have roundly criticized higher education for failing to honor the First Amendment on campuses. Administrators generally need not seek out First Amendment challenges, as the conflicts find them in their capacity as hall directors, student conduct staff, and senior student affairs officers. Such incidents may involve offensive posters in residence halls, campus preachers spewing their version of religious bigotry at passersby, controversial issues and speakers that ignite protests and counterprotests, offensive fraternity and sorority theme parties that are racist or otherwise degrading, perceived discrimination by club and organizational membership, recognition of controversial or ultraconservative student groups, vulgar fan behavior, comments made by controversial faculty, and racist, homophobic, or sexist slurs directed at any number of individuals or groups. One thing is certain: the offended party or parties will call for immediate action. Even if the speech or behavior in question is indeed protected (albeit offensive or hurtful), immediate action will be demanded! For the uninitiated, the pressure to redress such incidents is palpable and often leads to the development of new policies (sometimes called hate speech codes) and limiting the areas in which expression may occur to tiny, out-of-the-way "zones." Too often, the feel-good, knee-jerk, well-intended responses to stop or prevent perceived harmful expression result in clear violations of the First Amendment.

Kermit Hall (n.d.), president of the University of Albany, State University of New York, writing for the *First Amendment Center* website, said: "[Speech codes] are the most controversial ways in which universities have attempted to strike a balance between expression and community order" (p. 2). "Efforts to restrict the viewpoint or message of anyone on a campus puts the institution at odds with its primary educational mission: to give students the opportunity to sort through opposing ideas" (p. 5).

Guidelines for Policy Development and Analysis

Faced with the dichotomy of providing an educational environment that represents the "marketplace of ideas," rich in challenge, discourse, and, of course, disagreements, alongside a commitment to diversity and acceptance, college educators and administrators often seek guidance in developing, applying, and analyzing their policies in a manner that balances competing rights and interests and minimizes the risk of legal challenge. Creating policies that incorporate the college mission, support free expression, address access, and balance competing interests poses great challenges. The U.S. Supreme Court has held, time and time again, that the mere fact that someone might take offense at the content of expressive activity is not sufficient justification for its prohibition.

Private colleges and universities have broader latitude in restricting both access to campus property and topics for public speech, because they generally are not bound by First Amendment limitations that are imposed on government entities. Although First Amendment restrictions are not a factor in the development and implementation of their policies, private institutions are, nevertheless, bound by federal nondiscrimination laws, which are imposed on all institutions that receive federal funding. Therefore, these nondiscrimination laws must be a consideration in policy development related to inclusion, exclusion, and public speech, often posing similar confounding challenges to private institutions as those presented to public institutions.

The standard by which the constitutionality of a policy that regulates speech or other forms of expressive activity on a public college or university campus must be evaluated is based on the character of the "property" (for purposes of this chapter, "property" refers to both physical space and the conceptual space represented by other venues of expressive activity, such as student press, student organization regulations, and campus policies) at issue. The Supreme Court, through many First Amendment decisions, has created an analysis framework referred to as "forum analysis" as a means to determine the nature or special characteristics of the "property" in question in relation to the degree of restrictions that may be imposed on expressive activity for that specific "property." Thus, a public college or university must apply the forum analysis for each policy that involves speech or other forms of expressive activity.

The extent to which the First Amendment permits a college or university to restrict speech depends on the character of the forum the institution has created. In applying the forum analysis, a public college or university must first identify the type of forum, based on special characteristics. The type of forum establishes the appropriate category of "scrutiny" that must be applied to any limitation. "Scrutiny" refers to the level of analysis required by law that must be applied to the "governmental interest" in establishing a limitation on a constitutionally protected right—such as speech. The courts apply an analysis to the forum, which identifies a "rational basis" standard and a "strict scrutiny" standard—as a part of a hierarchy to weigh the asserted government interest in limiting expression against an individual or group's right to speak. Once the category of forum and level of appropriate scrutiny is identified, colleges and universities may impose content neutral "time, place, and manner" limitations to expressive activities consistent with forum type.

Traditional Public Forum

A place that has immemorially been held in trust for use by the public and has always been used for purposes of assembly and to communicate thoughts between citizens and discussion of public questions is the traditional public forum. Examples include public streets, sidewalks, and parks. This type of forum is subject to the highest level of scrutiny; any time, place, and manner regulations imposed on expressive activity in this type of forum must be "content neutral" and "narrowly tailored" to serve the specific government interest. "Content neutral" means that one cannot impose limitations on expressive activity based on the topic, and "narrow tailoring" means that any limitations the college imposes on expression must be sufficiently limited to achieve the "compelling government interest" involved without encompassing more expression than is necessary in doing so. Any restrictions must also leave open ample alternative channels of communication.

Public colleges and universities may never prohibit all expressive activity in this type of forum, and any limitations must be drawn narrowly to meet the "compelling government interest" standard. A "compelling governmental interest" refers to something necessary or crucial, as opposed to something merely preferred or imposed as a preference or convenience. For example, the public sidewalks surrounding a campus, a public parking lot adjacent to the campus, and sidewalks or paths that are primary routes of travel through the campus, used by the public and the campus community, are considered "traditional public forums." In areas such as this, any limitation on expression must meet the "compelling government interest" standard, such as protecting the educational environment from disruption in support of the college's mission, or ensuring the public safety of the college community's members. The college cannot regulate the topics for discussion, but it can apply regulations such as no amplified sound or restrictions on groups convening in a way that limits ingress or regress of the campus buildings or walkways.

Designated Public Forum

This type of forum is created specifically by the government entity (college or university) as a place for expressive activity that generally is not necessarily identified for this purpose, and is not by default a traditional public forum. Generally designated public forum areas are not created by inaction or simply permitting limited discourse in the designated area; instead, they must be created by both the institution's policy and practice. In the designated public forum area, there is an automatic assumption that expression may not be restricted unless it meets the high standards of scrutiny in balancing the right of the institution to create limitations with the rights of the speaker, as described for the traditional public forum.

Examples of designated public forum areas include the "free speech zone," the "gazebo," the "oval," or the student newspaper. This type of forum is not required to remain so designated indefinitely, but as long as it is designated as a public forum, all restrictions on expressive activities are subject to the same analysis as a traditional public forum.

Designated Limited Public Forum

This type of forum is created by the government entity (college or university) for public expression, but is limited to particular groups or particular topics. This type of forum is not the same as a "designated public forum" because this type has additional limitations related to restricting expressions of specific kinds or by specific groups. Although the institution may not discriminate on the basis of viewpoint, it may limit the forum to certain speakers or for discussion of certain topics. Examples of this type of forum are a student organization, athletic arenas, meeting spaces, or auditoriums. In this type of forum, the institution may give priority for use to one form of expression over another (e.g., a college auditorium may have priority for campus theater productions, or meeting space may be limited to student or faculty groups only).

Designated limited public forum areas must be governed by a written use or membership policy that includes the stated purpose of the forum and the basis for any limitations on that use. The standard to be applied for creating limitations is "reasonableness." That is, the restriction or limitation must be consistent with the purpose of the location, the college mission, or the historical use to meet the reasonableness test. However, the institution cannot impose more limitations than are necessary to reasonably support the purpose of the forum. In this type of forum, the college may give priority to college entities over noncollege entities as long as that standard is applied consistently.

Nonpublic Forum

Any public property that is not, by designation or tradition, a public forum is, by default, considered a nonpublic forum. This type of forum is created when there is clear evidence that the public body did not intend to create a public forum, or where the nature of the property at issue is inconsistent with expressive activity. One example is where a public college or university is acting as a "proprietor," managing its internal operations. In this type of forum, the public body may restrict expressive activity for its intended purposes as long as the restrictions are not based on viewpoint. Limitations on expression must only be "reasonable," but may not limit the expressive activity based on a disagreement with the speaker's viewpoint. Examples of nonpublic forum areas include campus offices, classrooms, and residence hall rooms. These locations have the lowest standard for restricting expression. For example, a college may restrict all posters on residence hall walls because of the environmental impact, but may not restrict only those posters that communicate a certain message, nor may it limit categories of posters.

The most important point is that in the past decade, courts have been clear about the fact that public college and university campuses should not consider themselves entirely public forums in nature; however, neither can they identify themselves as completely nonpublic or limited in nature. Therefore, college administrators are faced with the challenging task of identifying the appropriate forum areas for their specific campus and applying the appropriate level of "scrutiny" when creating the limitations that will establish the legal balance between the type of forum and the rights to expression.

Categories of Unprotected Speech

Of course, not all forms of expression enjoy First Amendment protection, no matter the forum in which they occur. In addition to the restrictions that may be implemented using the forum analysis, the courts have determined that some forms of expression may be prohibited, but these particular categories are small in number, and their scope is fairly narrow.

Fighting Words

Perhaps the most misunderstood category of unprotected speech on the college campus is that of "fighting words." This term is often applied liberally to any speech that someone may find offensive or that someone considers to be "hate speech." In reality, the concept of fighting words is so narrow that it would be difficult to comprehend what truly meets that definition in modern society.

The "fighting words" doctrine was defined by the Supreme Court in the 1942 case, *Chaplinsky v. New Hampshire* (1942), where Chaplinsky was arrested for calling someone "a God-damned racketeer" and "a damned Fascist." The Court reaffirmed that the right of free speech is "not absolute at all times and under all circumstances" and that "fighting words" represented a class of speech that could be prevented and punished. The Court defined "fighting words" as "those which by their very utterance inflict injury or tend to incite an immediate breach of the peace" (pp. 571–572).

Inherent in this definition is the notion that such words, when spoken, would be so inflammatory that a reasonable person hearing them would have no recourse but to react with immediate physical violence. This doctrine is an old one and reflects the times in which it was written. No Supreme Court decision since has upheld this doctrine, and it certainly could be argued that any reasonable person on a college campus should be able to contain his or her violent reaction, no matter how offended he or she is.

Obscenity

Modern college campuses are fraught with profane messages on clothing, tasteless cheers at sporting events, political cartoons of a sexual nature, and a host of other messages that some people find offensive. It is rare, however, that any of these rise to the level of true "obscenity" as defined by the Supreme Court.

The 1973 Supreme Court case, *Miller v. California* (1973), related to sexually oriented adult materials and provided the test for measuring obscenity by modifying the formerly used *Roth* test. According to the Court, the determination of obscenity must take into account:

- whether "the average person, applying contemporary community standards" would find that the work, taken as a whole, appeals to the prurient interest;

- whether the work depicts or describes, in a patently offensive way, sexual conduct specifically defined by the applicable state law; and
- whether the work, taken as a whole, lacks serious literary, artistic, political, or scientific value (p. 429).

Given this very narrow definition, the majority of offending messages on college campuses do not constitute "obscenity" and, thus do not lose their First Amendment protection.

Threats

Administrators often grapple with complaints by students and staff alike that they have been threatened on campus. "True threats" certainly may be prohibited or punished, but it may be difficult to discern between a casual or sarcastic statement and a "true threat." Several court cases have attempted to define such a threat, and the common thread running through all of them seems to be the intent of the speaker and the interpretation of a "reasonable person."

In *Virginia v. Black* (2003), the Supreme Court said, "Intimidation in the constitutionally proscribable sense of the word is a type of true threat, where a speaker directs a threat to a person or group of persons with the intent of placing the victim in fear of bodily harm or death" (p. 360). The intent in this language is to protect a victim from the fear of violence and does not rely on the speaker's plan to carry out the threat.

The court, in *Planned Parenthood v. American Coalition of Life Activists* (2002), defined a threat as, "a statement which, in the entire context and under all the circumstances, a reasonable person would foresee would be interpreted by those to whom the statement is communicated as a serious expression of intent to inflict bodily harm upon that person" (p. 49, 1077).

Thus, such a statement that is made in an offhand fashion, is uttered as a joke or prank, or does not seem likely to be carried out may not rise to the level of unprotected speech.

Incitement

Just as difficult to determine as a "threat," "incitement" can be an unprotected category of expression that may be difficult to identify precisely. In *Brandenburg v. Ohio* (1969), a Ku Klux Klan leader was arrested after a KKK rally featured a speaker who said, "if our President, our Congress, our Supreme Court, continues to suppress the white, Caucasian race, it's possible that there might have to be some revengeance [sic] taken" (1829, p. 446).

The court said that the arrest in Brandenburg punished the mere advocacy of violence, as well as assembly with others to advocate, rather than actual incitement of violence. The court did define unprotected expression, however, when it stated, "Freedoms of speech and press do not permit a State to forbid advocacy of the use of force or of law violation except where such advocacy is *directed to inciting or producing imminent lawless action and is likely to incite or produce such action*" (emphasis added) (1969, p. 434). Thus, expression that actually incites or produces lawless action is prohibited, while expression that simply advocates violence or lawless action is protected.

Racial and Sexual Harassment

Much confusion has arisen regarding racial and sexual harassment as those concepts intersect with First Amendment freedoms of expression. Muddled expectations and directives from the Office for Civil Rights (OCR), along with imprecise language in Title VI and Title IX, have made these terms difficult to define. In a 2003 "Dear Colleague" letter, however, the OCR attempts to provide clarity regarding expectations for dealing with harassment and in defining such. As stated in the letter,

> Harassment of students, which can include verbal or physical conduct, can be a form of discrimination prohibited by the statutes enforced by OCR. Thus, for example, in addressing harassment allegations, OCR has recognized that the offensiveness of a particular expression, standing alone, is not a legally sufficient basis to establish a hostile environment under the statutes enforced by OCR. In order to establish a hostile environment, harassment must be sufficiently serious (i.e., severe, persistent or pervasive) as to limit or deny a student's ability to participate in or benefit from an educational program. OCR has consistently maintained that schools in regulating the conduct of students and faculty to prevent or redress discrimination must formulate, interpret, and apply their rules in a manner that respects the legal rights of students and faculty, including those court precedents interpreting the concept of free speech. OCR's regulations and policies do not require or prescribe speech, conduct or harassment codes that impair the exercise of rights protected under the First Amendment. (OCR letter, 2003)

The letter further states that prohibited harassment "must include something beyond the mere expression of views, words, symbols or thoughts that some person finds offensive. Under OCR's standard, the conduct must also be considered sufficiently serious to deny or limit a student's ability to participate in or benefit from the educational program." In addition, the letter clarifies that the questionable conduct must be "evaluated from the perspective of a reasonable person in the alleged victim's position, considering all the circumstances, including the alleged victim's age."

Given this more precise definition, it is incumbent on the administrator to determine if the expression in question is truly so severe, persistent, or pervasive as to "limit the student's ability to participate in or benefit from the educational program." Since this test must also be applied from the "perspective of a reasonable person," it does not depend simply on the reaction of the specific victim; especially one who might be overly sensitive.

Racial and sexual harassment are serious concerns on campus, and their impact is significant. To combat such intolerance, many institutions have implemented speech codes that prohibit "hate speech" and other expression that offends, marginalizes, or stigmatizes others. It is important to note that "hate speech" has no substantive legal definition and, in and of itself, is not a category of unprotected speech. Many such speech codes have been found to be unconstitutional in that they are either vague (a reasonable person could not easily discern exactly what is prohibited) or overbroad (they prohibit constitutionally protected speech in their sweep). Although there are many effective ways to deal with such intolerance on campus, implementing a speech code is generally not one of them.

Defamation

A final category of speech that is not constitutionally protected is "defamation." Typically, defamation requires that a false statement be made about a person (either orally or in writing) to someone other than the person to whom it is likely to cause harm. In *New York Times v. Sullivan* (1964), the Supreme Court further stated that if the victim is a public official, actual malice must be present (p. 696).

As defamation cases are generally reserved for civil courts, however, it may not be prudent for an institution to routinely interfere with such expression.

How to Respond: The Educator's Challenge

When faced with a minor or major First Amendment challenge the first step is to analyze the facts of the case or incident and determine if disciplinary action is warranted. If action may be taken, it is prudent to document all steps and ensure that involved parties understand the rationale behind what is being done. If action is not warranted, the administrator still has the opportunity to meet with the student(s) involved and engage in a meaningful conversation about the impact of the behavior. Most students have no idea how they have affected others or even the consequences of their behavior on the larger community. When confronted with these realities, students begin to learn invaluable life lessons about fundamental responsibilities associated with foundational rights. It is also critical that administrators engage the entire community in similar discussions. Most students (even those associated with most college and university newspapers) know little about the First Amendment. The opportunity to teach about this right often leads naturally to a discussion of community expectations regarding civility and the need to educate ourselves about intolerance, ignorance, and arrogance. It is amazing how transformational these conversations can be. Some members of the community, especially those most affected by, for example, (protected) "hate" speech, will likely not be satisfied with perceived inaction of university administrators. They may be angry and rightly so. First Amendment discussions are difficult but necessary. Following difficult incidents, administrators can share their shock and disappointment with the speech or behavior in question to facilitate broader campus discussions. Some campuses have hosted forum days and speak-outs following particularly offensive incidents.

Bird and Mackin (2006a) note,

> From the very beginning, it is important to continually try to identify those who may be experiencing a negative impact from the incident and to provide as much institutional support as possible. This may include meeting with students or groups who were affected by the speech to assess their welfare, listen to their issues, offer campus support sources, inform them about the institution's plans for action, and simply let them know that their concerns are being heard. The needs of faculty and staff should also receive close attention. (p. 162)

Successful administrative interventions depend on excellent communication channels, the ability and willingness to successfully "take the pulse" of the campus, and crafting timely, thoughtful responses. This can be particularly difficult when media are involved because attempts to ignore them are rarely effective. Every spokesperson for the university should collect his or her thoughts and be prepared to provide the three most important messages the campus wants readers or viewers to understand about the incident. According to Bird and Mackin (2006b),

> Although there are many principles and precedents to guide administrative action in incidents related to free speech, seldom will an event lend itself to a single easy resolution. Instead, various perspectives and approaches may need to be blended with the nature of the specific incident and the culture of the campus. In addition, any free speech issue on campus will likely blossom quickly, with the campus finding itself in the center of controversy, media attention, and opinions, including criticisms. (p. 140)

The old adage that one should "fight speech with speech" is clichéd but true. Higher education administrators need to understand the rights and responsibilities guaranteed by the First Amendment and take every available opportunity to teach and model them.

References

Bird, L. E., & Mackin, M. B. (2006a). Healing communities and stakeholders. In L. Bird, M. B. Mackin, & S. K. Schuster (Eds.). *The first amendment on campus: A handbook for college and university administrators.* Washington, DC: National Association of Student Personnel Administrators.

Bird, L. E., & Mackin, M. B. (2006b). Practical and political realities of a first amendment crisis. In L. Bird, M. B. Mackin, & S. K. Schuster (Eds.). *The first amendment on campus: A handbook for college and university administrators.* Washington, DC: National Association of Student Personnel Administrators.

Brandenburg v. Ohio, 395 U.S. 444 (1969).

Chaplinsky v. New Hampshire, 315 U.S. 568 (1942).

Hall, Kermit L. (n.d.). *Free speech on public college campuses—Overview.* Retrieved March 31, 2007, from www.firstamendmentcenter.org

Miller v. California, 413 U.S. 15 (1973).

New York Times v. Sullivan, 376 U.S. 254 (1964).

Office for Civil Rights (2007). *"Dear Colleague" letter.* Retrieved March 10, 2007, from http://www.ed.gov/about/offices/list/ocr/firstamend.html

O'Neil, R. M. (1997). *Free speech in the college community.* Bloomington, IN: Indiana University Press.

Virginia v. Black, 538 U.S. 343 (2003).

13

ADDRESSING STUDENT WELL-BEING AND MENTAL HEALTH

Gary Dickstein and Annie Nebeker Christensen

Introduction

Information about the mental health crisis among today's college students is disconcerting. The numbers of students who are involved in incidents of inappropriate behavior and who also suffer from some form of psychological illness or diagnosed disability are on the rise. Numerous authors have noted that there is an increase in the severity and complexity of students experiencing mental health issues (Benton, 2006; Benton, Benton, Newton, Benton, & Robinson, 2004; Eells, Rando, Gartner, & Rodolfa, in press). Moreover, on college campuses today, "the number of freshmen reporting less than average emotional health has been steadily rising since 1985" (Shea, 2002, p. 1). Nearly 50% of all college students self-reported feeling so depressed at some point in time that they had trouble functioning (American College Health Association [ACHA] Survey, 2004). Two years later the ACHA conducted the same study, and it was discovered that 62% of students reported feeling hopeless at times; more than 9% had seriously considered suicide, and 1.3% had actually made a suicide attempt (ACHA, 2006).

As a result of the documented increase in mental health issues among students, college and university administrators are challenged more than ever to respond to these issues; however, they are finding them complex in their composition and challenging to resolve (Dickstein & Rando, submitted for publication). How do administrators strike the delicate balance between protecting the rights of the individual and considering the safety and/or tranquility of the larger campus community? Should a university administrator contact the parents of a student who is in crisis? If the decision is made to contact parents, what steps are appropriate to follow to release information from that student's educational record and still comply with federal privacy laws? What factors need to be considered with respect to the impact of the federal Health Insurance Portability and Accountability Act (HIPAA) on disclosing information to parents and others? These questions represent just the tip of the iceberg. Additional concerns include what process should be followed if the student's behavior is so egregious that removal from the residence halls or dismissal from the institution is warranted? Conversely, if the student is allowed to continue, what resources are available to monitor the student and ensure that he or she does not "fall through the cracks"? Does the institution even have the resources necessary to monitor the student in such a manner? All of these questions present huge challenges for college administrators.

As tragedies such as the random shootings at Virginia Tech University in 2007 demonstrate, the consequences of failing to address students' mental health issues can be dramatic not only for the students themselves, but for the institutions they attend as well. Students with untreated mental health issues can struggle to function, learn, live in a community, and be productive and engaged members of the campus community. They may fail a class or, worse yet, leave the institution prematurely because of poor academic performance. One of the most tragic consequences of poor mental health is when a student attempts to commit or commits suicide. This chapter, which seeks to answer some of the preceding questions, is intended to help university administrators to identify students who are struggling with mental health issues and to connect students with the appropriate support and treatment intervention.

Mental Illness on Campus

Conducted since 1981, the National Survey of Counseling Directors includes data provided by the administrative supervisors of college and university counseling centers throughout the United States and Canada (Gallagher,

2006). In 2006, the survey included data from 367 counseling center directors who reported that 40% of their student clients had severe psychological problems. Of these, 8% had such serious psychological difficulties that they could not remain enrolled in school, or they suffered from a degree of illness that necessitated extensive psychological/psychiatric help. This study also reported that 32% of students experienced severe problems associated with their mental health, but they were treated successfully with available treatment modalities (p. 5). Another study, by a psychologist at Kansas State University, examined trends among college students seeking mental health counseling and found that the percentage of students seen with depression had doubled, and the number of students seen with suicidal ideation had tripled within the last 13 years (Benton, Robertson, Tseng, Newton, & Benton, 2003). This same study also found that four times as many college students had sought counseling as a result of sexual assault; 6% of college students reported serious problems with substance abuse or an eating disorder; and the proportion of students taking psychotropic medication rose from 10 to 25% (Benton et al., 2003). Another study also found "a sharp rise in the number of college students taking psychiatric medication" (Young, 2003, p. 1).

College health experts report that the most common mental health issues presenting in college students are mood disorders, followed by developmental issues such as establishing identity, independence, family issues, and formulating a plan for the future. Anxiety disorders are also commonplace, and these include social phobias, obsessive compulsive disorder, posttraumatic stress disorder, and general anxiety disorders (Arehart-Treichal, 2002). Manifested behaviors such as substance abuse problems and eating disorders are also prevalent in students who seek assistance from college counseling centers. As is the case with most areas of mental health, students may be struggling with dual challenges, such as coping with one or more developmental issues coupled with a mental health disorder (Arehart-Treichal, 2002).

The Mental Health Needs of Today's College Student

From depression to bipolar disorder, eating disorders to self-harming incidents, campus officials across the country report that today's college students are arriving on campus with histories of mental illness and are already on psychotropic medications. We also know that psychological conditions, including depression, bipolar disorder, and schizophrenia, typically manifest themselves at ages 18–25, making college campuses the prime location for the first occurrence of a student's mental illness (Chisholm, 1998). At times, these illnesses can be severe and complicated to manage. To understand the increasing rate of mental illness in the student population, it is essential to understand the demographic changes that have transpired on campus.

Today's college students are vastly different from their counterparts from previous generations. Baruth and Manning (2007) advise that persons of color will constitute the numerical majority somewhere between 2030 and 2050. A recent article by noted demographer Harold Hodgkinson (2000) indicates that 57% of the first-year class of college students for the year 2010 will be from non-White backgrounds. The proportion of nontraditional-age college students (25 years and older) has increased significantly in recent years. From 2005 to 2015, the National Center for Education Statistics (NCES) (NCES, 2006) projects a rise of 18% in enrollment of persons 25 and over. Whereas college was once a place of privilege, current students are more representative of the population as a whole (Marano, 2002).

As the demographics of college students change, so do their mental health needs. In the last 10 years, campus counseling centers have reported a significant change in the concerns of students who seek counseling. The psychological difficulties of students have shifted from more benign developmental issues and informational needs to more severe and complex psychological problems (Gallagher, 2000; Gallagher, 2006; Pledge, Lapan, Heppner, & Roehlke, 1998). Students are increasingly coming to college "overwhelmed and more damaged than in previous years" (Levine & Cureton, 1998b, p. 95). Research on college students who participated in counseling indicates that they consistently present with medical histories that include psychiatric treatment, psychiatric hospitalization, depression, substance abuse, eating disorders, and personality disorders that interfere with their social and academic functioning (Gallagher, 2001; Pledge et al., 1998). A 13-year study about the changes seen in college counseling centers found that the number of students with depression doubled and the proportion of students taking psychiatric medication rose from 10 to 25% (Benton et al., 2003). The same study concluded that 18–20% of students who sought counseling were already on psychotropic medication.

Family dysfunction has also contributed to the increase in psychological difficulties. Many students come to campus without a supportive or stable family base (Marano, 2002). Divorce, disordered interpersonal attachments, and poor parenting skills have led to greater instability in the psychological lives of students (Gallagher, 2001). Additionally, U.S. college students experience adolescence earlier, and it lasts longer (Marano, 2004b). As a result, many young people have been exposed to sex, drugs, and violence long before they have the cognitive and emotional abilities to cope with such pressures (Marano, 2004b). Earlier experimentation with drugs, alcohol, and sex has also been associated with higher rates of mental illness in college students (Gallagher, 2001).

The enormous developmental tasks facing traditional-age college students should not be overlooked or minimized as contributors to students' stress level, yet they often are. The transition to college is extremely difficult for many students and it creates numerous emotions that are new to these postadolescent individuals. One crucial developmental milestone that we know takes place during this period is identity formation and establishing independence from parents. For the first time in their lives, many college students are away from home living in unfamiliar surroundings and must learn to rely almost entirely on themselves. In addition to gaining independence, students confront the burdens of college life, including increased academic pressure, little adult supervision or structure, exploration of their sexuality, and availability of alcohol and drugs. Research has demonstrated that the developmental transition from adolescence to adulthood can exacerbate existing psychological difficulties or trigger the emergence of new ones (Voelker, 2003). These factors, coupled with advances in the mental health field such as better treatment plans and earlier diagnosis; make the increased number of psychological disorders on campus a logical outcome.

While serious mental health conditions have always been present, a generation ago, students affected with these disorders were rarely diagnosed and treated, making it difficult for them to attend college (Marano, 2004b). Medical technology has provided new psychotropic medications with fewer side effects and greater effectiveness, allowing students to function at levels not previously attainable. Also, the stigma of mental illness has lessened, and seeing a therapist or psychiatrist is more common and acceptable. Now, many more young people who have experienced mental illness succeed in school and perform well enough to manage the challenges of higher education, making college an option that had not been available to them previously (Gallagher, 2001).

Suicide and the College Student

The third suicide at New York University (NYU) in less than five weeks was met with sadness, shock, and concern across college campuses. In the fall of 2003, three students leaped to their deaths from the 6th, 9th, and 10th floor balconies at the NYU library (Scelfo, 2003). In response to the deaths, NYU administrators told students that access to the internal balconies at the Elmer Bobst Library would be restricted, and extra security guards would be posted to keep people away while glass panels were installed to prevent future suicides (Lipton, 2003).

When a death occurs such as those at NYU, and authorities believe that a psychological illness may have been a contributing factor, a psychological autopsy can be performed. This procedure includes investigating a person's death through reconstructing what the person may have thought, felt, and did preceding his or her death. This reconstruction is based on information gathered from interviews with families and friends and collected from personal documents, police reports, medical reports, and coroner's records. Psychological autopsies that have been performed among youth and adults who have committed suicide attribute more than 90% of those deaths to a psychiatric disorder, most often a mood disorder (Haas, Hendin, & Mann, 2003). The results of these psychological autopsies raise valid questions. Are colleges and universities doing enough to create climates on campuses that assist in the healthy promotion of "self" for students? What safeguards and precautions can a university put into place to protect students at risk for suicide? How should institutions of higher learning respond to behaviors that are a direct result of mental health issues? Can colleges and universities prevent suicide? Are conduct administrators doing all they can to help students with deep developmental challenges?

The suicide of a college student represents a devastating loss that affects many different individuals, including the student's family, friends, witnesses, roommates, faculty members, campus personnel, and professional staff. In the last 50 years, suicide rates for the general population in the United States have been fairly stable (Kachur, Potter, James, & Powell, 1995. In contrast, suicide rates for college students in the United States have tripled (Peters, Kochanek, & Murphy, 1998).

Suicide is now the second leading cause of death among American college students following automobile accidents (Jamison, 1993; Silverman, 1993). A study on college suicide conducted between 1991 and 2004 found that there were 1,404 student suicides and an estimated at-risk population of 33,412,350 students. This translated into a rate of 6.5 suicides per 100,000 students each year (Schwartz, 2006). With 8 million students ages 18–24 currently attending college, this translates into approximately 935 student suicides each year (Schwartz, 2006). Another study estimated that approximately 1,100 college students commit suicide in the United States each year (Suicide Prevention Resource Center, 2004). However, these figures may be low or inaccurate because they do not account for the number of students who are asked to leave college or who leave voluntarily or the number of suicides that occur off campus and are unaccounted for (Applebaum, 2006).

The three leading causes of death for young adults age 15–24 are all injury-related and include unintentional injury, suicide, and homicide. The literature describes suicide as a cluster injury-related risk that tends to correlate with other high-risk behaviors. Increased risks for all three of these causes of deaths have been associated with suicide ideation (Cheng et al., 1999). The 1995 National College Health Risk Behavior Study, conducted by the Centers for Disease Control and Prevention (CDC) found that nationwide, 10.3% of college students had seriously considered attempting suicide during the year prior to the study, and 6.7% of these students had made a specific plan to attempt suicide (CDC, 1997). The study also found that 1.5% of college students nationwide had actually attempted suicide, and 0.4% of college students had made a suicide attempt, such as an overdose, injury, or poisoning, that required medical treatment. Regardless of the fact that most of the literature suggests that college students are still less likely to kill themselves than are their nonstudent peers, even one suicide involving a college student is too many (Silverman, Meyer, Sloane, Raffel, & Pratt, 1997).

The act of suicide is a complex behavior and is generally attributed to a series of events, rather than to a single experience. A study published in the *Journal of American College Health* (Barrios, Everett, Simon, & Brener, 2000) indicated that suicide ideation runs along a continuum and can be linked to unintentional injury and homicide, which are the first and second leading causes of death among college-age students. Specifically, the authors state:

> Suicide has been described as the end point of a continuum that begins with suicide ideation [consideration of suicide], followed by planning and preparation for suicide and finally by threatening, attempting, and completing suicide. Although some young people make impulsive suicide attempts, many experience thoughts and engage in behaviors along this continuum. (p. 229)

The study further reported that students with suicidal ideation were more likely to carry a weapon, engage in a physical fight, boat or swim after drinking alcohol, ride with a driver who had been drinking alcohol, drive after drinking alcohol, and rarely or never use seat belts (p. 229). In campus officials' efforts to manage dangerous behaviors among college students, it is essential to pay attention to suicide because it is correlated so closely with other dangerous behaviors that endanger the health and well-being of college students.

Today's college climate demands that higher education officials establish comprehensive and collaborative programs that educate the campus about mental illnesses and injury-related risk behaviors. Researchers attribute lower rates of suicide to the resources and support services available on college campuses, specifically, more low- or no-cost mental health treatment services and supportive peer and advising centers to help students navigate through developmental challenges (Haas et al., 2003). Suicide prevention programs that promote student safety, understand and discourage potential risky behavior, and use community and campus resources to address mental health issues and injury-related behaviors should be developed.

In addition to proactive programs and services that should be available for students, conduct administrators can serve as a vital resource in identifying a student's developmental challenges and needs. A broken heart, rejection in a social setting, financial problems, etc., may be considered typical developmental challenges in a student's life. But to some, these challenges may be overwhelming. Conduct administrators should approach each intervention with an eagerness to listen to the student's story. Students, as with most other human beings, need to be heard and understood. Since conduct administrators are in a unique situation to listen and discuss with students what is happening in their lives and the motivations for their behavior, this personal connection may make a profound difference in a student's mental health.

Responding to Increased Student Needs

College counseling center directors report that their biggest challenge today in treating college students is the fact that students are facing developmental and environmental stressors in addition to more urgent psychological problems (Kadison & DiGeronimo, 2004). These stressors include leaving home and being on their own in a new environment, establishing intimate relations, planning a career, managing time, learning study skills, and dealing with financial responsibilities.

In the highly structured and supervised environment of many homes, today's parents attempt to raise their children with every opportunity to enrich themselves, to excel, and to achieve. With a record number of high school students applying for a limited number of admission spots at both public and private institutions, the expectation for these students to distinguish themselves academically continues to rise (Kadison, 2004). Once in college, pressure from home can continue to mount for students as parents push them to achieve so they will get into a top graduate school or get a high-paying job. Even with the best of intentions, parents with unrealistic expectations of their children may unknowingly contribute to the mental health crises college students experience today (Kadison & DiGeronimo, 2004).

In large part because of these stressors, many students who come to college are already receiving treatment in high school, and by the time they arrive at school, have been taking medication. However, once at school, students on medication can face even more challenges. The sheer stress of attending college may require their physicians to readjust their medication. Students who are on their own for the first time also have no one to remind them to take their medication and may decide to take a "vacation from meds" or simply forget to take them. Students also have been known to go off their meds so they can drink to fit in with what they perceive is the campus culture.

The prevalence and severity of mental illness in college students has resulted in a staggering increase in the demand for mental health services on college campuses. Sixty percent of senior student affairs professionals reported a record number of students using university counseling centers and the need for those receiving services for longer periods (Levin & Cureton, 1998b). A 2002 study found that that nearly 45% of campus counseling centers had problems with waiting lists (Gallagher, 2002).Two years later, Gallagher's study (2004) found the average ratio of mental health professionals to students was 1 to 1,511. The study also reported that 40% of counseling centers have limited the number of counseling sessions for each student, with an average number of 5.6 sessions.

It is imperative for campus officials to understand the relationship of students' mental health status to their emotional, physical, and academic well-being. Students who experience mental health illness may find it difficult to concentrate and focus on their coursework, which often results in their dropping out of school or being expelled because of poor academic performance. Moreover, they can also be very disruptive to the residential communities in which they live and/or in the classroom. However, university personnel need not wait for a disruption to take place before they take action.

Educational programming for students and training for faculty and staff are positive, proactive ways to reduce mental health crises on campus. Offering workshops to students on topics such as healthy lifestyles and stress management can provide them with the tools and resources necessary to lead a more balanced life. Programming that educates about mental illness; sleep deprivation, respectful relationships, and responsible drinking has been shown to benefit the campus community as well (Kadison & DiGeronimo, 2004). Initiating training for resident assistants, academic advisors, staff, student panelists, and faculty about the signs and symptoms of mental health illness and where to get assistance is also beneficial. A well-trained staff that can differentiate between disruptive, unhealthy behavior and behavior that is merely disturbing or eccentric is also beneficial. Providing prompt and professional access to mental health care is another important resource that all college campuses need to make available to students. Students are more likely to seek help and talk openly about their problems when they are distressed. However, if there is a delay in getting a student an appointment with a mental health professional, the likelihood that the student will ever get treatment is reduced. Counseling centers that offer group and short-term therapies can extend counseling resources during high-traffic times, such as midterms and final exams, to meet the additional demand.

Proactive prevention measures are also an important aspect of promoting mental health wellness and reducing incidents of inappropriate behavior.

Conduct administrators can be of great assistance in designing and implementing such prevention strategies. In many cases, they may be the first administrators to learn of a student's behavior that could be a signal that he or she needs assistance. A conduct officer's willingness either to mandate a referral or simply walk a student over to the counseling center for an assessment is one of the first proactive steps that can be taken to determine whether a student needs help. Also, identifying and communicating where evening and weekend access to mental health services for residential students are available is another way conduct administrators can be proactive.

Developing collaborative relationships with the staffs of multiple departments on campus before an incident takes place is also a positive prevention tool. A collaborative, well-defined relationship with staff from other departments can be instrumental in providing a coordinated response to students in crisis. Departments such as disability services, police/security, office of residential services, and the counseling center are just a few of the offices on campus with which a conduct administrator should take the time to develop collaborative relationships.

Legal Issues and Student Conduct Administration

"Institutions of higher education in the United States have been engaged in the practice of student discipline for more than 300 years" (Dannells, 1997, p. v). As stated elsewhere in this book, administrators and faculty have long been concerned about student misbehavior that takes place both inside and outside the classroom. To respond to student disruption and hold students accountable for their behavior, codes of student conduct were developed. As noted in chapter 4, codes of student conduct also communicate to the student body the institution's values as well as the behavioral expectations of students if they are to remain members of that community. It is these behavioral expectations that students with psychological disorders are at times at odds with. When a student displays behavior that violates the code of student conduct, institutions must respond to that student in a timely fashion and address the inappropriate behavior. This task becomes especially challenging when the behavior appears to be driven by a psychological disorder.

During the development of the earliest codes of conduct, policies and procedures addressing mental health concerns were not addressed. A review of two of the earliest codes of conduct that originated in the 1800s, those of

Harvard University and the University of Connecticut, found no policies or procedures addressing inappropriate student behavior due to mental distress or disorder (Harvard University, 2007; Roy, 1998). Today however, it is very common to find such policies in numerous college and university codes of student conduct. Examples can be found by looking at Wright State University, Eastern Illinois University, and Ohio University, all of whose codes of student conduct have portions specifically addressing mental health-related issues (Eastern Illinois University, 2007; Ohio University, 2007; Wright State University, 2007).

It is essential that colleges and universities develop and implement clear and comprehensive policies and practices to ensure fair and appropriate treatment of students who are experiencing these problems. There are many issues to negotiate when an institution is developing such policies. What is the most appropriate response to a student who threatens suicide or actually attempts it? Is it appropriate to require the student to have a mental health assessment or evaluation? What short- or long-term action should be taken if the student poses a risk to himself or herself or others? Is it acceptable to allow a student to obtain a medical leave of absence if the student is mentally ill? What, if any, academic or financial consequences should the student bear as a result of leaving? Colleges and universities are being taken to task over the practice of simply banning students from residence halls or campus properties because the student has exhibited self-injurious behavior or threatened suicide. Campuses that do not have sound policies and processes in place to address such issues run the risk of exposing themselves to serious legal consequences.

Policies that address student misbehavior must strike a balance between protecting community interests and offering a compassionate and nondiscriminatory approach toward the individual. An excellent resource for developing fair and appropriate policies is the model code presented in chapter 4; a full copy of this model code is included in the chapter's appendix. This resource cannot simply be cut and pasted into your code; rather, it offers multiple examples of best practices that each practitioner can review and decide whether they are appropriate to meet their respective campus needs.

There are several advantages to colleges and universities having a well-scripted policy in place that deals with students whose inappropriate behavior may be the result of a mental health-related issue. When the decision to implement such a policy is based on the inappropriate behavior of the student and not on the psychological disorder the student may be experiencing, the institution runs a much better chance of not being challenged by provisions included in Section 504 of the Rehabilitation Act of 1973 (Pavela, 2002, p. 2), which states in part:

> [n]o otherwise qualified handicapped individual . . . shall, solely by reason of his handicap, be excluded from the participation in, be denied the benefits of, or be subjected to discrimination under any program or activity receiving federal financial assistance [29 U.S.C. 794, 1982]. . . . The act describes "handicapped" as any person who has a mental impairment which substantially limits one or more of such person's major life activities [29 U.S.C. 706 (7)(B), 1982].

The court case involving Jordon Knott, who sued George Washington University for suspending him after he threatened to harm himself, reaffirms the need for universities and colleges not to take disciplinary action against a student simply because that student may suffer from a mental illness (Capriccioso, 2006; Hoover, 2006). Creating a policy that dictates that action be taken against a student who has been found responsible for violating the code and who may suffer from a psychological disability must be crafted with great care and consideration. It is essential that the language focus on the alleged inappropriate *behavior* as the cause of the violation and not the associated mental health issue(s) that may be present. When an incident is reported to a conduct administrator, before taking action against a student, it is critically important to determine if the behavior is truly an alleged violation of the code or is simply behavior that others find disturbing. This distinction is important as disruptive behaviors, such as outbursts in class, purposefully injuring oneself, or threatening bodily harm, would be considered violations of most codes of conduct. However, disturbing behavior such as talking to oneself or dressing in a manner that draws attention may make others uncomfortable but would not normally constitute a violation of the code. In the event that a student does participate in behavior that may be in violation of the code, and you are concerned for the student's mental health well-being, a process that incorporates many of the same rights that any other student is entitled to when being accused of violating the codes should be in place, but the process may be altered slightly by considerating mitigating circumstances.

The following are some examples of issues to address when crafting such a policy. The student should have a right to receive notice that he or she must appear before the appropriate university official (usually the conduct administrator) to discuss the behavior in question. Any notice should include the time, date, and place the student is expected to appear as well as the ramifications of the student's choice if he or she does not attend. This notice should be given in writing whenever possible, but may be given verbally if circumstances dictate. The student should also be told where he or she can locate a copy of the policy and/or procedures governing the process so the student will be informed of his or her rights and responsibilities.

When the conduct administrator meets with the student, the administrator should allow the student an opportunity to discuss the reliability of the information concerning the student's behavior; whether that behavior poses a significant danger of causing harm to self or others, and/or if the behavior substantially affects or prevents activities of other members of the campus community. The student should also be allowed, if he or she chooses to, to bring an advisor to the meeting. The role of the advisor should be clearly defined; he or she should not be permitted to speak on behalf of or "represent" the student, but to provide support and guidance if the student so desires. If the outcome of the process may result in the suspension or expulsion of the student, an appellate process may be appropriate. By having a well-written and established policy in place, the student and the university both know how the process should be implemented and each party's rights and responsibilities.

Sanctioning

Sanctioning in cases where a student has been found responsible for violations where there may be mitigating circumstances due to a student's mental health can be challenging. Student conduct administrators commonly believe that the sanctioning phase of the student discipline process should be educational, not punitive. The goals of helping students understand how their behavior affects themselves and others and motivating the student not to repeat the inappropriate behavior in the future are two optimal outcomes of the sanctioning process. Moreover, effective sanctions should be appropriate to the nature of the violation and in proportion to the seriousness of the violation. There are usually several different sanctioning options available in codes of conduct.

A frequent sanction mandated in cases where a student has violated the code and there is concern for his or her mental health well-being is a mandatory assessment by a mental health professional. The purpose of this sanction is to provide the conduct administrator, who likely is not professionally trained to make such determinations, with information necessary to determine whether psychological issues are involved and what, if any, future treatment is necessary. This information can be very useful in assisting the university to determine what support and structure is necessary for a student in an attempt to maximize the student's chances of success. It is customary to offer the student a choice of obtaining this assessment through either the institution's counseling center or a private mental health provider. In either case, release of information is typically required in conjunction with the assessment so the results and any recommendations for future treatment (if any) can be communicated to the appropriate university official. In cases where an assessment is completed and a determination is made that the student cannot function appropriately in an educational setting, a discussion should take place to determine whether the student will withdraw voluntarily from the institution or the institution should take additional action to remove the student from campus. In either case, the student should not be permitted to return until written evidence is provided by a licensed mental health professional that the student's mental health status has stabilized, and returning to school will not be psychologically harmful to the student.

In the event that a withdrawal must take place, there are two ways to facilitate such action. The most obvious choice is if the student initiates the process to leave school and withdraws voluntarily. The second, sometimes referred to as "involuntary or mandated withdrawal," is a policy institutions have used when the student does not leave voluntarily, but the information available suggests that the student should be separated from the institution to enable him or her to focus on his or her mental health and well-being before continuing in school.

It is prudent in cases of involuntary or mandated withdrawal for a policy of this nature to contain multiple safeguards for both the institution and the student. If a school is considering withdrawing a student for psychiatric reasons, it should only be done if, on the basis of clear and convincing evidence that the student has engaged or threatens to engage in behavior, staying in school poses a significant risk of causing substantial harm to him or herself, to others, or to property (University of Illinois, 2007, p. 1; Eastern Illinois University, 2007, p. 1). An example of a significant risk or "direct threat might include a student who, more likely than not, may cause substantial harm to the health or safety of the student or others and where that harm cannot be eliminated or reduced to an acceptable level through the provisions of reasonable accommodations" (Pavela, 2006, p. 18).

There has been much discussion since the 2007 Virginia Tech mass shooting tragedy about whether to contact the parents of a student who is in crisis. In the absence of a release of information signed by the student permitting information to be shared with others, there are few legal ways a university can share information about a student without that student's permission. Restrictions and exceptions pertaining to sharing information contained in a student's educational record can be found in the Family Educational Rights and Privacy Act of 1974 (FERPA). Initially signed into law by President Gerald Ford on August 21, 1974, FERPA was originally designed to

> provide parents with the right to inspect and review any and all official records, files, and data directly related to their children, including all material that is incorporated into each student's cumulative record folder, and intended for school use or to be available to parties outside the school or school system. (U.S. Department of Education, n.d., p. 1)

However, as a result of many amendments to the higher education act since 1974, FERPA has been modified significantly to allow information to be released to others without the consent of the student only under certain conditions.

There are two FERPA exceptions that university officials use most commonly to release information without a student's approval. The first allows for the release of information when the maintainer of the record (e.g., the university) is trying to protect a student's health and safety. FERPA Reg. 99.36 states, "An educational agency or institution may disclose personally identifiable information from an education record to appropriate parties in connection with an emergency if knowledge of the information is necessary to protect the health or safety of the student or other individuals" (U.S. Department of Education, 2007). Therefore, when an incident takes place that results in the student's health or safety being jeopardized, it is legally acceptable to contact the parents or any other individuals when sharing such information will help protect the student from harm. What constitutes a health and/or safety concern can be interpreted broadly. For this reason, some administrators have been willing to take the chance of being found in violation of FERPA for contacting the parent of a student in crisis because they believe it is the right thing to do.

The second exception allowing for the release of information to a parent or guardian is contained in Reg. 99.31(a)(8) of the statute: when a student is financially dependent on his or her parents, as defined in section 152 of the Internal Revenue Service (IRS) Code of 1986, the institution may, *but is not required to*, release information contained in the student's educational record (U.S. Department of Education, 2007). The person requesting the information must provide proof to the institution of such dependency in the form of a copy of the most recent IRS tax form that proves the parent claimed his or her son or daughter as a dependent. Releasing information in this manner is more common after the parent initiates contact with the institution for more information about an issue, but no waiver has been signed by the student. It is important to note that, under this exception, the institution does not have to share the information, but may choose to do so if it wishes. This is an important distinction because the philosophy regarding contacting parents for any reason may vary from institution to institution.

There are multiple factors to consider when determining whether it is appropriate to contact the parent(s) of a student who is in acute distress. How old is the student? Is the student a resident or commuter? How serious is the crisis? Is it possible contacting the parents could do more harm than good? Noted author Gary Pavela, in his recent book on student suicide, writes, "absent a history of parental abuse or neglect" notifying parents is a sound practice, especially when the student is at risk of suicide (2006, pp. 15–16). Many student affairs professionals agree with Pavela's philosophy.

If contact with the parents is being considered, college and university administrators seem to operate under one of two schools of thought. Many institutions promote the philosophy that parents (especially those of traditional-age students) should be viewed as a partner who has a very significant investment (financial as well as in other ways) in the success of the student, and as such, should be contacted when the student's success is in jeopardy. The second typical stance is that, once the student is at college, he or she is an adult and should be responsible for giving permission for and determining whether, with whom, and when information is shared about them. Regardless of which philosophy an institution chooses to endorse, its stance on the issue should be communicated to both parents and students. Finally, the decision to release information comes down to administrators trying to synthesize all the facts available and make the best decision possible with the information available at the time.

A second piece of legislation affecting the release of certain types of information pertaining to college students is the federal Health Insurance Portability and Accountability Act (HIPAA). In 1996, Congress enacted HIPAA to create standards of privacy and security in the exchange of health information and to establish continuous health coverage for people who change jobs (Campbell, 2004; Office of Civil Rights, 2002, 2003).

HIPAA's privacy rules protect all individually identifiable health information held or transmitted by a "covered entity" or its business associate in any form or media, whether this health information is communicated via paper, orally, or by electronic means. HIPAA's privacy rule refers to this information as "protected health information." A covered entity is a health care provider that submits claims electronically, a health plan, or a health care clearinghouse (Woods, 2002). With the exception of academic medical centers, most colleges and universities do not consider themselves to be heath care providers. Nevertheless, if these institutions provide any services, care, or supplies related to the health of the individual, they may qualify as health care providers under HIPAA (Woods, 2002).

While HIPAA may not have a dramatic affect on how conduct officers accomplish their job tasks, the legislation has changed the way conduct officers interact with health care professionals in their educational and local communities. Similar to FERPA's purpose to protect educational records, HIPAA's privacy rules regulate that only a HIPAA-covered entity can disclose private health information as permitted by the privacy rule or as authorized in writing by the individual or the individual's "personal representative" (Rowe, 2005). While HIPAA is too complicated to be addressed here, there are some best practices that can assist conduct officers as they try to obtain student information from HIPAA-covered entities.

One best practice includes having a basic understanding of HIPAA and how it may affect how a conduct officer interacts with health care professionals within the college or university community. It is also important to understand how the health care services affiliated with an institution have chosen to manage and disclose student health and treatment records. This entails learning which health care components qualify as covered entities under HIPAA. Some of these entities may include campus counseling centers, hospitals, private physicians, ambulance services, and student health clinics. Because these interactions often occur when there is a student emergency, it is useful to understand how these health care entities can lawfully share student health information before a crisis arises. Also, HIPAA protocols can vary by entity, so it is useful to know who serves as the privacy officer of a particular health care provider and to consult with that individual when questions about HIPAA arise. Another best practice includes fostering productive relationships with local area hospitals to establish processes that are legal and protect a student's health and privacy. Conduct officers should not request information from a health care provider without obtaining the appropriate authorization.

Experts say that there is nothing in HIPAA that prevents an educational institution from requesting or requiring a student to authorize a HIPAA-covered entity to release private health information to the student or the institution as a requirement for a student's admission or continued attendance (Rowe, 2005). However, once this health information is shared with the institution at the student's request, it falls under FERPA protections and cannot be disclosed without the student's permission or as permitted by FERPA. In protecting a student's health and educational information, another best practice is following FERPA meticulously in maintaining and disclosing student information (Rowe, 2005). If a conduct officer requests health information from a student, be mindful that forms generated within an institution may not meet HIPAA requirements. In these situations consulting with legal counsel is advisable. Conduct officers who want more specific information about HIPAA are encouraged to go the U.S. Department of Health and Human Services website, http://www.hhs.gov/ocr/hipaa.

A United Front: The Importance of Collaboration on Campus

Recent litigation in student suicide on college and university campuses has exposed the problems associated with departments not communicating effectively with one another about students about whom they have concerns. Levels of bureaucracy have also inhibited effective communications. These legal cases point to instances in which a lack of communication with and coordination of care for students who were in distress failed in part because of organizational formalities and bureaucracies. This is very problematic since it is suggested that mental health issues may best be addressed via a systemic approach that requires the collaboration of offices such as student conduct, counseling, police/security, housing, and other departments (Owen, Tao, & Rodolfa, 2006). A prudent approach would be to establish a proactive crisis response team made up of representatives of staff from units such as residential life, student conduct, campus police/security, student health, disability services, and the counseling center. This response team can be invaluable in developing protocols and procedures to manage crisis.

Since most student affairs professionals do not have formal counseling training and may not know how to respond appropriately to a distraught student, it is essential that such individuals collaborate with mental health professionals on their campus to support students who have emotional difficulties. Collaboration with counseling centers also enables the administrator to gain insights into the psychological issues the student may be experiencing so that the most beneficial intervention plan can be formulated.

Conclusion

For many young adults, the college years are the best times of their lives, but too often these critical years of adjustment are undermined by mental health issues that can lead to serious problems for the student, the campus community, and the institution at large. It is essential that college campuses have processes and policies in place to address inappropriate student behavior and mitigating mental health concerns while incorporating safeguards for both the student and university.

Student conduct administrators have a unique opportunity to contribute personally to student persistence and success when they work to establish multifaceted, collaborative, and coordinated policies and procedures to address the complex mental health needs of today's college students. Assisting students with addressing and getting treatment for their mental health issues contributes not only to their academic success but also creates emotionally sound college graduates who are healthy and ready to be productive and responsible members of their families, the workforce, and their communities.

References

Applebaum. P. (2006). Law & psychiatry: "Depressed? Get out!" Dealing with suicidal students on college campuses. *Psychiatric Services*, (7), 14–16.

Arehart-Treichal, J. (2002). Mental illness on rise on college campuses. *Psychiatric News*, 37(6), 6.

Barrios, L. C., Everett, S. A., Simon, T. R., & Brener, N. D. (2000). Suicide ideation among US college students. Associations with other injury risk behaviors. *Journal of American College Health*, 48(5), 229–233.

Baruth, L. G., & Manning, M. L. (2007). *Multicultural counseling and psychotherapy: A lifespan perspective* (4th ed.). Upper Saddle River, NJ: Pearson.

Benton, S. A., Benton, S. L., Newton, F. B., Benton, K. L., & Robertson, J. M. (2004). Changes in client problems: Contributions and limitations from a 13-year study. *Professional Psychology: Research and Practice*, 35, 317–319.

Benton, S. A., Robertson, J. M., Tseng, W. C., Newton, F. B., & Benton, S. L. (2003). Changes in counseling center client problems across 13 years. *Professional Psychology*, 34(1), 66–72.

Campbell, E. (2004, February 19, 2007). *Testimony on the intersection of the Health Insurance Portability Act of 1996 and the Family Educational Rights and Privacy Act before the National Committee on Vital and Health Statistics Subcommittee on Privacy and Confidentiality*. Retrieved June 16, 2007, from http://nacuaorg/documents/Testimony_EllenCampbell_HIPPA_PrivacyRule.pdf

Capriccioso, R. (2006). *Counseling crisis*. Retrieved July 19, 2007, from http://www.insidehighered.com

Cheng, T. L., Wright, J. L., Fields, C. B., Brenner, R. A., Schwarz, D., O'Donnell, R., & Scheidt, P. C. (1999). A new paradigm of injury intentionality. *Injury Prevention*, 5, 59–61.

Chisholm, M. S. (1998, May 15). Colleges need to provide early treatment of students' mental illnesses. *The Chronicle of Higher Education*, pp. B6–7.

Dickstein, G., & Rando, B. (submitted for publication). The Health and Wellness Conference Process: A tool for addressing mental health related disruptive behaviors. *NASPA Journal*.

Eastern Illinois University. (2007). Mandated withdrawal for psychological reasons. *Student Code of Conduct*. Retrieved April 21, 2007, from http://www.eiu.edu/~auditing/IGP/policy63.html

Eells, G., Rando, R. A., Gartner, M., & Rodolfa, E. (in press). The Association for University and College Counseling Center Directors Campus Mental Health Survey: Executive summary. *NASPA Journal.*

Gallagher, R. P. (2000). *National survey of counseling center directors.* Alexandria, VA: International Association of Counseling Services Inc.

Gallagher, R. P. (2001). *National survey of counseling center directors.* Alexandria, VA: International Association of Counseling Services Inc.

Gallagher, R. P. (2004). *National survey of counseling center directors.* Alexandria, VA: International Association of Counseling Services Inc.

Gallagher, R. P. (2006). *National survey of counseling center directors.* Alexandria, VA: International Association of Counseling Services Inc.

Gehring, D. D. (2002, November/December). To prevent tragedy, understand the laws of liability. *NASPA Forum, 5.*

Haas, A. P., Hendin, H., & Mann, J. J. (2003). Suicide in college students. *American Behavioral Scientist, 46*(9), 1224–1240.

Harvard University. (2007). Standards of conduct in the Harvard community. *General regulations and standards of conduct* (Sec. 4). Retrieved April 21, 2007, from http://webdocs.registrar.fas.harvard.edu/ugrad_handbook/current/

Hodgkinson, H. (2000). An interview with Harold Hodgkinson: Demographics—ignore them at your peril. *Phi Delta Kappan Online, 82*(4), 304. Retrieved July 3, 2007, from http://www.pdkintl.org/kappan/kgo10012.htm

Hoover, E. (2006). Student dismissed after seeking treatment for depression claims George Washington U. violated his rights. *The Chronicle of Higher Education.* Retrieved April 1, 2007, from http://chronicle.com/daily/2006/03/2006031302n.htm

Jamison K. R. (1993). *Touched by fire: Manic depressive illness and artistic temperament.* New York: Viking.

Kachur, S., Potter, L., James, S., & Powell, K. (1995). *Suicide in the United States, 1980–1992.* Violence Surveillance Summary Series, 1. Atlanta, GA: Centers for Disease Control and Prevention, National Center for Injury Prevention and Control.

Kadison, R., & DiGeronimo, T. F. (2004).*College of the overwhelmed: The campus mental health crisis and what to do about it.* San Francisco: Jossey-Bass.

Levine, A., & Cureton, S. (1998). *When hope and fear collide: A portrait of today's college student.* San Francisco: Jossey Bass.

Lipton, E. (2003, October 12). Second suicide leap leaves New York University shaken. *The New York Times*, p. N39.

Marano, H. E. (2002). Lessons for college. *Psychology Today*. Retrieved from http://psychologytoday.com/articles/index/php??????20030501.000064???? = 2

Marano, H. E. (2004). The campus crisis. *Psychology Today*. Retrieved May 5, 2005, from http://psychologytoday.com articles/index.php?term = pto3395.html&from Mod = popular_p

National Center for Educational Statistics (NCES). (2006). *Digest for educational statistics*. Retrieved July 3, 2007, from http://nces.ed.gov/programs/digest

Office of Civil Rights. (2002). *Standards for privacy and individually identifiable health information*. U.S. Department of Health and Human Services. Retrieved June 16, 2007, from http://www.hhs.gov/ocr/hipaa/finalmaster.html

Office of Civil Rights. (2003). *Summary of the HIPPA privacy rule*. U.S. Department of Health and Human Services. Retrieved June 16, 2007, from http://www .hhs.gov/ocr/privacysummary.pdf

Ohio University. (2007, September 1). Statement on Emotional Stability Relating to Conduct. *Student code of conduct*. Retrieved April 21, 2007, from http://www .ohio.edu/judiciaries/conduct_procedure.cfm#CP_JUMP_252131

Owen, J. J., Tao, K. W., & Rodolfa, E. R. (2006). Distressed and distressing students: Creating a campus community of care. In S. A. Benton & S. L. Benton (Eds.), *College student mental health: Effective services and strategies across campus*. (pp. 15–33). Washington, DC: National Association of Student Personnel Administrators.

Pavela, G. (Ed). (2002, February 1). Disabilities law: Defining protected disabilities under the ADA. *Synfax Weekly Report*, 02.4.

Pavela, G. (Ed.). (2006). *Questions and answers on college student suicide: A law and policy perspective*. Ashville, NC: College Administration Publications, Inc.

Peters, K. D., Kochanek, K. D., & Murphy S. L. (1998). Death from final data for 1996. *CDC National Vital Statistic Reports*, *47*(9).

Pledge, D., Lapan, R., Heppner, P., & Roehlke, H. (1998). Stability and severity of presenting problems at a university counseling center: A 6-year analysis. *Professional Psychology Research and Practice*, *29*(4), 386–389.

Rowe, L. (2005). What judicial officers need to know about the HIPAA privacy rule. *NASPA Journal*, *42*(4), 1. Retrieved June 16, 2007, from http://nvweb.hwwilson-web.com/hww/results_single_ftPES.jhtml.

Roy, M. J. (1998, November 2). *Social changes reflected in university's evolving student conduct code*. Retrieved April 5, 2007, from http://advance.uconn.edu/1998/981102/110298hs.htm

Scelfo, J. (2003). Preventing suicide. *Newsweek, 18*, 10.

Schwartz, A. (2006, May/June) Are college students more disturbed today? Stability in the acuity and qualitative character of psychopathology of college counseling center clients: 1992–1993 through 2001–2002. *Journal of American College Health, 54*.

Shea, R. H. (2002, February 12). *On the edge on campus: The state of college student's mental health continues to decline. What's the solution?* Retrieved February 12, 2002, from http://www.usnews.com/usnews/issue/020218/education/18education.htm

Silverman, M. M. (1993). Campus student suicide rates: Fact or artifact? *Suicide and Life Threatening Behavior, 4*, 329–342.

Silverman, M., Meyer, P., Sloane, F., Raffel, M., & Pratt, D. (1997). The Big Ten student suicide study. *Suicide and Life Threatening Behavior, 27*, 285–303.

Suicide Prevention Resource Center. (2004). *Promoting mental health and preventing suicide in college and university settings*. Newton, MA: Education Development Center, Inc.

University of Illinois. (2007, August 1). *Code of policies and regulations applying to all students*. Retrieved April 21, 2007, from http://www.admin.uiuc.edu/policy/code/

U.S. Department of Education. (2007). *Family Education Rights and Privacy Act*. Retrieved April 21, 2007, from http://www.ed.gov/policy/gen/reg/ferpa/rights_pg17.html#subpartd

U.S. Department of Education. (2007). *FERPA general guidance for parents*. Retrieved March 8, 2007, from http://www.ed.gov/policy/gen/guid/fpco/ferpa/index.html

U.S. Department of Education. (n.d.). *Legislative history of major FERPA provisions*. Retrieved April 21, 2007, from http://www.ed.gov/policy/gen/guid/fpco/ferpa/leg-history.html?exp=0

Voelker, R. (2003). Mounting student depression taxing campus mental health services. *Journal of the American Medical Association, 289*(16), 2055–2056.

Woods, G. (2002). *HIPPA privacy rule primer for the college or university administrator*. American Council on Education Division of Government and Public Affairs. Retrieved June 16, 2007, from http://www.acenet.edu

Wright State University. (2007, September 1). Health and Wellness Conference Process. *Code of student conduct* (sec. 9). Retrieved April 21, 2007, from http://www.wright.edu/students/judicial/mhcc.html

Young, J. R. (2003, February 14). Prozac campus: More students seek counseling and take psychiatric medication. *The Chronicle of Higher Education*, pp. 1–5.

14

DEALING WITH STUDENT GROUP MISCONDUCT

Judith M. Haas and James L. Street Jr.

I t is likely that every student development practitioner has once thought, "What if that happened on our campus?" upon receiving frightening news from another campus via the newspaper or the television. Marching bands make headlines for hazing, fraternities for unruly community behavior, group sports teams have stirred up controversy on occasion, and even less likely culprits have mismanaged funds or stolen property from campus or community members in the name of a prank. When these situations are brought to light on another campus, do you feel prepared to handle the same misconduct on your own college campus? Or do you breathe a heavy sigh of relief that this event did not occur on your watch, and wonder what you would do in the same circumstance? Events in 2007 at two universities made headlines—one, a scandal involving false allegations against lacrosse players at Duke University and, two, the catastrophic mass shootings at Virginia Tech. The manner in which campus administrators addressed them was scrutinized by the world. The reputations of students and universities are both "out there" for the others to critique, condone, or condemn.

This chapter helps prepare you for the time when your campus makes headlines—even in the local newspaper—for a situation involving group misconduct, an often trickier situation to manage and discipline than conduct by an individual. Taking the time to develop a response and process for such events before they are needed can give you the peace of mind of knowing that if and when a student organization is involved in misconduct on your campus, you have a course of action.

Consider the following:

Example A: A male student is engaged in underage drinking and is found passed out in the bathroom of his residence hall. The student is referred to the Office of Student Conduct. The behavior is addressed, the student is made aware of his rights and responsibilities, and a process is followed to resolve the concern. In this example, it is clear who is responsible and who needs to learn from the experience through the conduct process.

Example B: There is an off-campus party where more than half of the guests are from the same organization. The police arrive because someone complained about the noise, and underage drinking is identified. We later learn that the party was posted on Facebook.com. More than 200 students attended the party, and the nonstudent neighbors are upset. In this case, who is responsible? Who needs to learn from this experience? Do you have a responsibility? Or do you assume that you have no responsibility to address group behavior on or off campus? Should we educate all members of organizations, and if so, how? If it is true that discipline is about teaching, how do we take a group-related incident and make it a learning opportunity? Most student development practitioners would agree in addressing individual misconduct. We would argue that organizationally related student misconduct should be dealt with at the group level as well. Let's go deeper, and explore the reasons why.

Ronald F. Tunkel, from the National Center for Analysis of Violent Crime Behavioral Analysis Unit at the Federal Bureau of Investigation Academy and the Department of Alcohol Tobacco and Firearms, discussed the connection between school dynamics (norms, interpersonal relations) and the behavior of its individual students (Tunkel, 2007). A similar connection can be made between the campus environment and the behavior of clubs and organizations. Questions regarding campus climate and student organizational behavior should be asked, including the following:

- What are the group dynamics within and between groups?
- What are the student organization's values and is their behavior consistent?
- What issues should get our attention?
- Whose voices are being/should be heard?
- Is this a group behavior we can or should regulate?

- Are inappropriate behaviors being overlooked?
- Is there a tolerance for hazing, bullying, or marginalizing by or of the organization's membership?
- Why do students leave or quit the organization? Is there a pattern?
- Does an informal code of silence exist in the organization?

Colleges and universities have to be aware of how they respond to organizational misconduct. They must be responsive, consistent, and fair to all parties. Inappropriate behavior of any kind that happens repeatedly without a consistent and fair response can potentially lead to more serious behaviors.

For a long time universities had a "hands-off" mentality about dealing with student organizational misconduct. What happened off campus, behind closed doors, during recruitment or initiation was not their concern. Bickel and Lake (1999) refer to this period from the 1970s to the mid-'80s as the bystander era. Times have changed; the pendulum is now swinging the other way in regard to disciplining students and organizations. Bickel and Lake (1999) refer to this movement as the facilitator model—the university is mutually responsible with the organization and must balance rights and responsibilities. Our constituents are asking questions about how conduct is being addressed, in what way we hold our organizations accountable, and what specifically we are doing to ensure that our students and our communities are safe. Many believe this mentality drove Duke University's administration to respond too reactively in the 2007 lacrosse case. In the midst of change and uncertainty in the relationship between student and university, we must somehow find that voice of reason. We must seek a balance that is ethical for both.

The philosophy of organizational conduct resolution that follows applies equally to public and private institutions. Unless otherwise noted, where case law is cited, especially related to constitutional issues, the cases refer to public, not private institutions. In either case, the question remains, "What if this happened on my campus?"

Context for Action

Whose Job Is It to Respond When Organizations Act Up?

To demonstrate the complexity of disciplining campus organizations, consider the following example. A business fraternity has a party in its meeting room in an academic building. The next morning, the housekeeping staff find beer cans everywhere in the room. In this example, it is very likely that the office that reserves rooms will take away the privilege of meeting space for a given amount of time; however, this information may or may not get back to the office that works with advising student organizations. On a collaborative campus, information regarding student organization behavior is systematically shared between all constituents.

When a student organization misbehaves, who should respond? The answer most likely depends on the type of infraction the club has committed. A club advisor may address inappropriate behavior, whereas a formal hearing process may be in place for a more serious infraction. In all cases, though, a coordinated focus for administrative response to such incidents may be helpful to a campus in ensuring that all clubs ultimately are treated equally in the discipline process. This means that while the College of Business in the preceding example may take away club meeting room privileges, there should also be a system in place to inform a central campus administrator of that action. Who this central staff member may be depends on what works best for each campus. A starting point in determining the key staff member to handle these issues is to take a look at the history of club discipline on your campus and determine which office has typically played a central role. Additionally, though a key staff member will likely take the lead, depending on the situation, other people or groups may have a role in the process, such as the club faculty advisor, the student conduct office, the dean of students office, a committee of peers, or, in this case, the College of Business central office or the fraternity's national headquarters. Determining who should respond and in what order is a necessary step in dealing with these situations.

Legal Precedence

While student organizations' rights are protected by the freedom of association and expression concepts under the U.S. Constitution's First Amendment, educational institutions do have the authority to revoke university recognition and, therefore, to discipline these groups in certain cases. The legal foundation for this balance of student rights and institutional authority can be found in the case of *Healy v. James* (1972, p. 408 U.S. 169, 193). In this case, the U.S. Supreme Court determined that Central Connecticut State College had no valid grounds for denying recognition to a local chapter of Students for a Democratic Society. Although the Court sided with the organization in this case, the decision did clarify under what conditions the institution could regulate organizations and their behavior.

> Just as in the community at large, reasonable regulations with respect to the time, the place, and the manner in which student groups conduct their speech-related activities must be respected. A college administration may impose a requirement, such as may have been imposed in this case, that a group seeking official recognition affirm in advance its willingness to adhere to reasonable campus law. Such a requirement does not impose an impermissible condition on the students' associational rights. Their freedom to speak out, to assemble, or to petition for changes in school rules is in no sense infringed. It merely constitutes an agreement to conform with reasonable standards respecting conduct. This is a minimal requirement, in the interest of the entire academic community, of any group seeking the privilege of official recognition. (*Healy v. James*, 1972, p. 408 U.S. 169, 193)

As long as rules created by the administration do not violate constitutional rights and are fair, just, and applied equally to all student organizations, those organizations must abide by them. In *Healy*, the Court made it clear that if an organization is seeking recognition and states clearly that it refuses to abide by campus rules and regulations, recognition by the institution can be denied. But the mere possibility of violation of policies, rather than actual violation, cannot serve as a basis for denial of recognition. Of course, in the event of a recognized organization's proven violation of campus rules, the organization can be put on probation or suspended for a reasonable period.

While the courts have paved the way for colleges to establish rules of conduct for student organizations, they have also indicated that such rules should be printed and accessible. Unfortunately, some universities have dealt with group conduct issues from a historical perspective rather than from a written code. It is essential to create a codified, fair process that is transparent, that has no surprises, and that the practice of which ensures students' voices are heard and respected and that reasonable process is followed. The process should be fully presented in the code of conduct. Since there are major differences between public and private requirements for process, see chapters 4 and 5.

Registration Versus Recognition

A quick Internet search involving clubs and organizations quickly shows there are a few common words universities use to describe the relationship between the club and the school. Often these words include registration and recognition. While some campuses use the words "recognition" and "registration" interchangeably (Maloney, 1988), others separate the two. Milani and Nettles (1987, p. 62) suggest, "Being registered connotes the groups' existence is simply recorded with the institution, but it does not suggest approval in the same sense that recognition might." A good discussion of the issues inherent in recognition and registration of student organization and special relationships/duty can be found in the *Rights and Responsibilities of the Modern University: Who Assumes the Risks of College Life?* by Robert Bickel and Peter F. Lake (1999). For simplicity's sake, we use the words interchangeably, but it is wise to become familiar with the language of your college or university and exactly what responsibility the term carries.

An online review of numerous universities revealed that most do require some sort of registration or process for clubs and organizations to be officially recognized. This type of affiliation often allows the use of campus facilities and in some cases it allows access to funding and to certain campus resources (e.g., parking, game-day tailgating, leadership opportunities, and the ability to have information included in publications without cost). To be recognized officially some schools may require constitutions, by-laws, or written policies defining the club's role and purpose.

At schools that require such recognition, a clearly articulated conduct process can work well. At universities where clubs and organizations do not need to be recognized or registered, the student organization's written policies and the university's code of conduct prevail, and it may only be possible to address the behavior with the students directly involved in the incident. Keep in mind that universities are responsible for reporting certain types of incidents based on infraction and location in their annual Clery Report. (See chapter 5 for more information.)

Individual Versus Group

Developing and enforcing a group misconduct policy does not necessarily eliminate the need for individual students to be held accountable. Individuals can be held accountable for their own actions as well as their actions as part of a recognized organizational entity under the code. They can also be held liable through criminal and civil charges. An example: Three band members take three new band members to a bridge and explain that every new band member over the last 10 years has proven his or her commitment by jumping off the bridge. All three new band members jump off the bridge, and one is seriously injured. An investigation revealed that the practice of pressuring new band members to jump off the bridge had been passed on for years, so a review board held all current band members responsible and recommended that the band be placed on probation and the three members most active in this event be suspended from the band for one year. In addition, the three students who took the individuals to the bridge were referred to the Office of Student Conduct for violations of the code of student conduct, and all three were sanctioned by the Office of Student Conduct for their individual roles in carrying out this misconduct. Finally, the students may also face criminal or civil liability based on the seriousness of their behavior and harm to the injured student.

What Constitutes Student Organizational Misconduct?

To address group conduct and determine accountability there must be clearly defined guidelines outlining the relationship of the conduct to the organization. The following criteria, taken individually or as a whole, suggest grounds on which to proceed with organizational discipline:

1. The behavior is committed by one or more members of a student group and is sanctioned by the organization and/or its officers.
2. The behavior is committed by one of more members of a student group during the course of an activity financed by the organization and/or on property owned by the organization.
3. The behavior is committed by one or more members of a student and is supported by its members.
4. The officers of the organization had prior knowledge that the incident would take place.
5. Members of the organization lied about the incident.
6. The test most conduct officers use is: Would a reasonable person understand the behavior to fall within the scope of the organization's activity? (University of Georgia, 2007; Indiana University–Bloomington, 2006).

Policies, Procedures, and Protocols

When creating codes of conduct for student organizations, the policies and practices of several schools should be reviewed, possibly including those of your school's benchmark institutions. By reviewing the guidelines of others, a template can be created for those working with student organizations. Review this information and make it applicable to your own university or college. As it is updated, modified, or in some cases created, this information can then become the basis for the disciplinary procedures to address organizational misconduct on your campus.

In developing this policy, the lesson of *Occam's Razor* should be heeded. William of Occam, a 14th-century Franciscan friar, philosopher, and logician, was credited with developing the notion that "Entities should not be multiplied unnecessarily." Further simplified, this means "All things being equal, the simplest solution tends to be the best one." How many times have we campus administrators sat down to create a policy, only to end up creating a much more in-depth document than we ever intended, covering every possible scenario within the confines of one policy?

Conversely, a cookie cutter approach does not allow flexibility for the multiple paths necessary to address diverse group concerns. If the established system does not allow the best resolution possible, it will discourage both students and administrators from participating in it in the future. Practitioners will feel hindered and frustrated by an overly bureaucratic approach, rather than feeling they have made the most of a teachable moment by helping those involved learn about community standards, community development, or group decision making. Thus, creating a system that is simple yet allows for multiple resolutions based on the situation is what we should strive for in this process.

What Process Is Due?

How much process is due or required in addressing organizational misconduct? How much is enough, and is there such a thing as too much? Going back to Occam, keep it simple. In most cases universities provide more than necessary. Universities are not bound by the same due process as the criminal system; however, the stronger the possible penalty, the more process is due (Kaplin & Lee, 1997).

Similar to requirements for dealing with individual conduct, a club or an organization's officers must be informed of the charges being made against the organization; the organization's officers must be informed in writing of the date, time, and location of the hearing; they must be given adequate time to prepare and be allowed to provide evidence that they were not responsible for the behavior in question. Those given the responsibility to review the information must be impartial (*Dixon v. Board of Education*, 1961).

The Complaint

In most cases when an incident occurs involving an organization, it is brought to the university's attention through a third party via a telephone call, e-mail message, or personal visit. One or more of the following sources may try to make the staff aware: a concerned/frustrated or upset parent; an individual who was present and is familiar with risk and safety who thought you ought to know what he or she observed; a member's significant other concerned or worried about the behavior or even more specifically about their personal friend; or by a member of another club or organization. The worst method of learning about an incident is from the media, followed by learning from your chancellor or president of the university or from the local police. It is necessary and helpful to get the complaint in writing. This allows creation of a timeline and a paper trail as officials determine the next step in the process. It may also help those reporting such allegations to clarify the facts of the case for themselves and for the conduct office. Universities can choose to take no action if there is not enough evidence to support the allegation.

Determining Resolution Process

After a complaint has been made and a preliminary investigation has been completed, the person or group of people designated to address organizational misconduct has to determine whether no further action will be taken or the incident will continue through the organizational conduct process. Neither of these options precludes an initial conversation with the club or organization about appropriate behavior and making good choices. In the event that the process continues, several resolution methods can be used at this point, based on the scope and seriousness of the allegations.

After meeting with the person designated to work with clubs and organizations, the next steps in the resolution process must be determined. Using as much information as is available, the best method for addressing the misconduct must be chosen. A list of possible resolution processes follows:

- Informal administrative process: The club or organization meets with its advisor/and university official. The club or organization takes responsibility for the misconduct and either sanctions itself or helps create the sanction or outcome. This usually applies to a low-level conduct concern.

- Mediation: The club or organization may be having difficulty with other groups on campus. Both parties agree to come together and work out their differences. If either group refuses to participate, or, as the process unfolds, it becomes clear that common ground cannot be found, the issue may need to be referred to a more formal process. Mediation must be voluntary and may not be appropriate to use in addressing all conduct concerns. Consider reviewing chapter 6 for a more in-depth review of dispute resolution and its limitations.

- Restorative justice/trust circle: Though little research supports this type of process for groups, it may be the most appropriate in teaching organizations about the impact of their decisions. Representatives of the organization (those most involved and appropriate leadership) are invited to a circle with campus and community members most affected by the misconduct. This type of resolution is only used when the organization takes responsibility and those affected are willing to participate. At the conclusion of such a process, the organization accepts the outcomes set forth by the group because its members helped in creating the sanction or outcome. With this process the organization is trying to repair or rebuild the relationship/trust/integrity that may have been damaged by the misconduct.

- Formal hearing process: The club or organization is given an opportunity to have the allegations against them heard before a review board. This peer review board can consist of organizational membership alone or a broader representation of campus clubs or organizations and may be either centralized or decentralized. The club or organization has the opportunity to dispute the alleged behavior, provide information, and confront those who are making the complaint. In this process, the hearing board determines if the club or organization is responsible and determines the sanction or educational outcome. It is assumed that an organization is not responsible unless proven so through the process. Earlier complaints are not shared unless the organization is found responsible and the information is used to assist with sanctioning. The decisions of this board may be conclusive or may come in the form of a recommendation to a third-party decision maker such as the dean of students. An appeal to this process may be made to the next higher ranking person above the individual responsible for clubs and organizations or through a panel designated to hear an appeal, depending on your campus structure. Appeals can be based on three issues: (1) it did not follow process, (2) the outcome was too severe, and (3) new information has become available.

Types of Outcomes (Sanctions)

Through the resolution process, an educational outcome or sanction can either be agreed on by participants or mandated by the university. Organizations should understand potential sanctions when facing misconduct charges. Again, sanctions are educational tools and/or natural consequences to help students and organizations become better decision makers. Here is a typical list of sanctions:

1. Loss of privileges (meeting space, social functions, intramurals)
2. Reprimand (verbal or written)
3. Probation (time frame to demonstrate appropriate decision making)
4. Suspension (severs organization's relationship with the university for a determined period)
5. Expulsion (permanent removal of the organization)
6. Restitution (payment for property damages)
7. Service to others (related to the misconduct)
8. Educational programming (related to the misconduct)
9. Apology
   Always include as well:
10. Other appropriate sanctions, which allows for creative educational sanctioning

Best Practices

Based on success and failure, trial and error, and subsequent conversations, we offer the following advice to practitioners who are evaluating their approach to student organizational discipline.

Develop a Fair and Transparent Process

A fundamentally fair process is honest, consistent, impartial, reasonable, and easy to use, and the constituents being held to the organizational standards understand it. Students are respected and feel as though they have a voice. By using a fundamentally fair process as the standard for addressing behaviors on a college campus, students, faculty, and staff are less likely to confuse it with the legal system. It can also allow for alternative methods of resolution. It is important to include student group membership in the creation, development. and integration of the process.

Include Process in the Code of Conduct

Typically, written codes outline rules and regulations and the various consequences of violating those rules and regulations. In addition to this fundamental portion of the code, we believe it is important to be clear about the entire process—start to finish—and include this in a written format as part of your code. All that occurs between the complaint and the resolution should be very clear to student organizations to avoid any misunderstanding or questions of fairness along the way. The benefits of taking the time to include the process in the written code include heightened transparency with the student organizations and avoiding a misstep by the team working on the case. When this type of detailed information is written into the code, one must be careful to update the code of conduct whenever a revision is made to the process.

Build Relationships With Those Who Share Responsibility

To deal effectively with matters of student organization conduct, one needs to ask who else on the campus or in the community needs to sit down at the same table and discuss the what, why, and how regarding organization discipline. Once the key staff member has been identified, a team needs to be formed to share this responsibility. The adage, it takes a whole village to raise a child, fits well here. This is especially important if your campus is creating a new, formal process for student organization conduct hearings.

Who should be on your team? While each campus has to determine the best people to fill this role, here are some suggestions to start the process. It is likely that either a staff member from student activities or the judicial affairs/ student conduct office will be the key coordinator of the team, but each should clearly be included as part of the team. On some campuses, a separate office or staff member might advise a certain classification of organizations, such as a Greek life office for fraternities and sororities or a recreation office for club sports teams. These staff members may be smart choices to invite as members of this team as well, given their direct affiliation.

Another important group of people to consider are those who are in a position to find violations of university rules, including the campus security/ police department, the intramural office, and the office that reserves rooms for student organizations. Occasionally, you may even need to communicate with the local police and sheriff's office when local, state, and federal laws have been violated.

Why wait until a crisis for those who share responsibility to get together? Meet regularly with all constituents of the student organization judicial process. It is good practice to form your core team, and then involve other relevant members of campus on an as-needed or case-by-case basis.

Educate Students and Organizational Advisors

If student organizations are going to be held responsible for misbehavior, then it is imperative that students become educated regarding the expectations, rights, and responsibilities of student groups and the consequences of behavior. They need to know that the university can deal with organization-related behavior problems from an individual or group approach or both. Organizations, members, and officers can be held accountable for the actions of their members. They need to know and understand the consequences for behavior—benefits withheld, reprimand, probation, suspended activities, and organizational suspension or expulsion.

Be Informed of Current Legal Issues and Trends

To deal effectively with student organization conduct, it is imperative to be aware of current issues and trends, including changes to federal, state, and municipal laws; state and federal court decisions; and issues and trends identified by professional associations that deal with student conduct.

Here are some resources to consider in staying current: Publications may include *The Chronicle of Higher Education, Pavela Report, Fraternal Law*, the Association for Student Judicial Affairs' *Law and Policy Report*, Association of Fraternity Advisors' quarterly publication, *Perspectives,* and/or its monthly educational e-newsletter, *Essentials*, and the Counsel on Law in Higher

Education's *Student Affairs Law and Policy*. Organizations to consider include the Association for Student Judicial Affairs, the American College Personnel Association, the Association of Fraternity Advisors, the Fraternal Information and Programming Group, and the National Association of Student Personnel Administrators.

Be Aware of Your Campus Climate and Be Proactive

A pound of prevention: perhaps the best advice we can give you is that you must be aware of what is going on around campus. This means getting out of the office, meeting with student leaders, attending events on campus, and being more visible to students on campus than your job calls for. Being visible and approachable will make it easier for students to trust you. Of course, it is important to have formal policies and procedures so when unfortunate things happen the mechanisms are in place to deal with the situation. It is equally important to respond to questionable or volatile situations *before* they turn into a formal student organization conduct case.

Likewise, being in touch with what is happening on campus can assist you to proactively advertise the campus misconduct process. For example, if your campus has an annual spring celebration that you know includes a heavy degree of partying into the night, it might be a good opportunity to reinforce student organization misconduct policies before this event. Some other events to consider for your campus may include an annual Greek week and Greek recruitment period (aka pledging); the football calendar, including home games and tailgating; exam time; and other campus-specific competitions or celebrations of which you need to be aware.

Consider the following scenarios:

1. Tensions arise on the intramural playing field between two student organizations. There is not sufficient evidence of university violations for a conduct case. The intramural office could suspend playing privileges of certain players or the whole team, but lingering tensions might follow the groups off the field.

2. An anonymous phone call from a concerned parent or significant other suggests that a student may be involved in hazing activities during an organizational pledging process. There is insufficient evidence to bring charges of hazing against the organization, but the information might be enough to call some officers into the office to discuss university policy.

In both of these situations, there is insufficient evidence to pursue a conduct hearing, but far worse consequences can be avoided by taking a proactive and educational approach to events like these. On hearing rumors or reports of misconduct such as the ones listed, we suggest that taking the time to discuss the matter with the president of the club will not only likely resolve the situation at hand, but will also spread the word that your policies matter and that you mean business!

Establish a Network of Colleagues/Mentors at Other Institutions

Very often, the responsibility for dealing with conduct on a college campus falls to one or two people. Due to confidentiality and the policies involved with conduct, this can be stressful, and one can feel isolated or alone in the work he or she does. You need allies and you need support. When student organization-related misconduct occurs, it is likely that someone at another college has dealt with a similar incident. It is important to have colleagues, friends, and mentors at other institutions who are just a phone call away. Group-related misconduct, by its nature, can be more difficult to investigate, determine responsibility for, and resolve. Having an objective, uninvolved peer walk through the situation with you, with due regard for the confidentiality of individuals involved, can be invaluable. Don't be afraid to pick up the phone or send an e-mail; learning from other people's experience is a valid method of helping to determine your own course of action.

Allow Time for Legal Counsel to Review

We also suggest that you always allow time for your campus's legal counsel to review your code and comment on it before it becomes official policy. This often forgotten step could save you time and difficulty in the long run. Remember that legal counsel does not determine policy but should have a keen critical eye for risk and can ask probing questions that may point out areas in the system that are weak and need to be improved or modified. The process of review by legal counsel should be repeated regularly, especially after changes to the conduct process have been considered.

Revision Is Okay

Remember that it is okay to revise a written policy. We often fall victim to outdated policies and bemoan the old ways instead of taking on the challenge of revising or modernizing a policy based on current needs. Many times we realize this need after a situation occurs, and the process prevents the most effective/appropriate resolution because it was not written in the code. Timely evaluation of the process is a key component. Take notes throughout the year when something happens and navigating the process is difficult. Each year, when processes are reviewed, make appropriate revisions. Make sure that all constituents are invited to the table when it is time to review, including student leaders, campus police, Greek advisor, club and organization advisor, and anyone else who works with groups on campus.

Keep It Simple

Using the analogy of *Occam's Razor*, when dealing with conduct and conduct-related issues, it is best to keep the process simple. What *really* needs to be done to address organizational or group conduct? If students and others learn that the system is fair and can be trusted, they will use it more often than they would a cumbersome, confusing process. Your team must develop the simplest policy that allows for multiple resolutions based on the situation.

Like the old *Master Student* (Ellis, 2005) cliché, having "tools in your toolbox," or faculty members having the ability to call on diverse teaching strategies and activities to reach all the different types of students in their classes, personnel responsible for organizational conduct need multiple resolution options to address organizational misconduct. If the process does not allow for multiple methods of clear resolution, then you need to change the process to meet your needs.

Final Thoughts

Student group misconduct can occur at any time, on a large or a small scale. This chapter has equipped you with the means for putting a process in place to handle group misconduct fairly. The final advice in this chapter is simply, "Do not wait." It is tempting to view policy creation as time-consuming and difficult to sift through in the beginning stages. Play it safe on this one and be proactive. Knowing that you have a policy in place will save you time in the long run when misconduct does occur. Creating that process in the thick of things will likely result in a less planned, more harried attempt to reach resolution. Resist the urge to wait until things slow down to begin creating your policy; the proverbial "things will slow down this summer" may just be too late. Begin to handle it now, and you will feel significantly better the next time you hear about misconduct at another institution, knowing that you have a fair process in place at your own school. Remember, issues and people can and will always be challenging; navigating the resolution system should not be.

References

Bickel, R., & Lake, P. (1999). *The rights and responsibilities of the modern university: Who assumes the risks of college life?* Durham, NC: Carolina Academic Press.

Dixon v. Board of Education, 294 F.2d 150 (5th Cir. 1961).

Ellis, D. (2005). *Becoming a master student.* Boston: Houghton Mifflin.

Healy v. James, 408 U.S. 169, 193 (1972).

Indiana University–Bloomington. (2006). *Code of student rights, responsibilities, and conduct.* Bloomington, IN: Dean of Students Office, Indiana University.

Kaplin, W., & Lee, B. (1997). *A legal guide for student affairs professionals.* San Francisco: Jossey-Bass.

Maloney, G. (1988). Student organizations and student activities. In M. Barr (Ed.), *Student services and the law* (pp. 284–307). San Francisco: Jossey-Bass.

Milani, T., & Nettles, W. (1987). Defining the relationship between fraternities and sororities and the host institution. In R. Winston, W. Nettles, & J. Opper (Eds.), *Fraternities and sororities on the contemporary college campus* (pp. 57–73). New Directions for Student Services, No. 40. San Francisco: Jossey-Bass.

Tunkel, R. (2007, May). *Understanding school violence and threat management.* Presentation: Boone, NC.

University of Georgia. (2007). *UGA student handbook.* Athens, GA: Vice President of Student Affairs Office, University of Georgia.

15

ACADEMIC INTEGRITY

Models, Case Studies, and Strategies

Patrick Drinan and Tricia Bertram Gallant

Acts of academic dishonesty such as cheating and plagiarism have plagued colleges and universities for almost as long as student alcohol abuse. The persistence and durability of academic dishonesty have been measured since the 1950s, with most studies revealing that 70% of undergraduate students cheat occasionally, and about 20% do so regularly (honor code schools have lower rates). Even more worrisome, more than half of undergraduates do not see cheating as a deeply troubling issue, and technology such as the Internet and cell phones can facilitate plagiarism or unauthorized collaboration (McCabe, 2005). While the problem of dishonesty is often framed in higher education in terms of preventing cheating and developing student morality, most recent work has focused on creating organizational cultures of integrity and examining student honesty in a broader context of integrity (e.g., Bertram Gallant & Drinan, 2006b). The formation of the Center for Academic Integrity (CAI) in the early 1990s coalesced this work by: (1) promoting the dissemination of best practices; (2) identifying the common values across higher education in support of academic integrity; and (3) stimulating research and discourse on more sophisticated organizational approaches to advancing academic integrity.

The CAI's publication of *The Fundamental Values of Academic Integrity* in 1999 was a signal event in defining the values of academic integrity and distinguishing honesty from integrity. It "defines academic integrity as a commitment, even in the face of diversity, to five fundamental values: honesty, trust, fairness, respect, and responsibility. From these values flow principles of behavior that enable academic communities to translate ideals and action" (1999, p. 4). CAI goes on to say that "integrity is built upon continuous conversations about how these values are, or are not, embodied in institutional life" (p. 4). Integrity, then, is broader than honesty and involves the whole of the organization of higher education, not just individual campuses.

Within each campus, however, students, faculty, administrators, and student affairs professionals must begin to ascertain how they can institutionalize academic integrity and discourage academically dishonest behaviors. Student affairs professionals are integral to successful institutionalization of academic integrity because they are at the center of college governance and administration, particularly in the arena of student conduct. This is true even within the arena of student academic conduct, despite the fact that such an involvement brings the student affairs professional into the formerly protected territory of the academic classroom. Two events in the history of higher education have led to this blurring of territory lines: (1) the mid-20th-century massification of higher education made disciplining students burdensome for faculty whose focus was teaching and research, and (2) in the latter half of the 20th century, the introduction of due process rights for students in disciplinary matters, including academic misconduct, removed full disciplinary authority under *in loco parentis* from the faculty, and disciplinary processes were devised around more systematic, regular administrative functions and structures (Hardy & Burch, 1981). As a result of these two historical processes, student academic misconduct is now often relegated to disciplinary procedures and socialization measures for students directly conducted, supervised, or monitored by student affairs professionals or students themselves. The rapid growth of administrative personnel over the last 35 years has reflected these and other modernization processes in the academy and is not limited to student affairs.

What is surprising about this phenomenon is that faculty prerogatives and faculty jurisdictional sensitivities might seem to inhibit a significant student affairs professional role in regulating academic dishonesty and promoting academic integrity in the student body. However, several factors have contributed to students and student affairs professionals filling a vacuum that faculty left or, in many cases, had never inhabited, including: (1) adoption of honor systems that are historically student-run with minimal faculty involve-ment; (2) complaints by students that faculty judge and adjudicate miscon-duct within the classroom domain without providing students proper due process; (3) faculty fears of litigation, time-consuming procedures, or nega-tive effects on student academic and career futures that lead them to ignore misconduct; and (4) faculty denial and anger.

Honor systems and honor codes have a long and distinguished history at several dozen private colleges and universities and at some public universi-ties and military academies as well. There are important variations in how these are designed and operated, yet they share the common characteristic that students are in the primary position to orient the student body and adju-dicate cases. Student affairs professionals are often asked to give advice and coordinate logistical support to students running these honor systems. Al-though faculty may also have some advisory roles, they find themselves at a greater distance from the hub of activities than students or student affairs professionals. The largest debates about honor codes nationally among stu-dent affairs professionals tend to revolve around two issues: (1) whether there should be a "single sanction," that is, expulsion for a first proven offense, and (2) what should the obligation for student reporting of academic integ-rity violations be, and how should it be enforced. The first issue is exagger-ated since very few schools have a single sanction rule or are even considering it. Most schools use progressive discipline, and there is little sentiment for single-sanction systems, given enforcement problems, a lack of develop-mental maturity of younger undergraduate populations, and a general loss of flexibility in responding to cases of academic dishonesty within a single-sanc-tion system. The second issue often reveals more fundamental strains: stu-dents do not usually believe in a "rat rule," that is, students' obligation to turn in their peers who have engaged in academic misconduct. Without some sense of obligation, it is difficult to detect cheating, since student par-ticipation in monitoring cheating and using peer pressure is exceptionally valuable. Even the strongest honor code schools have difficulty in developing this sense of obligation (McCabe, Trevino, & Butterfield, 2001).

More problematic on both legal grounds and consistency of administra-tion has been the avoiding or even denying of due process. This typically occurs if faculty do not report academic dishonesty according to policy, but yet apply academic sanctions in response to alleged cheating. When this oc-curs, the matter can escalate into a more public issue on campus, and threats of litigation become more likely. Since student affairs professionals have more experience dealing with students in matters like this, they often are called in to help manage the student spillover concerns. This can further alienate faculty, who may interpret administrative involvement in classroom conduct as a threat to academic freedom. Although it is usually neither wise nor rewarding to debate with faculty about this, there is an important role for student affairs professionals in helping academic deans and vice presidents understand and deal with the issue of academic integrity within its broader context.

Related to the preceding issues, and even more endemic, is faculty ignoring academic dishonesty because of their fear of litigation, perceptions of time-consuming procedures, or perceptions of negative effects on student academic and career futures. At one level, this may seem less problematic for an institution, yet sweeping cheating "under the rug" can easily be seen as rewarding it, so it may stimulate hypocritical feelings among students. Student affairs professionals will find it hard to be proactive in such situations and normally have to wait for academic or administrative leadership on campus to "bell the cat" of academic dishonesty; this frequently occurs when a program has experienced a serious violation of academic integrity. Once this begins to occur, student affairs professionals can demonstrate their knowledge of how comparable institutions approach the matter of confronting academic dishonesty (see the longer discussion of institutional readiness that follows).

Of decisive importance in understanding how faculty have disengaged from building stronger academic honesty structures is for student affairs professionals to recognize the psychology of faculty denial and anger. Faculty denial refers to the phenomenon of instructors' inability to believe that cheating or plagiarism could occur in *their* classes (although they could see it happening in others' classes!) because of the special bond or rapport they believe they have with their own students. When denial no longer works, faculty anger can be severe because the bonds they had idealized in the faculty-student relationship have been broken. This anger can lead to punitive behavior or highly controlled classroom and evaluation systems that minimize learning opportunities, especially in those moments when a student is caught cheating, or, in some cases, draconian behaviors intended to prevent future cheating or plagiarism can diminish possibilities for a creative and positive classroom learning environment. More often, anger cannot be maintained, and the faculty member reverts to hope in student redemption or denial that cheating is recurring.

For student affairs professionals, understanding faculty psychology is as important as designing effective procedures. Because faculty are central to the academic integrity process, even with the involvement of student affairs professionals, it is virtually impossible to design a solution to the dishonesty problem without faculty's involvement (even in schools with student-run honor systems). Faculty have to feel that the policies and procedures support them in their teaching role, and that they are partners with the university rather than adversaries who have to defend themselves, their pedagogy, and their assessment practices. The very intimacy of the classroom-laboratory environments and the idealism of faculty in their educational goals mean that it will be difficult to design a strong academic integrity system without significant peer support from other faculty and academic administrators, especially deans.

Given these scenarios, the role of student affairs professionals in handling student academic misconduct, as well as education of students to the norms of academic integrity, can differ by institution. We suggest that there are five distinctive patterns for student affairs professional involvement:

1. as the lead group in dealing with academic misconduct in support of an honor council or similar student-run body;
2. as a regulatory and disciplinary body that handles all student misconduct, academic and nonacademic;
3. as a support group to academic administrators and faculty who manage academic misconduct allegations;
4. no role whatsoever because student affairs professionals are prohibited from intervening in any academic matter; or
5. there are no policies for the institutional handling of academic misconduct.

Each pattern poses different issues and opportunities for student affairs professionals. The first one requires maintenance, socialization, and leadership development for those running honor councils with the usual attention paid to ensuring that procedures are workable and followed. The second involves an array of related responsibilities that must be coherent across both academic and nonacademic misconduct. Typically, students are the players in the first and second patterns, and responsiveness to their voices is essential. This is an area of expertise for student affairs professionals and does not substantially differ in the academic integrity arena from other arenas in which there is strong student involvement. In the case of student-run honor councils, strong advisement and mentorship are often needed, especially in the beginning stages, because of the challenges associated with getting the university community, faculty and students alike, to address something as "undiscussable" as academic misconduct. And, in the second pattern, as with nonacademic misconduct, involving students on hearing panels and in writing and reviewing policy can go a long way in gaining cooperation from student constituencies such as student government and Greek organizations.

The third and fourth patterns are often more difficult for student affairs professionals, not because of leadership responsibilities but because deference to faculty interest is required when there is a perception of an unfilled need. While the first and second patterns require more routine and technical activities, the third, fourth, and fifth involve creative and adaptive responses. Following are five case studies that probe some of the implications within each of the five patterns.

Case Studies

Case Study: Pattern #1

College X is a private, liberal arts college formed in the 1840s. It is moderately selective and has 2,400 undergraduate students. The mission of the college has shifted from predominantly religious to that of a well-regarded regional school known for supplying highly qualified students to prestigious law and doctoral programs nationally. An honor code, in place since the 1920s, is revered on campus and requires the Office of Student Affairs to support the Honor Council and give it nonbinding advice and counsel.

The Situation. A student who has been found guilty of plagiarism for the second time is expelled and sues the college for a violation of due process because there is no method for appealing the Honor Council's decision to university administration. Although the college wins the case, it seems like a close call. The outside attorney for the college, herself an alumna, advises the president to revise the honor code to permit an on-campus appeal. The president sees wisdom in this and asks the Honor Council to review its procedure and seek an all-student vote following a recommendation for or against a campus appeal. However, the honor code has not been changed in 30 years, and the Honor Council does not want to change it because they disagree with the premise of an appeal. The student body does not feel strongly and tends to support the president.

The Challenge. As a student affairs professional, whose primary role is as liaison to the Honor Council, you seem caught between strong opinions of both the president and the Honor Council. The issue: How do you pursue your duties as advisor and counsel to the Honor Council without being seen as a tool for the president or as "captured" by the Honor Council?

Case Study: Pattern #2

Well-Known University (WKU) is a large, private, research-intensive institution with a traditional-age undergraduate population oriented predominantly toward future professional lives in business, medicine, or law. The Greek societies are a powerful presence contributing to the party atmosphere on campus despite the reputation of an academically serious student body. The student affairs staff spends a significant amount of time on student activities and programming in addition to student discipline for both academic and nonacademic misconduct. Student Judicial Affairs (SJA), the central administrative office for student misconduct, is primarily charged with regulating and disciplining student behavior through enforcement of policy and enactment of disciplinary sanctions. For cases of academic misconduct, faculty are expected to report students directly to SJA and not handle cases on their own.

The Situation. The 75 academic misconduct cases reported to SJA are minor, given that student surveys reveal that 55% of the 18,000 undergraduates admit to cheating at one time or another. The worry is that faculty are adjudicating cases on their own and are penalizing students academically without proper due process. The second concern is the unwillingness of faculty to discuss or participate in a centralized administration (e.g., on hearing panels) because they see student academic misconduct as requiring swift and final reactions, not education or development.

The Challenge. A disgruntled faculty member, who reported a case to SJA that did not result in a student's dismissal as he had hoped, has gone to the Faculty Senate to complain about student affairs staff's handling of student academic misconduct cases. As a result, the Senate requested a report from SJA on the academic integrity policy, including the number of cases, length of time for processing and sanctioning, and outcomes. The report shows that the 75 cases of academic misconduct take a significant amount of time to reach resolution because the majority go to hearing and SJA has difficulty securing the necessary three faculty members to sit on hearing panels. Despite these problems with faculty, the Senate, convinced that the fault lies with SJA, becomes more heavily involved in the policy process. The issue: How do you, as the traditional regulatory disciplinary body, seize the opportunity to increase faculty interest and participation, yet ensure that due process and fair sanctioning remain central priorities?

Case Study: Pattern #3

Masters College is a medium-size midwestern college with master's-level graduate programs in business and education and 48% of the undergraduates majoring or minoring in business. Half the undergraduate students are traditional 18- to 22-year-olds, while the other half are commuter students, whose average age is 29. The college's mission declares service to region and career formation as central. Masters College has a strong student affairs professional staff, which has been recognized for its alcohol reduction programs, fraternity/sorority programming, and multicultural programming. Academic misconduct cases are handled by standing faculty committees in each academic unit, which include a voting student representative elected by the student government. Each of the five academic units has had an average of three cases a year referred to it by faculty. Athletic programs are prominent, and coaches are quite assertive in monitoring the progress of student-athletes.

The Situation. Recognition of academic integrity as a priority on campus is not in evidence. The number of cases referred to the standing faculty committees is abysmally low, particularly given that schools of business have some of the highest rates of cheating as according to national reports. Student affairs professionals are preoccupied with other matters and have deferred to the academic units on student academic misconduct.

The Challenge. One of the star football players is accused of cheating and given a failing grade in the course, which jeopardizes his status on the team. The faculty member submits the case to the faculty hearing committee, and the coach comes to plead mercy. Although the evidence is not substantially strong, there is a preponderance of evidence to suggest that it is more likely than not that the student cheated. When the decision is reported, however, the student is declared not responsible, which subsequently requires that the faculty member not fail the student for academic misconduct. Although the voting record of the panel is normally not known, the student on the hearing panel, who opposes the decision, is incensed and publicizes the perceived lax treatment of the student athlete. A campus furor results, which is picked up by the local newspapers. The president is forced to make a public statement defending the hearing panel for following procedures, but the student and faculty member who are in the minority do not let the matter lie and stoke unrest among students and faculty, especially those who are less supportive of athletic programs. The issue: How do you, as a student conduct professional, begin to turn this into an institutional learning opportunity?

Case Study: Pattern #4

Land-Grant University is a large institution, with over 25,000 undergraduates and 10,000 graduate students in all disciplines, from the arts and sciences to engineering, agriculture, architecture, education, and business. Lower division general education and science classes typically have 200–500 students enrolled, with several undergraduate and graduate teaching assistants. The student affairs division is large and handles the typical portfolio, including residential life, new student orientation, health and wellness, and student discipline. The university, however, has a strong tradition of faculty shared governance, and the faculty takes great pride in and responsibility for anything academic, including all educational policies pertaining to classes. The provost's office, with a part-time faculty director and full-time professional staff, handles academic misconduct centrally. The academic integrity policy is a separate document from the student conduct code, which is administered by student affairs staff. According to policy, faculty can handle uncontested student academic misconduct allegations on their own as long as they report the case to the central academic integrity office. If students request a hearing or are facing suspension or dismissal, academic integrity cases are referred to the academic integrity office for further adjudication.

The Situation. Although the academic integrity policy is established, the academic integrity (AI) office has some difficulty educating students about policy outside of individual faculty announcements in classrooms. Student affairs staff are responsible for new student orientation, counseling, and advising, but because the AI office is an academic affairs unit, academic integrity is often excluded from student affairs handouts and presentations. There is great difficulty communicating across the academic-student affairs boundary, given the clear territorial line faculty have drawn on academic integrity as an academic issue. As a student affairs professional, you would like to ensure students are educated about the policy, but the Faculty Senate has yet to approve any material you have proposed.

The Challenge. A group of first-year students in one of the introductory biology classes of 500 + students is accused of unauthorized collaboration on a take-home exam. The process takes place according to policy, and the students are found responsible for misconduct. However, the students and their parents are furious because they believe they were not properly or fully made aware of university policy and argue that, in large classes, students need to help one another since faculty or their undergraduate teaching assistants provide little help. The issue: As the unit responsible for admissions, new student orientation, and residential life (where all first-year students live), how do you step in to help academic affairs deal with this issue and improve academic integrity education?

Case Study: Pattern #5

Spirit College is a liberal arts institution that draws its small student population from local communities. There are no graduate programs at the school, and very few students go on to further education elsewhere, but when they do, it is usually to the local state university a few miles away. Academic misconduct is considered so rare that there is no academic integrity policy. It is assumed that faculty will handle academic misconduct in the same manner as other inappropriate classroom behaviors such as perpetual lateness or cell phone use. Because class size is small (fewer than 20 students), faculty develop relationships with the students and become quite familiar with their writing skills and general capabilities, so opportunities for cheating are uncommon. The college does have a community principles statement, and student affairs staff represent a small but significant body working with academic staff and students on upholding principles such as integrity, honesty, compassion, and service. Student affairs staff spend little time on discipline—very few students live on campus, and there seem to be few situations requiring significant involvement beyond handling the occasional rambunctious young adult behaviors.

The Situation. As a student affairs professional, you try to stay active and up-to-date in your profession—both regionally and nationally. You know that academic misconduct is a hot button topic at many of your peer institutions, but no one on your campus seems particularly interested in talking about it. In fact, you often hear, "But our students don't cheat!" However, you are concerned that: (1) there is no explicit talk about the importance of academic integrity to counter the larger cultural message that cheating is acceptable, and (2) if a serious case of academic misconduct does occur, the college is not prepared to handle it.

The Challenge. A former student, who did not finish her degree with Spirit College, claims in a letter to the college and local media that while at the college, she wrote all of the papers for another student who happens to be the daughter of a local and very successful businessman and college contributor. The local media contact the president's office to inquire, but no one on campus is sure how to respond to their request regarding academic misconduct policies and the procedures for handling this particular case. Because the businessman is known within the state, the story is picked up by other outlets, and you find your small college regularly on the evening news. The president looks to student affairs for help because the matter is partly about student discipline. The issue: How do you as a key student affairs professional help to mobilize the community to handle this case and implement an academic integrity policy that fits your college community culture?

Summary

These five case studies suggest common patterns for student affairs professional involvement in academic misconduct, which varies by institutional type and organizational culture. These case studies illustrate that if academic integrity cases are viewed as just another form of student misconduct, student affairs professionals may mismanage the sensitive terrain that surrounds such cases. The commonality in all patterns of student affairs involvement in academic misconduct cases is the necessary and intimate involvement with faculty who have traditionally been the caretakers of everything within the academic terrain. Increased public scrutiny of academic affairs and the expansion of student rights require student and academic affairs to work closely together to manage academic misconduct and enhance cultures of academic integrity on campuses.

Institutional Readiness

To understand the possibilities for student affairs professionals in academic integrity, it is also essential to go beyond *pattern* and comprehend the *pace* and *direction* of change on a given campus. We call this institutional readiness. How does one ascertain an institution's readiness to make progress on significant structural improvements of its academic integrity systems? We have three suggestions: (1) by using self-assessment tools; (2) by specifying the stage of academic integrity institutionalization on campus; and (3) by diagnosing tactics and strategies.

Several possibilities for self-assessment are available, from homegrown surveys to extensive and intensive self-assessment coordinated in partnership with CAI. A quick survey instrument is provided as an appendix to this chapter. There are several propitious moments on a given campus to pursue self-assessment: as a regular part of reaccreditation, during strategic planning and assessment of learning, and as a response to a perceived crisis. Partnership with faculty and student leaders and academic administrators in conducting assessments is essential, of course. Understanding the stage of institutionalization of academic integrity on a given campus is vitally important in developing strategies and tactics for advancing academic integrity (Bertram Gallant & Drinan, 2006a). Studies (e.g., Bertram Gallant & Drinan, 2006a; Bertram Gallant, 2007) have shown four likely stages of academic integrity institutionalization on a continuum:

1. Recognition and commitment
2. Response generation
3. Implementation
4. Institutionalization

Movement from one stage to another can be problematic since there are points of organizational resistance between each. And although achieving full institutionalization of academic integrity is extremely difficult, the stages of response generation and implementation are achievable for most colleges and universities and fall within the normal range. Patience and persistence of the champions of academic integrity on campus are necessary, and setbacks can be expected. Simple awareness of what stage a campus is on can be a powerful stimulus to coordinate expectations of the campus and prevent serious miscues about how to proceed.

There are diagnostic tools to help develop strategy and tactics for progress on campus. Institutional readiness can have powerful implications for robust strategies for change. One useful diagnostic, the PRINCE system (Coplin & O'Leary, 1998), is described here, and an example of how to use it follows.

- Start with a contested question that can be answered on a yes-no basis.
- Identify actors on campus who have a stake, even a small one, in an answer.
- Specify the current answer of the actor to the contested question on a numerical scale, with " +3" being the strongest possible yes and "-3" the strongest no (avoid "0").
- Specify the power of the actor on campus on the question with "3" being high power, "2" being modest power, and "1" being some power.
- Specify salience (i.e., how important is the given issue to this actor): "3" is high salience; "2" is modest salience; and "1" is low salience.
- Multiply the scores for each actor and total them.

A Hypothetical Application of the PRINCE System

Contested question: Should our college/university make a large organizational effort to reduce academic dishonesty? Table 15.1 illustrates the hypothetical numerical analysis of the power and salience of each relevant actor.

Even though the campus community seems divided in this case, the " +7" total indicates a fairly strong readiness to move to a large organizational effort. Additionally, the diagnostic indicates several possibilities to increase the positive score:

1. if the president can be persuaded to make the issue more prominent in his/her speeches, and
2. if faculty and student leaders each can be persuaded to change their issue position to just a " +1."

The combination of these seemingly small changes would add 11 positive points to the total and suggest a much more receptive environment for a large organizational effort.

TABLE 15.1
Hypothetical Application of the Prince System to the Contested Question

Actors	Issue Position	Power	Salience	
President	+2	2	1	+4
Deans	−1	2	1	−2
Faculty Leaders	−2	2	1	−4
Student Leaders	−1	1	1	−1
Trustees	+3	1	2	+6
Student Affairs Administrators	+2	1	2	+4
			Total	+7

The value of the PRINCE diagnostic is that it provides a realistic appraisal of the "politics" of an institution on the issue and a methodical device to focus strategy and tactics. Intuitive understandings of these politics may lead to similar conclusions, but the discipline of the diagnostic can be powerful if it is commonly held and understood by the champions of academic integrity. Of course, those opposed to a large organizational effort could take advantage of the same diagnostic to prevent change!

Conclusions

Institutional change on a persistent issue such as academic dishonesty can seem daunting. Student affairs professionals should be alert for possibilities for change on a given campus, even if it seems that cheating and plagiarism fall primarily in the academic area of faculty governance. There are more moments for insinuating academic integrity into campus discourse than seemed likely even just 15 years ago; increased media attention to academic integrity, the formation of CAI, and the proliferation of centers for teaching and learning are three of the most compelling. Media reports and cheating have spiked in recent years and have been connected with business fraud. (See especially Daniel Callahan's (2004) book, *The Cheating Culture,* for the connections.) The rise of CAI also indicates growing national attention to integrity. And proliferation of centers for teaching and learning as platforms for improvement of teaching means that campuses are focusing on the teaching mission; strengthening faculty-student connections is a proven way to create a greater radius of trust in the classroom and beyond.

On a given campus, the normal rhythms of reaccreditation and strategic planning provide opportunities to raise the issue. And, of course, cheating cases that break out publicly on campus provide a crucial opportunity to stimulate discourse. We caution you against waiting to exploit these moments to pursue a stronger academic integrity system, however; it is much better to be proactive in organizationally developing more sophisticated and durable approaches. If that kind of thinking and planning is already in place, the reaction to a campus cheating or plagiarism crisis can be a genuine catalyst for change.

Author Note

Correspondence concerning this chapter should be addressed to Tricia Bertram Gallant, University of California, San Diego, 9500 Gilman Drive Dept 0067, La Jolla, CA 92093–0067. Phone: 858–534–2715. E-mail: tbg@ucsd.edu

References

Bertram Gallant, T. (2007). *A multi-case study investigation into the institutionalization of academic integrity*. Paper presented at the Annual Meeting of the American Educational Research Association, Chicago, IL.

Bertram Gallant, T., & Drinan, P. (2006a). Institutionalizing academic integrity: Administrator perceptions and institutional actions. *NASPA Journal, 44*(1), 61–81.

Bertram Gallant, T., & Drinan, P. (2006b). Organizational theory and student cheating: Explanation, responses, and strategies. *The Journal of Higher Education, 77*(5), 839–860.

Callahan, D. (2004). *The cheating culture: Why more Americans are doing wrong to get ahead*. Orlando, FL: Harcourt, Inc.

Center for Academic Integrity (CAI). (1999). *The fundamental values of academic integrity*. Retrieved February 22, 2006, from http://www.academicintegrity.org/pdf/FVProject.pdf

Coplin, W. D., & O'Leary, M. K. (1998). *Public policy skills* (3rd ed.). Croton-on-Hudson, NY: Policy Studies Associates.

Hardy, R. J., & Burch, D. (1981). What political science professors should know in dealing with academic dishonesty. *Teaching Political Science, 9*(1), 5–14.

McCabe, D. L. (2005, Summer/Fall). It takes a village: Academic dishonesty and educational opportunity. *Liberal Education,* 26–31.

McCabe, D. L., Trevino, L. K., & Butterfield, K. D. (2001). Dishonesty in academic environments: The influence of peer reporting requirements. *The Journal of Higher Education, 72*(1), 29–45.

Institutionalization Self-Assessment Survey

SECTION 1.					
A. Read the following statements in the context of your institution. Place a check in the appropriate box; leave blank if unsure.					
		Not at all	Minimally	Adequately	Substantially
1	We use the phrase "academic integrity."				
2	We talk about trying to create a culture of integrity.				
3	We have a committee that works on promotion of and education about academic integrity.				
4	We have a designated budget for promotion of and education about academic integrity.				
5	We have staff who are responsible for promotion of and education about academic integrity.				
6	We have a designated office space where university members can go to obtain information about academic integrity.				
7	We have a tradition of academic integrity within the institution.				
8	Undergraduate students are committed to transforming institutional culture.				
9	Graduate students are committed to transforming institutional culture.				
10	Faculty are committed to transforming institutional culture.				
11	Student affairs administrators are committed to transforming institutional culture.				

		Not at all	Minimally	Adequately	Substantially
12	Academic affairs administrators are committed to transforming institutional culture.				
13	The chief academic officer is committed to transforming institutional culture.				
14	The president/chancellor is committed to transforming institutional culture.				
15	The board of trustees/governors is committed to transforming institutional culture.				
16	Faculty comply with the policies, procedures, and/or codes.				
17	Students comply with the policies, procedures, and/or codes.				
18	Staff are consistent in the application of the policies, procedures, and/or codes.				
19	Schools/colleges/programs are consistent in the application of the policies, procedures, and/or codes.				
20	The policies, procedures, and/or codes can adapt to respond to new forms of student cheating or plagiarism.				
21	Deans are held accountable for reducing student cheating and plagiarism.				
22	Vice presidents are held accountable for reducing student cheating and plagiarism.				
23	The president is accountable for reducing student cheating and plagiarism.				
24	Students recognize academic dishonesty as a problem and are committed to addressing it.				
25	Faculty recognize academic dishonesty as a problem and are committed to addressing it.				

		Not at all	Minimally	Adequately	Substantially
26	Student affairs administrators recognize academic dishonesty as a problem and are committed to addressing it.				
27	Academic affairs administrators (including deans) recognize academic dishonesty as a problem and are committed to addressing it.				
28	The president/chancellor recognizes academic dishonesty as a problem and is committed to addressing it.				
29	Students are addressing the problem.				
30	Faculty are addressing the problem.				
31	Student affairs administrators are addressing the problem.				
32	Academic affairs administrators (including deans) are addressing the problem.				
33	President/chancellor is addressing the problem.				
34	Board of trustees/governors is addressing the problem.				
B.	**Add the check marks in each column.**				
C.	**Multiply each column total by the number indicated.**	× 0	× 1	× 2	× 3
D.	**Enter the new total for each column.**				
E.	**Add all 4 totals from Line D.**		= Section 1 Grand Total		

SECTION 2.

F. Read the following statements in the context of your institution. Place a check in the appropriate box. Leave blank if unsure.

		Not an Obstacle	Somewhat an Obstacle	Fairly Strong Obstacle	Very Strong Obstacle
35	There is internal conflict over *the importance* of the policies, procedures, and/or codes.				

		Not an Obstacle	Somewhat an Obstacle	Fairly Strong Obstacle	Very Strong Obstacle
36	There are disparities in the implementation of the policies, procedures, and/or codes among colleges, schools, programs, and/or departments.				
37	There is difficulty in educating faculty and students on the policies, procedures, and/or codes.				
38	There is a lack of central authority for the management of the policies, procedures, and/or codes.				
39	A peer culture (i.e., campus norms) supports student cheating.				
40	There are faculty who do not mention or enforce policies, procedures, and/or codes to students.				
41	There are gaps between policy/procedure development and policy/procedure implementation.				
42	There is a lack of support from deans.				
43	There is a lack of support from vice presidents.				
44	There is a lack of support from the president/chancellor.				
45	There is a lack of support from board of trustees/board of governors.				
46	There are cumbersome policies or procedures.				
G.	**Add the check marks in each column in Section 2.**				
H.	**Multiply each column total by the number indicated.**	× 3	× 2	× 1	× 0
I.	**Enter the new total for each column in Section 2.**				
J.	**Add all 4 totals from Line I.**		= Section 2 Grand Total		

		Not an Obstacle	Somewhat an Obstacle	Fairly Strong Obstacle	Very Strong Obstacle
K.	**Add the two Grand Total Scores together.**		**= Total Institutionalization Score**		
L.	**Institutionalization Stage**	**Score**	**Stage**		
		0	No Stage		
		1–44	Recognition & Commitment		
		45–88	Response Generation		
		89–133	Implementation		
		134–176	Institutionalization		

16

FINDING OUR VOICE
AS A PROFESSION

James M. Lancaster and Diane M. Waryold

I t is uncertain where and when the first student conduct violation was resolved. Equally unknown are the identities of the individual who was charged and the individual responsible for bringing resolution to the allegation. Perhaps Prometheus's theft of fire from the gods as a gift to mankind qualifies as the first youthful offense. More likely, the first offense came in a much more familiar and earthbound scene—one or more students faced allegations concerning their actions. Perhaps they were given some rudiments of being heard before discipline was imposed. Surely the individual imposing that action was a dean or someone very dean-like. While early colonial colleges usually were governed by religious and moralistic rules, until quite recently in the history of colleges and universities in this country, any conduct decision was made without the *legal* requirement of minimal fairness, although the dean may have felt ethically bound to some notion of fairness.

But those days are history at this point in the evolution of the profession of student conduct resolution. As John Lowery has portrayed in chapter 5, the case of *Dixon v. Alabama* began the slow but unrelenting process that has moved the role of those involved in student conduct resolution from the position of *in loco parentis* to an approach based at least in part on providing fairness, which, while not constitutional due process, is certainly closer to that concept than to the notion of serving in absence of the parent.

We are more aware of when this work of administrators in student conduct began to be perceived as a potential profession. Such recognition came with the meeting of the first such administrators, convened by Don Gehring in the Coral Room of the Holiday Inn-Surfside in Clearwater Beach, Florida, in 1987 (Association for Student Judicial Affairs [ASJA], 2007d). Our written history tells us this much. We have learned much from this and other events in the years since 1987. An international conference of the Association for Student Judicial Affairs (ASJA), attended by hundreds, convenes annually in Florida. A fledgling training institute designed to provide conduct officers with the minimum competencies necessary to complete their responsibilities successfully has evolved to the Donald D. Gehring Academy for Student Conduct Administration, encompassing not only training in competencies but advanced sessions for professional development and two levels of alternative dispute resolution education as well. Frequent teleconferences, publications, and other professional development opportunities have also been offered in this period. It is clear that this work of conduct administration is becoming a true profession that encompasses a "specialized body of knowledge, set of skills, group mission or identity [and] standards of behavior and practice" (Plaut, 2007).

It is a reasonable conclusion that we are *finding our voice as a profession.* Yet, after 20 years of development toward the goal of professionalism, we find that the search for that common voice goes on; it is a journey that longs for a final destination. We know much about what is ethically, legally, developmentally, and educationally significant in our work. However, we are still discovering what combination of those sometimes divergent elements can lead us to speak with a voice that at once is recognized as harmonious with our principles while intelligible to even the least developmentally ready of our constituents.

In the past we have sometimes worried about process and procedures to the detriment of the humanness of the process—we have been legalistic when we might more appropriately have been luminous—holding students in the light of our concern as readily as we have held them accountable for their conduct. We have worried about current issues that raise liability and safety concerns on our campuses while too often failing to recognize them as threads that, left unresolved, can destroy the larger fabric of community that we seek to weave. These concerns for liability, risk, and other "problems" have been and continue to be real and challenging to those who work in this profession. They are our most frequent source of immediate risk for our students and institutions as well as the most likely cause of the outcome some fear more than all others—a summons to face the civil or criminal court as a defendant in a wrongful action or tort case.

But in this same period of learning and development as a profession, we have also begun to perceive that many things are more devastating than a court appearance—among them the loss of a student who, in some way, we might have reached or helped if only we could have discerned more clearly the disparate themes of their lives and actions that coalesced into trouble or tragedy. And perceiving the opportunities we may have missed, we increasingly have sought new ways of hearing and understanding the stories that students have to tell us. From a profession that began with the goal of student development but sometimes ended with a resort to the rule book, we have begun to ask the Aristotelian question, What really matters here? And in asking that question, we have grown to engage our students and colleagues in what our colleague Gary Pavela has frequently termed the "ethical dialogue" (Pavela, 2003). We more frequently ask ourselves and our institutions the important questions about meaning and mattering in student conduct—in the process of over 20 years, we have begun to create a real profession, to find our voice in a practice that can justify the term "professional."

In seeking and discovering that voice, we have often looked to the past for portents about the future. Indeed, Thomas Jefferson's letter to Thomas Cooper is frequently taken as evidence of the historic and ongoing challenges we face as conduct officers. In that document, Jefferson warned that "premature ideas of independence, too little repressed by parents, beget a spirit of insubordination. . . . I look to it . . . as a breaker ahead . . ." (Stoner & Lowery, 2004, p. 1)

Don Gehring, founder of ASJA, is fond of telling newcomers about Joe Kavanaugh's characterization of conduct officers as members of the "besieged clan" (personal communication, 2006). Kavanaugh coined this term during the first discussion of a strategic plan for ASJA in which he heard the leadership speak of a special camaraderie that is formed in our work in which only those who practice it can really understand it. And, as time has passed, members of that clan have come together to support one another in a variety of forums. In 1998, on the 10th anniversary of the founding of ASJA, a group of authors, all past presidents of the association, remained concerned with looking to the future of our practice. They too feared, in Jefferson's words, "a breaker ahead" that might cause our educational institutions to flounder on the rocks. In *The State of Student Judicial Affairs: Current Forces and Future Challenges* (ASJA, 1998, pp. 22–23), they warned of these, among other, future challenges:

- Hate speech and violent behavior
- Racial tensions
- Consumerism
- Federalization (proliferation of government mandates)
- Technology in the form of homepages, free speech, and regulation of such activities
- Deferring campus criminal activities to campus prosecution

In hindsight, those authors were quite right. Each of the preceding issues has grown in magnitude on our campuses. More significant, however, is their observation in the same publication that "[s]tudent judicial affairs administrators will be caught in the middle between local governments deferring cases to the campus and news media and lobby groups pushing to open campus hearings. . . . The future demands that student judicial affairs administration can no longer be 'just discipline'" (ASJA, 1998, p. 23). What these authors could not foresee was the extent to which their predictions, especially those related to technology, would threaten to overwhelm our campuses and our practice of conduct resolution. This was not a failure in vision but a natural consequence of what David Edgerton has described as a failure to anticipate how technology will be applied, and changed through use (Shapin, 2007).

New Yorker magazine book reviewer Steven Shapin interprets Edgerton's book as telling us that

> no one is very good at predicting technological futures; new and old technologies coexist; and technological significance and technological novelty are rarely the same—indeed, a given technology's grip on our awareness is often in inverse relationship to its significance in our lives. Above all, Edgerton says that we are wrong to associate technology solely with invention, and that we should think of it, rather, as evolving through use. A "history of technology-in-use," he writes, yields "a radically different picture of technology, and indeed of invention and innovation" (Shapin, 2007).

Edgerton's warning is clear and pertinent: as John Zacker illuminates in chapter 10, while we may predict in a general sense that technologies such as

Web pages or cell phones may prove problematic, we are not very successful in predicting how students and other consumers will use these devices, sometimes in a manner their inventors never anticipated. Ten years ago, when we worried about the future of student Web pages, we did not conceive that Web technology would result in virtual communities such as Facebook and MySpace. In turn, their creators did not realize how quickly their creations would be co-opted by third parties for purposes other than social networking. Nor could we or they foresee that what some have described as "Generation Me" (Twenge, 2007), in which narcissistic students believe everything about themselves to be of interest to the larger community, would post unimaginable and uncensored personal data and photos, which in turn, could make them unintended subjects for stalking and pornographic display of personal photos. Or how cell phones, equipped with cameras, might be used to take intimate photos of students who otherwise believed they were assured of privacy in locker rooms or bathroom facilities. All of this has left conduct administrators scrambling to deal with the implications of such technology for their students and their institutions. How, for example, do you attempt to provide a safe environment when so much of that environment is accessible through transmission via cell phones and the World Wide Web? As satellite technology is refined further and, with the assistance of imaging technology, routinely available even to average computer users, how will products such as Google Earth, which provides satellite views of virtually any mapped zone on the planet, be used or misused in campus settings? How soon might one be able to gaze into a residence hall window or apparently private backyard using the satellite and imaging technology now emerging? Voyeurs who once relied on field glasses and telescopes will undoubtedly discover new uses for this technology that we have not yet fully considered. Despite warnings about the fallacy of attempting to forecast what will happen next—we believe it is important to examine "threads" that may, without sufficient mending, unravel the fabric of our communities.

Threads

Technology

Technology amplifies and accelerates the general trends of our society—and students are particularly innovative in their response to such changes. As discussed, we seldom anticipate fully the uses to which our society will put new technology and the manner in which users will adapt existing technology. But we know that technology, once it has emerged, is unlikely to be successfully banned or long retarded. Instead, it may be possible to apply human values and general community expectations wisely to shape the application and outcomes of using this technology. For example, if we believe as a community that respect is an important value, we would not engage in or tolerate the use of technology to spy on or invade privacy of individuals engaged in lawful, daily conduct.

Diversity

Human relationships will be more challenging in an increasingly multicultural society on and off campus—Byrne (2005) has projected that

> [t]he number of white high-school graduates is predicted to fall from more than 1.77 million in 2005 to 1.58 million by the end of the decade. The number of black, non-Hispanic high-school graduates will rise slightly during the same period, but it will be far outpaced by growth in the number of Hispanic high-school graduates. . . . In 2005 the number of black high-school graduates—359,033—is only slightly greater than the number of their Hispanic counterparts—358,762. But by 2015, the number of black high-school graduates will be only 367,407, while the number of Hispanic students predicted to be in the college-admissions pool will be 546,885. The Asian American population also represents a rapidly growing population in the United States.
>
> Baruth and Manning (2007) point to the 2005 U.S. Census, which captured the 231,000 Asian children under 14 years of age. Many of these children will be entering college in the coming years.
>
> Projections of how many people will graduate from high school can be inaccurate. But the overwhelming evidence is that the face of higher education will change greatly over the next decade in favor of more diversity.

Byrne (2005) goes on to suggest that pessimists may see these changes as a growing competition for resources and position in higher education. Surely such competition, should it come to pass, will result in conflicts among community members that conduct officers again will need to anticipate and will likely be asked to resolve.

Complexity

One-size-fits-all processes will likely fit none; given the likely diversity of higher education cited, it is unlikely that a single, linear procedural approach to every form of student misconduct will be successful. Full-time traditional-age students reflect one range of cognitive and developmental behavior, while nontraditional-age, part-time students with extensive life experience reflect another. In reality, our future populations will be represented by a wide range of points along the continuum of human development—conduct officers and their institutions will need to have a wide understanding of and appreciation for differing worldviews and cultural relativism will be key to successful practice.

Ethics

Ethics will continue to grow in importance as the growing complexity of human society defies management by simple rules. Rushworth Kidder, founder of the Institute for Global Ethics, has long suggested that we cannot solve 21st-century challenges and problems with 20th-century rules. "What matters most? The creation of a moral and social culture where core values, articulated in a common language and promoted from the very top, are defended courageously and consistently. You can't buy a better 21st century risk-management policy than that" (Kidder, 2001).

Freedom

With greater freedom comes greater responsibility. Eleanor Roosevelt has been credited with saying, "Freedom makes a huge requirement of every human being. With freedom comes responsibility. For the person who is unwilling to grow up, the person who does not want to carry his own weight, this is a frightening prospect" (Roosevelt, 1960). No sentiment could better describe the increasing divide between student freedoms and increased opportunities for harm. Today's students enjoy unprecedented individual accommodation, unparalleled access to resources and technology, and a "hands-off approach" to student oversight (by many campuses). Institutions today enjoy fewer opportunities to "control" their students; such control likely will not increase in the future, so institutional personnel will need to enhance and share community expectations while not unduly infringing on individuality and creativity. This concern is heightened when one considers the ongoing dilemma posed when the need for control is expressed by "helicopter parents" who feel comfortable sweeping in at every point in their children's development. Kibler and Paterson describe the "pros and cons" of parental involvement in greater detail in chapter 11. This is exacerbated by the emergence of a narcissistic student generation that does not recognize fully the need for individual accountability.

Assuming that we are correct in predicting some of these future "threads," how should our practice evolve to meet these challenges? We are charged legally and ethically with meeting the demands of student conduct resolution. But our response cannot simply be to conduct "business as usual" and expect that we will be successful. In this challenging future, conduct administrators must be "of their world" as well as "in their world." We must move beyond our traditional role in which we focus solely on the process of conduct resolution after it has occurred. We must be proactive in anticipating future areas of concern and in helping to create community expectations among our institutional citizens that will be relevant regardless of future innovative misconduct. We must accept that we will never outguess or "outinnovate" the ways our students can use technology, among other resources, for purposes that were originally unintended or unanticipated. More rules will not suffice. Instead, we must be agile and flexible, knowledgeable about the fundamentals of our practice, and thoughtful about our response to new challenges. We must be "of their world," anticipating the future of student behavior even if we are able to make only generalizations about that future. We must develop a clear self-awareness about what we value, understand the values of our institutions, and learn to appreciate the culture and values emerging in each successive generation of our students. We must move beyond considering ourselves a "besieged clan" and reach out to our community as institutional experts and advocates for student behavior. We must affirm our professional and personal voices to use our education, experience, and intuition to help resolve the various challenges and crises of the future.

There is good evidence that the conduct administration profession is moving toward these goals. When this chapter was written, the annual Gehring Academy for Student Conduct Administration was meeting in Salt Lake City, Utah. During that meeting, many faculty presenters spoke of what have previously been termed alternative forms of adjudication. But from their presentations and the reactions of many participants, it became clear that those involved with this academy no longer considered these alternatives as "new" or "radical." Instead there appeared to be a consensus that these were reasonable and thoughtful approaches for seeking alternative routes to resolution of different forms of student misconduct. Social justice, mediation, restorative justice, ethical and development models, all were discussed and appeared to be acceptable in some manner as forms of conduct resolution. This demonstrates two important examples of how we have found our voice as a profession: first, we no longer routinely assume that student misconduct is resolved through a process that mirrors the courtroom. We know from the development of case law, most of which has been well-defined for more than 20 years (personal communication with John Lowery, 2007), that we are required to offer "minimal due process," largely consisting of notice and hearing. We also know that this "minimal process," while it should grow less minimal as the likelihood of suspension or expulsion for the student increases, is far from the traditional criminal court standard. What has truly changed over the last 20 years, as we have synthesized existing case law with developmental and cognitive theory and experience, is that we now embrace a rich array of alternatives to that courtroom model. Second, we have an international organization, the Association for Student Judicial Affairs (ASJA), which, through 20 years of study and scholarship, conferencing, programming, and development has become an international voice and advocate for the professional student conduct administrator. In the growth and development of this organization, many new professionals have found guidance and knowledge that has helped to shape the profession. Continuing professionals have found their practice shaped and refined through the programs and services of this association. A collegial and broad-based network of student development professionals as well as attorneys and scholars has emerged through membership in ASJA. The world of higher education has recognized that ASJA is a "go to" source for information on student conduct, culture, and the manner in which institutions should respond to both.

These developments at the individual, associational, and international level mean that student conduct administration has now become a career objective for many aspiring student development professionals. Indeed, where the role of being a "judicial officer" was once either part of a larger job portfolio or an assignment through which one passed on the way to higher-level administration, it is now a broader and richer professional career destination for many individuals. In turn, this has increased the demand for more professional development opportunities to which the leadership of ASJA has increasingly been focused on responding. The symbiosis between professional practitioners and the primary professional organization in conduct administration means that ASJA will continue to expand and develop offerings in response to this demand.

How should ASJA assist professionals in the future of conduct administration? After ASJA's 20 years as an organization, members have come to expect that it will routinely provide a yearly international conference, a summer academy or institute for professional development along several tracks, regular updates via the Web, a voice at the legislative table, and sponsored publications and virtual meetings on current topics. Beyond these events, what might the profession ask of its association? Quite obviously, current activities will continue and develop in a variety of manners in response to needs. For example, the Gehring Institute, which began in 1993 as a topical training institute for professionals, has evolved into a multipart annual summer academy presenting a training institute for new professionals based on core competencies; an advanced seminar focusing on mid-level professionals based on current topics and updates on fundamental competencies; and a two-level certification program for those interested in developing skills in mediation and mediation training.

Other discussion has focused on promoting more circuit or regional development opportunities, "podcasting" current hard-copy publications, updating information and "breaking" issues as they occur, and ongoing development of professional publications that serve the scholar and practitioner. But beyond these evolutionary changes, what are conduct professionals likely to need?

At the 2007 Gehring Academy, advanced seminar participants, that is, those with 5 to 20 years experience, were asked to suggest future "threads" that may be challenging for the profession. Among other comments, their most pressing concerns involved:

- students with multiple disabilities and/or mental health issues;
- stress and stress-related illnesses and behaviors;
- inappropriate parental involvement;
- increasing litigation;
- conduct issues related to technology use;
- applying technology to conduct processes;

- constructing appropriate educational outcomes/assessment for conduct processes;
- educating about multiculturalism on campus, including immigration;
- dealing with government mandates; and
- emergency and crisis response.

Participants also were asked to speculate about how ASJA might meet such future needs. Those professionals, with sufficient experience to understand many of the issues the profession faces, suggested the following areas for future professional development activities:

- continued training, seminars, and conferences;
- e-mail updates on breaking events;
- collaboration with other student affairs organizations;
- developing more publications and suggested professional library resources;
- providing professional liability insurance (although it should be noted that response to this idea was mixed);
- encourage/conduct research on outcomes;
- develop assessment instruments;
- updates on emerging technology;
- better networking/support of circuits;
- lobbying state and federal governments;
- help reduce focus on policy for every problem;
- continued diversity education;
- provide professional consultation;
- greater support for part-time administrators;
- more information on how to communicate with parents and students;
- more mentoring programs;
- ASJA should be the ethical standard bearer; and
- ASJA hotline for emergency assistance.

While professional development activities and prescient reflection on future challenges are important considerations for our work as a profession, conduct professionals need to continue developing assessable measures of individual and organizational effectiveness and success as a part of planning for the future. Just as student development professionals in the broader student affairs world have discovered, conduct administrators have begun to understand that the effectiveness of their work is not simply a measurement of how many students are adjudicated and what sanctions are assigned. ASJA's mission is "to facilitate the integration of student development concepts with principles of judicial practice" (ASJA, 2007a), and that "a primary purpose for the enforcement of such standards is to maintain and strengthen the ethical climate and to promote the academic integrity of our institutions" (ASJA, 2007b). These are reasonable expectations to pursue for our institutions and for the professionals who administer student conduct. They are not our only expectations, but they serve as a good beginning basis by which to assess our practice.

When considering such expectations, it is important to translate them into goal statements and work objectives that reflect what your office and you as a professional hope to accomplish in your work. These goals, in turn, should become part of yearly action statements containing objectives we expect to accomplish in the short- and long-term life of our practice. To be measurable, these objectives must have learning outcomes that measure our effectiveness in meeting goals. These expectations are the most difficult part of assessment for many professionals. How does one, in fact, measure "the integration of student development concepts with principles of judicial practice" or whether your office has been able to "maintain and strengthen the ethical climate and to promote the academic integrity of our institutions"? Here are some suggestions:

- The conduct officer who saw the student through the resolution process may choose to talk with the student after the conclusion of the process, seeking to make meaning but also to gather informal data concerning the student's view of the process. Or the conduct office may give the student a survey following conclusion and solicit feedback within a specified length of time.
- If your campus has an institutional research office, or if your division of student affairs houses a research component, you may work with them in creating an assessment project for your conduct office. The process should involve some follow-up with students who have been served recently by the conduct office.
- Students who have participated recently in the conduct process may be angry or may feel that any assessment is an opportunity to redress

their dislike for the general conduct process or outcome, regardless of the quality of that experience. Schuh and Upcraft (2001) are careful to note that "no other office, department, or service may be more difficult to assess than an office of student conduct since this student affairs function almost exclusively deals with students and clients who are unhappy and do not want to have anything to do with the office" (p. 426). This is especially true for students who may disagree with a finding of responsibility. One technique for dealing with this natural emotion involves contact by a third-party office with students who have received services from the conduct office. The third party may be perceived as sufficiently distant from the conduct office to invite students to respond honestly about their experience.

- The first question that needs to be answered is, Who are our clientele? Knowing and analyzing the demographics of the population that is adjudicated can provide important information for targeting student populations in a proactive manner. If, for example, White, first-year, male students majoring in general studies make up the majority of the caseload, special emphasis should be directed to where these students are housed and the programmatic efforts devised in engaging this "category" of student. Related to this, the extent to which repeat "offenders" frequent the system must be assessed with respect to educational outcomes. If the system is truly working, and students are learning and maturing through their interaction with the process, recidivism should be low.

- From whatever source such assessment comes, it must be based on a set of questions or topics that accurately respond to the expectations the conduct office has established and the culture of the campus. This may be as simple as a survey instrument students are asked to complete and return, or as complex as a qualitative study of student offenders involving focus groups and/or interviews while using content analysis to give meaning to the data gathered. But the importance of accurately defining what you want to assess is critical. Do you know what students need to be successful in the campus environment? Are you concerned about students' satisfaction with their outcome? Do you want to give students a voice in assessing their view of how fairly they were treated or whether they were treated with respect? Is it of interest to ask specific questions about conduct officers versus members of panels versus administrative routine?

- Whether using conduct office resources or third-party resources for assessment, another component of such a program should examine how you are meeting goals, objectives, and learning outcomes over the longer term. It should also involve a periodic (3- to 5-year), recurring assessment of professional and organizational outcomes in regard to benchmarks established by the Council for the Advancement of Standards (CAS) and ASJA. Do conduct professionals possess and practice the basic competencies identified by ASJA? What do students, faculty, and staff say about the function of the office and its personnel? How would colleagues from other institutions or from professional associations rate your performance?

Planning assessment is a subject for a whole other text and is beyond the scope of this chapter. It is critical, however, that we develop assessable measures of individual and organizational effectiveness and success as a part of planning for the future of our practice. How can one possibly look to the future without first assessing current effectiveness?

The conference theme for the 20th anniversary celebration of ASJA's founding was "honoring our past; embracing our present, empowering our future: The journey continues" (ASJA, 2007c). Nothing could better summarize the direction in which we as practitioners and as a professional association should move. Our students and our institutional environments are not static, closed systems. Instead, we should realize that we live in a dynamic world where change is constant and where our work is constantly evolving. While we may learn the "basics" of policy, law, and practical administration, we will always be discovering new ways to approach our work. In this respect, our work is a journey—a work in progress. Every student whom we meet on that journey demands the best that we can put forward each day.

Most of our students will fall within a normal bell curve—neither exceptional in achievement nor infamous in their failures. Most of our students will inhabit some part of whatever range our society defines as "normal." However, a small percentage of our students will always experience life outside the boundaries of the conventional. It is in assisting these students, and the support to community development that such assistance provides, that we find our best service to education and development. The assumptions we make about our students are important. Might we never forget that each and every student is unique and possesses his or her own life story. And each student has potential and every offender is redeemable in some fashion. Our work is both simple and complex, troubling and exhilarating; our results are sometimes of minor consequence and at other times of profound importance to individuals and communities. We no longer need be a beleaguered clan but a profession that speaks with the voice of education, hope, and resolution in the midst of great confusion and emotion. We are reasoned, thoughtful, and developmental in our practice. We balance justice with mercy and the individual with the community. We are the voice of student conduct professionals.

References

Association for Student Judicial Affairs (ASJA). (1998). *The state of student judicial affairs: Current forces and future challenges.* College Station, TX: Author.

Association for Student Judicial Affairs (ASJA). (2007a). *Constitution of ASJA.* Retrieved June 22, 2007, from http://asjaonline.org/attachments/files/1/ASJA Constitution.pdf

Association for Student Judicial Affairs (ASJA). (2007b). *Ethical standards and principles of practice.* Retrieved June 22, 2007, from http://asjaonline.org/en/cms/?60

Association for Student Judicial Affairs (ASJA). (2007c). *Events, annual conference.* Retrieved June 22, 2007, from http://asjaonline.org/en/cms/?42

Association for Student Judicial Affairs (ASJA). (2007d). *History of ASJA.* Retrieved May 29, 2007, from http://www.asjaonline.org/en/cms/?61

Baruth, L. G., & Manning, M. L. (2007). *Multicultural counseling and psychotherapy: A lifespan perspective* (4th ed.). Upper Saddle River, NJ: Pearson.

Byrne, R. (2005). How will the future shake out? *The Chronicle of Higher Education.* Retrieved June 20, 2007, from http://chronicle.com/weekly/v52/i14/14a00101.htm

Kidder, R. (2001, December). Ethics is not optional. *Association Management.* Retrieved June 20, 2007, from http://www.asaecenter.org/PublicationsResources/AMMagArticleDetail.cfm?ItemNu m ber = 6904

Pavela, G. (2003). *Using the college disciplinary process to promote student ethical development.* Retrieved May 29, 2007, from http://www.studentaffairs.com/onlinec ourses/fall2003course6.html

Plaut, S. M. (2007). *What does it mean to be a member of a profession?* Retrieved May 29, 2007, from http://www.medschool.umaryland.edu/Professionalism/professionalism_dmrt.pdf

Roosevelt, E. (1960). *You learn by living.* Philadelphia, PA: The Westminster Press.

Schuh, J. H., & Upcraft, M. L. (2001). *Assessment practice in student affairs: An applications manual.* San Francisco: Jossey-Bass.

Shapin, S. (2007). *What else is new? How uses, not innovations, drive human technology.* Retrieved June 1, 2007, from http://www.newyorker.com/arts/critics/books/2007/05/14/070514crbo_books esh apin

Stoner, E. N., & Lowery, J. W. (2004). *Navigating past the "spirit of insubordination": A twenty-first century model student conduct code with a model hearing script.* South Bend, IN: National Association of College and University Attorneys and Notre Dame Law School.

Twenge, J. (2007). *Generation me.* Retrieved June 20, 2007, from http://www.theatlantic.com/doc/print/200707/primarysources

ABOUT THE AUTHORS

Elizabeth Baldizan is currently director of the UNLV Jean Nidetch Women's Center. Her experience in higher education includes more than 20 years at both four-year and community colleges. She received an Ed.D. in higher educational administration from UNLV, an M.A. in education from the University of New Mexico, and a B.A. in communications and environmental studies from the University of Northern Colorado. Dr. Baldizan has served as assistant dean of students at the University of New Mexico, dean of student life at South Seattle Community College, and dean of student development at UNLV. She was also adjunct faculty and graduate intern coordinator at Seattle University and adjunct faculty at UNLV in the Department of Educational Leadership. Her professional involvement includes serving as president of the Association for Student Judicial Affairs, as a member of the Board of Directors of the National Association of Student Personnel Administrators (NASPA), on the Journal Editorial Board, and on the Council on Law in Higher Education's editorial board. She has also published and presented on ethical development.

Tricia Bertram Gallant is the academic integrity coordinator for the University of California, San Diego. Dr. Bertram Gallant's writings and research on academic integrity issues, which are framed most sharply by organizational, leadership, and institutionalization theories, are intended to encourage higher education practitioners and researchers to reconsider student academic misconduct beyond that of "students behaving badly" to a systemic and complex issue shaped by myriad organizational, institutional, and societal factors. In addition, Dr. Bertram Gallant is developing work that links the academic conduct of students with that of faculty, researchers, and higher education administrators.

Lee E. Bird, vice president for student affairs at Oklahoma State University, received a doctorate from the University of Arizona. She has worked in student affairs for 28 years, previously served as president of the National Board of Directors for the Association of Student Judicial Affairs, and continues to present nationally on topics related to student development, First Amendment rights of students, judicial affairs, sexual harassment, and staff training. She has volunteered with groups such as FEMA, American Red Cross–Disaster Relief Services, Habitat for Humanity, and the St. Cloud Hospital Emergency/Trauma Center, where she served as a liaison between patients and their families and the medical staff. Dr. Bird has co-authored several articles on disaster response and a book, titled *The First Amendment on Campus: A Handbook for College and University Administrators* (2006).

Gary Dickstein, who recently completed his class work requirements for his Ph.D. in higher education and expects to graduate in December 2007, earned a B.S.W. from Western Michigan University and an M.A. in college student personnel administration from Wright State University. Throughout his 19-year career in student affairs, Mr. Dickstein has held numerous positions on a variety of college campuses. Currently assistant vice president for student affairs and director of student judicial services at Wright State University, he has presented at numerous state, regional, and national conferences as well as served as a facilitator for LeaderShape Inc. and the Undergraduate Interfraternity Institute. Additionally, for the past three years, Mr. Dickstein has served as a faculty member at the Donald D. Gehring Academy for Student Conduct Administration and is currently president-elect of the Association for Student Judicial Affairs.

Patrick Drinan, a professor of political science at the University of San Diego (USD), served as dean of USD's College of Arts and Sciences from 1989 to 2006. He is a past president of the Center for Academic Integrity, which awarded him its Donald McCabe Lifetime Achievement Award for promoting academic integrity in 2006. He has published frequently on academic integrity in scholarly journals and is currently working on a book on academic integrity in collaboration with Tricia Bertram Gallant and Steve Davis.

Felice Dublon, vice president and dean of student affairs at the School of the Art Institute of Chicago, is a past president of the Association for Student Judicial Affairs (ASJA), and a charter member of the organization. She has been recognized for her exceptional individual contributions to the area of student judicial affairs with the Donald D. Gerhring award. She serves on the editorial board of the *NASPA Journal*, has taught in the Department of Leadership, Foundations, and Counseling Psychology at Loyola University and has held numerous leadership positions in both ASJA and the National Association of Student Personnel Administrators. Dr. Dublon earned bachelor's degrees in psychology and political science and a master's degree in counseling psychology from the University of Illinois. She received her Ph.D. in higher education administration from Florida State University.

William Fischer currently serves as associate dean of students and director of the Office of Student Conduct at Johnson & Wales University. His primary responsibilities are to oversee administration of the student conduct and conflict resolution system. He has 10 years of professional experience in higher education and holds an adjunct faculty appointment at Northeastern University, where he teaches law and higher education. Before his tenure in higher education, Mr. Fischer engaged in the private practice of law for approximately 10 years. He is an active member in the Association for Student Judicial Affairs (ASJA) and has served on its Board of Directors for 6 years. He currently serves as its president. He earned his B.A. from Villanova University and his J.D. from Seton Hall University School of Law.

Judith M. Haas, who has worked in the Division of Student Development at Appalachian State University for 17 years, is director of student conduct and also has responsibility for parent orientation. She received a bachelor's degree from Averett College and a master's degree from Appalachian State University in student development with an emphasis in counseling. In past years, she has served as the Association for Student Judicial Affairs Circuit 4 representative and has participated actively in the association for many years. Prior to her work with student conduct, most of her experience was in housing and residence life at Averett College, Appalachian State University, and The University of Tennessee–Knoxville.

William L. Kibler, vice president for student affairs and professor of counselor education at Mississippi State University, has also served in a variety of leadership roles in student affairs at the University of Florida and Texas A&M University. He earned a bachelor's degree in economics, master's and specialist degrees in counselor education from the University of Florida, and a doctoral degree in educational administration from Texas A&M University. He has served as the president of the Association for Student Judicial Affairs and of the Center for Academic Integrity and in a number of leadership roles in the National Association of Student Personnel Administrators, including national conference chair. He has co-authored a book on academic integrity and a book on student judicial affairs; has written several book chapters and articles and made numerous professional presentations in academic integrity, student judicial affairs, and student affairs administration; and has consulted with numerous leading universities on these topics. He also serves on the editorial board of *NASPA Journal.*

James M. Lancaster, assistant professor of human development and psychological counseling at Appalachian State University, was formerly associate vice chancellor for student affairs at The University of North Carolina at Greensboro. He has more than 30 years of experience in student development practice and teaching in higher education. He holds bachelor's (1972) and master's (1974) degrees in history and a doctorate (1979) in administration of higher education, all from The University of North Carolina at Greensboro and has written and presented widely on legal/developmental/ethical concerns in administration. He is a past director and current faculty member of the Donald D. Gehring Student Judicial Affairs Academy of the Association for Student Judicial Affairs, where he teaches the ethics track. He is also a past president of the Center for Academic Integrity and a past member of the editorial boards of the *Journal of College Student Development* and the *NASPA Journal.* He is a member of the International Leadership Association. Dr. Lancaster has written and spoken widely on integrity and ethics issues. He is the co-editor of a published monograph on New Directions in Student Services, titled *Beyond Law and Policy: Reaffirming the Role of Student Affairs*, and of the recently published book, *Exercising Power with Wisdom—Bridging Legal and Ethical Practice with Intention.*

Matthew Lopez-Phillips, acting vice president of student affairs and enrollment management, previously served as assistant vice president of student affairs and enrollment management and director of judicial affairs and special projects at Sonoma State University. His career path has included posts as director of judicial affairs at the University of Colorado at Boulder, campus community coordinator at George Mason University, residence life coordinator at the University of Vermont, and hall director at Northeastern

University and University of the Pacific. He earned a master's degree in college student development and counseling at Northeastern University and did his undergraduate work at the University of the Pacific.

Mr. Lopez-Phillips is a member of several professional organizations and is actively involved in the Association for Student Judicial Affairs. He has presented on traditional and alternative judicial programs and substance abuse issues in higher education, among other topics. He has served as a diversity curriculum instructor in the Department of Housing at Boulder, co-chaired the Student Affairs Diversity Committee, served as a member of the Chancellor's Standing Committee for GLBT issues at Boulder, and attended the National Social Justice Training Institute and the Visions Training Workshop. He has also been a trainer/guest speaker on diversity and social justice at University of Denver, University of Vermont, and Edinboro University.

John W. Lowery is associate professor in the School of Educational Studies at the Oklahoma State University and coordinates the college student affairs program. He previously served on the faculty at the University of South Carolina for six years and led its Higher Education and Student Affairs Program. He earned his doctorate at Bowling Green State University in higher education administration and has held administrative positions at Adrian College and Washington University. Dr. Lowery is actively involved in numerous professional associations, including the Association for Student Judicial Affairs; ACPA: College Educators International; the Association for the Study of Higher Education; and NASPA: Student Affairs Administrators in Higher Education. He has a master's degree in student personnel services from the University of South Carolina and an undergraduate degree in religious studies from the University of Virginia. He is a frequent speaker and author on topics related to student affairs and higher education, particularly legislative issues and judicial affairs, on which he is widely regarded as an expert. Included among the honors he has received during his career are the D. Parker Young Award for outstanding ongoing scholarly research contributions to the fields of higher education and student judicial affairs, at the Association for Student Judicial Affairs' 2007 Conference, and the Tracy R. Teele Memorial Award from the Commission on Campus Judicial Affairs and Legal Issues for "outstanding contributions to the area of judicial affairs and legal issues," at the 2005 meeting of the American College Personnel Association.

Vaughn Maatman, a veteran of 29 years in higher education, did his undergraduate work at Hope College and his graduate work in counseling and social ethics at Princeton Theological Seminary and The University of Pennsylvania, receiving his M.Div. in 1978. He has held positions at Princeton University, Bowling Green State University, and The University of Chicago. In 2006 he completed 19 years at Kalamazoo College as the dean of students (SSAO), where he was responsible for a unified (academic and social) student conduct system founded on the college's Honor System. He holds certifications in mediation and has consulted on issues involving crisis intervention and developing institutional crisis management plans. He has also frequently presented on academic integrity, ethics, and ethical decision making at Association for Student Judicial Affairs conferences. Currently he is executive director of the Lake Louise Christian Community, on the northern lower peninsula of Michigan.

Mary Beth Mackin is assistant dean of student life at the University of Wisconsin-Whitewater, where she is responsible for student conduct administration, ombudsmen, crisis management, alcohol education, and sexual assault prevention. She has been actively involved in the Association for Student Judicial Affairs for many years, serving as president, immediate past president, president-elect, treasurer, and conference chair. In addition, she has served for many years as a faculty member at the Donald D. Gehring Academy for Student Conduct Administration, and she has presented at numerous state, regional, and national conferences during her tenure in higher education. She also co-authored *The First Amendment on Campus.*

Annie Nebeker Christensen is the dean of students at the University of Utah, where she works with the crisis response team, student conduct administration, sexual assault prevention, and student advocacy. She has been active in the Association for Student Judicial Affairs and has worked for numerous years with the Donald D. Gehring Judicial Affairs Training Academy at the University of Utah and is currently serving on the ASJA Board of Directors. Ms. Nebeker Christensen earned her undergraduate degrees from the University of Utah and her master's degree in social work from the University of Pennsylvania. Currently, she is completing her Ph.D., which focuses on college student suicide intervention and prevention.

Brent G. Paterson, associate vice president for student affairs and clinical associate professor of educational administration and foundations at Illinois State University since 2001, was a member of the student affairs staff at Texas A&M University for 17 years serving in various roles, including dean of student life. He has been active in the National Association of Student Personnel Administrators (NASPA), the Southern Association for College Student Affairs (SACSA) and the Association for Student Judicial Affairs (ASJA), holding leadership positions in these associations. In addition to writing several publications, he received the D. Parker Young Award from ASJA for outstanding scholarly and research contributions in higher education law. He holds a B.S. from Lambuth University, an M.S. from the University of Memphis, and a Ph.D. from the University of Denver.

Gary Pavela teaches in the honors program at the University of Maryland and writes law and policy newsletters to which more than 1,000 colleges and universities in the United States and Canada subscribe. He was a law clerk to Judge Alfred P. Murrah of the U.S. Court of Appeals for the Tenth Circuit, a faculty member for the Federal Judicial Center in Washington, D.C. (the training arm of the U.S. courts), and a staff attorney for the State University of New York, Central Administration. He also served as a fellow at the University of Wisconsin Center for Behavioral Science and Law, taught at Colgate University, and is a member of the board of the Kenan Institute for Ethics at Duke University.

Identified by the *New York Times* as an "authority on academic ethics," Mr. Pavela has been a consultant on law and policy issues at many leading universities. In 2005 he received the National Association of Student Personnel Administrators' Outstanding Contribution to Literature and Research award, and in 2006 he was designated the University of Maryland Outstanding Faculty Educator by the Maryland Parents' Association.

Saundra K. Schuster, general counsel for Sinclair Community College and an assistant attorney general for the State of Ohio, was formerly senior assistant attorney general for the State of Ohio in the Higher Education Section and associate general counsel for the University of Toledo. Before practicing law, she served as associate dean of students at The Ohio State University. Ms. Schuster has more than 25 years experience in college administration and teaching and frequently presents nationally on legal issues in higher education. She has master's degrees in counseling and higher education administration from Miami University, a juris doctor from Moritz College of Law, The Ohio State University, and has completed her coursework for her Ph.D. in organizational development at Ohio State University.

Edward N. Stoner II, a founding member of the Association for Student Judicial Affairs (ASJA), teaches each year at ASJA's Donald D. Gehring Academy for Student Conduct Administration and is on the advisory board of the California Coalition Against Sexual Assault. He was a partner in the Pittsburgh, Pennsylvania, office of the law firm, Reed Smith LLP, and, over his 32-year career, has represented many colleges and universities. Mr. Stoner is a past president and chair of the Board of Directors of the National Association of College and University Attorneys.

James L. Street Jr., associate director in the Center for Student Involvement and Leadership at Appalachian State University (ASU), coordinates leadership programs, including a leadership studies minor. During his 16 years at ASU, he served as fraternity and sorority adviser; coordinator of student clubs and organizations; and adviser to the fraternity, sorority, and club governing bodies. Dr. Street received an Ed.D. in counseling and college student development from the University of Georgia, an M.Ed. in higher education and student affairs from Indiana University, and a bachelor of arts in psychology from the University of Florida. He is a member of the American College Personnel Association and the International Leadership Association.

Susan P. Trageser is associate director/senior conduct officer in student judicial affairs at the University of California, Berkeley. In the field of judicial affairs for 15 years, she has a master's degree in counseling and educational development from University of North Carolina at Greensboro. Ms. Trageser has served in many positions with the Association for Student Judicial Affairs, including chair of the 2006 ASJA International Conference, and is currently serving on the Board of Directors as Director at Large for Circuits 4 and 11. She has served on the Campus Conflict Resolution Resource Center Advisory Board and worked with the Best Practices Group. She is certified in mediation and is a Nationally Certified Counselor.

Diane M. Waryold, assistant professor in the College Student Development Program at Appalachian State University, was formerly executive director of the Center for Academic Integrity and Program Administrator for the Kenan Institute for Ethics at Duke University. She is an accomplished student affairs administrator, which she has served in various roles for over 20 years. She is a founding and charter member of the Association for Student Judicial Affairs (ASJA) and served as its president from 1995 to 1996. Dr. Waryold has presented programs, published, and consulted in campus judicial affairs, sexual assault, campus security/violence, campus policing, academic integrity, ethics, and group work methods throughout the country. She received a B.S. from the State University College at Cortland, N.Y., an M.Ed. from the University of Florida, and a Ph.D. in educational leadership from Florida State University.

Nona L. Wood, M.S.Ed., is associate director of student rights & responsibilities at North Dakota State University (NDSU), Fargo. She has been a student judicial affairs officer at NDSU since 1990 and has presented her research on a variety of topics to student judicial affairs personnel at the state, regional, and national levels for the Association for Student Judicial Affairs (ASJA). Ms. Wood has presented at ASJA on adjudicating campus sexual assault, advanced due process issues, psychological and other characteristics of sexual predators, search and seizure, stalking, and threat assessment. With her publishing partner, Dr. Robert A. Wood, associate professor of political science, North Dakota State University, she has also published works on applying student development theory to the academic classroom, moral and ethical development theory as applied to training student programming assistants, and stalking (single and co-authored) as well as two articles on due process in student conduct hearings. In addition, she has served as the 8th Circuit representative, president-elect, president, and immediate past president of ASJA.

John Zacker is director of student conduct at the University of Maryland, College Park, where he has been employed for 19 years within the judicial programs/student conduct office. He also holds a faculty appointment with the College of Education, College Student Personnel Program. Before coming to Maryland, he served as director of resident life at Occidental College in Los Angeles, California. He earned a B.S. from Plymouth State College, an M.Ed. from the University of Vermont, and a Ph.D. from the University of Maryland. He has been actively involved in professional associations, particularly the Association for Student Judicial Affairs (ASJA), having served on its Board of Directors for three years before being elected its president. Dr. Zacker currently directs ASJA's Donald D. Gehring Academy for Student Conduct Administration. He is a frequent consultant on student conduct administration and presents regularly at national association meetings, most recently on ethical development and assessment/learning outcomes.

Eugene L. Zdziarski, assistant vice president and dean of students at the University of Florida, provides overall leadership and direction to a variety of key programs and services in the university's Division of Student Affairs. The Dean of Students Office provides programs and services in disability resources, judicial affairs, leadership & service, multicultural & diversity affairs, new student programs, off-campus life, and student legal services. Before coming to the University of Florida, Dr. Zdziarski was at Texas A&M University, where he assisted in the development of the Student Conflict Resolution Center, which combined judicial affairs, student legal services, and mediation services into one campus dispute resolution center.

Dr. Zdziarski received a B.S. from Oklahoma State University, an M.S. from the University of Tennessee at Knoxville, and a Ph.D. from Texas A&M University. He serves as regional vice president for Region III of the National Association of Student Personnel Administrators (NASPA) and is also a member of the NASPA National Board of Directors. In addition, he has served as central office manager for the Board of Directors of the Association for Student Judicial Affairs. He also makes professional presentations at national, regional, and state meetings on such topics as crisis management, dispute resolution, and legal issues in higher education. He has also written two books and several articles and book chapters on similar topics and has served as a consultant to a variety of colleges and universities.